Multicultural Stepfamilies

Multicultural Stepfamilies

Susan Stewart and Gordon Limb, Editors

Iowa State University

SAN DIEGO

Bassim Hamadeh, CEO and Publisher
Amy Smith, Project Editor
Emely Villavicencio, Senior Graphic Designer
Stephanie Kohl, Licensing Associate
Natalie Piccotti, Director of Marketing
Kassie Graves, Vice President of Editorial
Jamie Giganti, Director of Academic Publishing

3970 Sorrento Valley Blvd., Ste. 500, San Diego, CA 92121

Brief Contents

Detailed Contents

3   African American Stepfamilies   45

Chalandra M. Bryant, PhD, University of Georgia

4   Hispanic Stepfamilies   77

Steven Hoffman, PhD, MSW
Bethany Breck, MSW, University of Texas at Austin
Lauren Beasley, MSW, University of Tennessee-Knoxville

5 American Indian Stepfamilies 111

Ryan Turner, MSW, Brigham Young University
Gordon Limb, PhD, Brigham Young University
Susan Stewart, PhD, Iowa State University

6 East Asian Stepfamilies 149

Shinji Nozawa, MA, Meiji Gakuin University

7   Religious Diversity in Stepfamilies   179

Todd M. Jensen, PhD, MSW, Jordan Institute for Families and University of North Carolina at Chapel Hill

8   Studying Diverse Stepfamilies: Conclusions and Future Directions   209

Gordon Limb, PhD, Brigham Young University
Susan D. Stewart, PhD, Iowa State University

CHAPTER ONE

Studying Multicultural Stepfamilies

WHY NOW?

Susan D. Stewart, PhD, Iowa State University
Gordon Limb, PhD, Brigham Young University

STEPFAMILIES HAVE ALWAYS been part of the family landscape. In the Plymouth Colony in the 17th century, it is estimated that 50% of men and 25% of women were remarried and one in six households contained stepchildren (Demos, 2000). Until the middle of the 20th century, stepfamilies were formed almost exclusively through remarriage after the death of a spouse. Over the last 50 years, there has been a death-to-divorce transition in stepfamilies, with divorce and remarriage replacing widowhood as the main pathway into stepfamily life. The divorce rate in the United States has been high and stable for decades aside from small dips related to economic recessions, which tend to depress the divorce rate. Roughly one in two marriages ends in divorce; however, there is huge variation in the divorce rate by education, income, and race/ethnicity (Payne, 2018a). Today, about 40% of new marriages are remarriages and the number of remarried adults has tripled since 1980 (Lewis & Kreider, 2015; Livingston, 2014). Two-thirds of remarriages include biological or adopted children from a previous relationship, thus forming a stepfamily (Lewis & Kreider, 2015; Livingston, 2014). Not all stepfamilies, however, are the result of remarriage, and stepfamilies come in a variety of forms. For example, since the early 1990s, there has been a 60% increase in births to unmarried mothers (National Center for Family and Marriage Research [NCMFR], 2017). The result is that in 14% of first marriages, at least one member of the couple has had children with someone other than their current spouse (Stykes & Guzzo, 2015).

Marriage and remarriage have declined as pathways into stepfamily life in favor of cohabitation (Allred, 2018). Between 2008 and 2016, the marriage rate declined 10% and the remarriage rate declined 15% (Payne, 2018b). Meanwhile, the percentage of women who reported ever having cohabited nearly doubled between 1987 and 2013, and two-thirds of married stepfamilies now begin with cohabitation (Kreider & Lofquist, 2014; NCFMR, 2017). Today, roughly half of children in stepfamilies are living with their parent's cohabiting partner (NCFMR, 2017). Overall, about three-quarters (78%) of U.S. children whose parents' union dissolved will acquire a cohabiting or married stepparent (Andersson, 2002; Andersson et al., 2016) and approximately 40% of all children in the United States will spend at least some of their youth living in a stepfamily household (Norris, Vines, & Hoeffel, 2012).

It is important to note that these figures do not include children in single-parent families who have stepfamily members who reside in a different household (i.e., the spouse or partner of a nonresident parent and/or half- and stepsiblings). Overall, 42% of all Americans report having at least one step-relative. This figure is 50% for people under age 30 (Parker, 2011). The effect of stepfamilies on the United States cannot be overstated and the increase in stepfamilies is a global phenomenon. Although the United States has the highest level of re-partnering in the industrialized world (Heuveline, Timberlake, & Furstenburg, 2003), every country in the world has some form of stepfamily, with divorce and remarriage increasing everywhere (Ganong & Coleman, 2017b).

Along with increasing complexity in family structure, the demography of the U.S. population is rapidly diversifying in terms of race, ethnicity, and religion. In 2015, two-thirds of Americans were White non-Hispanic, a decline of 14% since 2000 (U.S. Census Bureau, 2001, 2016). There has been corresponding growth in minority populations during the same period, especially Hispanics, and to a lesser extent, Eastern Indians, Africans, and Asians. Moreover, although roughly 70% of Americans identify as Christian, Christian religions are declining and the number of Americans who do not identify with any organized religion and non-Christian faiths (e.g., Jews, Muslims, Hindus) is increasing. There is also increasing racial and ethnic diversity within Christianity (Pew Research Center, 2015).

As the population of the United States continues to grow and change, scholars must incorporate different racial, ethnic, cultural, and religious groups into their teaching and research, including within family studies. This is especially true when it comes to stepfamilies. Stepfamilies are an important group to understand, if only because millions of Americans live in one. The number of married, two-biological-parent (and adopted) families has declined dramatically, especially in the last 50 years. Today, so-called "nontraditional" families, including families with single parents, cohabiting couples, and stepparents and stepchildren, now outnumber "traditional" ones (Coontz, 2015). Although percentages vary, this is the case in the United States and also in most European countries, Australia, and New Zealand.

Existing research indicates that race, ethnicity, religion, and culture matter to stepfamily structure and dynamics. In the United States, Hispanics, Blacks, and American Indians have higher rates of nonmarital childbearing and cohabitation than do Whites, which results in a higher percentage of stepfamilies formed through first marriage and cohabitation than remarriage among those groups (Lewis & Kreider, 2015). These patterns hold even when taking into account socioeconomic factors affecting family patterns such as education and income. Combined with higher divorce rates among African Americans and (native-born) Hispanics, a higher percentage of Black and Hispanic children than White and Asian children reside with step- and half-siblings (Pew Research Center, 2011). The result is that stepfamilies are disproportionately families of color (Pew Research Center, 2011). Remarriage rates also vary by race and ethnicity. Remarriage prevalence is highest among Whites and Asians and lowest among Hispanics and Blacks (Livingston, 2014).

Although stepfamily life may vary for different racial, ethnic, and religious groups, the number of studies on stepfamilies among different cultures is relatively few. For example, the role of religion in stepfamily life has been virtually ignored despite the fact more than three-quarters (77%) of mothers in the United States report that religion plays an important role in their daily lives (Mahoney, Lamidi, & Payne, 2015). Different religious groups can have vastly different family patterns and attitudes (Cornwall, 2013). Conversely, people from different family forms can have different views on religion (Mahoney et al., 2015).

The lack of information on racial, ethnic, and religious diversity in stepfamilies is unfortunate given the rapid increase in the racial, ethnic, and religious diversity of the U.S. population. Drawing upon the expertise and research of a diverse group of family scholars, *Multicultural Stepfamilies* explores similarities and differences in stepfamily life among different racial, ethnic, and religious groups in the United States. Moreover, these chapters contain original data analysis of stepfamily dynamics by race, ethnicity, and religion, providing information not currently available elsewhere in the literature.

Diversity, Inclusiveness, and Intersectionality

It's been a decade since the publication of Susan Stewart's book, *Brave New Stepfamilies: Diverse Paths Toward Stepfamily Living*, and two decades since Roni Berger's, *Stepfamilies: A Multi-Dimensional Perspective*. Both books contain chapters highlighting diversity in stepfamilies. Although Stewart's main focus was structural complexity, such as first-married and cohabiting stepfamilies and stepfamilies that extend across households, she included chapters on African American stepfamilies, stepfamilies with gay and lesbian parents, and stepfamilies with adult stepchildren. Likewise, Berger's book included chapters on Black, gay and lesbian, and immigrant stepfamilies. She also integrated research on cultural and religious variation by, for example, highlighting research on Israeli stepfamilies. More recently, Patricia Papernow, a leading expert on stepfamilies, in her 2013 book, *Surviving and Thriving in Stepfamily Relationships*, provides information on stepfamilies headed by gay and lesbian couples, African American stepfamilies, Latino stepfamilies, and later life cycle stepfamilies. Notably, she also tells the stories of real stepfamilies in these different groups. Aside from our own, we are aware of no other work that contains this level of stepfamily diversity.

The purpose of *Multicultural Stepfamilies* is threefold. Our first goal is to increase awareness of the growing population of non-White, non-Christian stepfamilies in an effort to stimulate research on racial, ethnic, and religious diversity in stepfamily life in the United States and around the world. This involves summarizing and critiquing the existing literature on stepfamilies among various groups and proposing avenues for future policy, practice, and research. The book is practical and informational, but also conceptual in the sense that it applies a multicultural perspective to stepfamily life. A second goal is to provide new data on stepfamily life within different groups. In contrast with studies that "control" for race and ethnicity and religiosity or religious affiliation, our book contains authors' original data analysis, providing much needed new information on cultural differences in stepfamily structure, attitudes, perceptions, and more. Third, each chapter contains a vignette designed to deepen readers' understanding of stepfamily life "on the ground" as opposed to relying on hypothetical, theoretical, and empirical models. Navigating stepfamily life has both rewards and challenges, and existing stepfamily research often misses the lived experiences of real people.

But highlighting diversity is tricky. We considered integrating racial, ethnic, and religious diversity across chapters divided by stepfamily structure, dynamics, and well-being. Given the lack of research on stepfamilies of color and the role of religion, however, we ultimately decided to create separate chapters for each. This is not without its pitfalls. There are incredible variations within these groups and they are not "monocultures" by any means. For instance, the American Indian population contains 566 federally recognized tribes, each with a distinct culture and tradition (Bureau of Indian Affairs, 2014). Remarried couples are also more likely to marry outside their race and ethnicity than are first-married couples (Shafer, 2013). For example, American Indians also have high rates of interracial marriage, leading to a large percentage of multiracial children among this population (Fu & Wolfinger, 2011; Kuroki, 2017). Interracial partnerships are becoming more common. In 2016, one in six (17%) of newlyweds (married less than one year) were married to a person of another race or ethnicity compared to 10% of those who were married longer (Wu, 2018).

Remarried couples are more likely than first married couples to marry someone of a different race, ethnicity, or religion, adding complexity to stepfamily life.

There is growing religious diversity in the United States as well. There are literally thousands of religions worldwide and hundreds of religions being practiced in the United States, if not more. In addition, increasing numbers of Americans do not identify with any one religion. A similar case can be made regarding any of the groups covered in this book, whether Hispanic, Asian, or lesbian, gay, bisexual, or transgender (LGBTQ+). A similar problem is that the language is constantly shifting. There is diversity and disagreement with respect to the way we refer to groups of various racial, ethnic, cultural, and religious backgrounds. Hispanic or Latino/a/Latinx? Native American or American Indian? African American or Black?

Given this, we do not highlight diversity alone. A necessary part of the discourse on diversity is *inclusiveness*. Rather than simply focusing on "otherness," we recognize that individuals and families, regardless of race, religion, and culture, are more similar that different. Some challenges of living in a stepfamily are universal. All stepfamilies grapple with adjusting to new relationships, living arrangements, and societal perceptions. Stepfamily membership increases children's stress, regardless of their race and ethnicity (Jensen, Shafter, & Holmes, 2017). Another aspect of adjustment has to do with labeling stepfamily members. The absence of terminology to refer to stepfamily members and finding words that "fit" is a problem across cultures. Moreover, what members of stepfamilies call each other can change over time (Kennedy & Fitch, 2018; Thosen & King, 2016). Stepfamilies worldwide are subject to stigmatization. In Hong Kong, stepmothers are referred to as "worn shoes" and in China "used goods" (Webber, 2003). Ganong and Coleman (2017b) asked a sample of U.S. undergraduates to list characteristics of stepfamilies versus nuclear families. Whereas nuclear families were described as "secure," "legitimate," and "caring," stepfamilies were described as "dysfunctional," "wicked," and "tumultuous." Attitudes are changing but progress is slow.

We are not able in this book to examine stepfamilies in all societies. For example, there is a distinct lack of research on stepfamilies in Africa, the Middle East, and Latin America. Divorce rates have increased among Muslims in North Africa and Indonesia (Cherlin, 2017). Even with piles of research on U.S. stepfamilies, our laws and policies concerning stepfamilies are ambiguous, conflicting, or nonexistent, and policymakers have been unresponsive to data showing the high prevalence of stepfamilies in society. Lacking clear laws and policies governing the rights and responsibilities of stepparents, disagreements are generally hashed out in court (Stewart, 2018). We are not the only country whose laws lag behind growth in nontraditional family forms. Associated with high levels of Catholicism, which takes a decidedly negative view of divorce, Ireland only legalized divorce in 1997, as did Chile in 2004. The Philippines bans divorce and remarriage outright (Cherlin, 2017). Therefore, studies should continue to examine diverse patterns of stepfamily formation among different cultures world.

Before delving into stepfamilies, it is important to define what we mean by "families." Although there are various definitions, they share some common functions: (a) they form an economic or otherwise practical unit and care for children and other dependents, (b) they consider their identity to be significantly attached to the group, and (c) they are committed to maintaining that group over time (Lamanna, Riedmann, & Stewart, 2018). We think readers will find after reading this book that stepfamilies of different races, ethnicities, and religious attachments are more similar than different. Robert Kettilz, in his 2014 Presidential Address at the annual meeting of the Association for Applied and Clinical Sociology, said, "As sociologists, our history is a history of doing studies focusing, either directly or indirectly, on the concept of inclusion. Much is known about the social factors that promote inclusion. We also know much about the social and personal consequences for categories of people when they are not fully included" (Kettlitz, 2016). In a socially stratified world, social inclusion highlights shared meanings and experiences. This is especially important when studying families other than families with married parents and their own biological children because despite their prevalence they remain controversial, especially in our highly polarized political climate (Allman, 2013).

A final theme of this book is *intersectionality*. We recognize that the stepfamilies are very likely members of multiple categories. Intersectionality highlights individuals' "multiple layers of social identity," which interact with one another to produce new forms of meaning and that shape social experiences (Smith, 2016). An example of intersectionality would be an African American lesbian stepfamily. Membership in each of these groups is associated with negative stereotypes in society and can be described as suffering from the "triple stigma" of difference (Berger, 1998). Intersections between race, ethnicity, and religion have been found to affect relationship trajectories. For example, Burdette, Haynes, and Ellison (2012) found that church attendance is important to African American's and Hispanics' perceptions on readiness for marriage but not Whites'. Therefore, we recognize that many of the stepfamilies in this book could be discussed in multiple chapters. Moreover, identities also interact with other statuses—education, income, rural versus urban residence, and others that are important in terms of accessing information and support services for stepfamilies.

Audience and Uses of This Book

There are many excellent books on stepfamily life and dynamics, such as Allan, Crow, and Hawker's (2011) *Stepfamilies*, Ganong and Coleman's (2017a) *Stepfamily Relationships*, Papernow's (1993) *Becoming a Stepfamily*, and Everett's (1993) *The Stepfamily Puzzle*; however, *Multicultural Stepfamilies* is unique in that it provides specific information on a wide variety of races, ethnicities, religions, and cultures. As noted previously, there are only three books to our knowledge that explicitly address stepfamily diversity. The first two are *Brave New Stepfamilies* (2007) by Stewart, and Berger's *Stepfamilies: A Multi-Dimensional Perspective* (1998). The most recent book that addresses stepfamily diversity is Papernow's *Surviving and Thriving in Stepfamily Relationships* (2013), which includes chapters on stepfamilies headed by lesbian and gay couples, African American stepfamilies, Latino stepfamilies, and later life cycle stepfamilies. We hope our book will serve as a complement to Papernow's work. In the absence of these resources, which are now between five and 20 years old, students and researchers desiring this information for comparative purposes would be required to conduct exhaustive searches of articles and books and individual groups. This book fills this gap.

Multicultural Stepfamilies is intended for a broad audience. The first audience is composed of researchers. This book contains new data on stepfamilies of different races, ethnicities, religions, and cultures. Each chapter contains a review and critique of existing studies and ideas for future research. Students make up the second audience, with the book serving as a supplemental text at both the undergraduate and graduate levels. Each chapter is self-contained so a specific chapter or chapters can be assigned. This book would be useful to researchers interested in expanding their work to understudied—but rapidly growing—subpopulations in the United States and internationally. Scholars have been calling for this type of work for decades (Weaver et al., 2001). The book would also be useful in social science courses on race and ethnicity, religion, and global and international perspectives. And it's intended to be helpful to professionals who work directly with families in social work and family and individual therapy, and helpful to church groups and religious institutions.

The book will facilitate "compare and contrast"-type discussions and assignments. Toward this end, each chapter will follow a similar, straightforward format that includes: (a) a vignette that provides an example of each group's experience of stepfamily life, (b) description of each group's demographic characteristics with attention to diversity therein, (c) discussion of each group's history and culture, (d) description of each group's overall marriage and family patterns, (e) review of research on stepfamilies pertaining to this group, (f) presentation of new or existing data conceptualized in a novel way, (g) implications of this knowledge for policy and practice, and (h) recommendations for future research. Each chapter contains a set of discussion and reflection questions and a list of additional resources.

Organization of Chapters

The book is organized in the following manner. The introduction includes our rationale for a book on a multicultural perspective of stepfamilies. We discuss our theoretical approach, our intended audience, and the book's potential uses. A brief summary of subsequent chapters follows.

Biases in Stepfamily Research

As discussed previously, the vast majority of what is known about stepfamilies comes from studies of White, middle-class, Christian families. While these stepfamilies make up a shrinking percentage of stepfamilies, they too have evolved, and therefore it is important to present a summary and critique of existing research. Chapter 2, "What We *Really* Know about Stepfamilies: An Elaboration on White, Middle-Class Biases in Stepfamily Research," by J. Bart Stykes of Sam Houston State University, does just that. This chapter includes a detailed discussion of stepfamilies' growing structural complexity, along with traditional theoretical perspectives of stepfamilies. The chapter, using the 2014 Survey of Income and Program Participation (SIPP), also shows how an expanded definition of stepfamilies—one that includes cohabiting stepfamilies, adult stepchildren, and same-sex couples—dramatically increases the number of stepfamilies in the United States nearly twofold. In addition, the chapter includes an important update on LGBTQ+ stepfamilies.

African American Stepfamilies

Chapter 3, by Chalandra M. Bryant of the University of Georgia, explores stepfamily life among African Americans. African American and Black family life is affected by their unique history of slavery, poverty, and discrimination (Raley, Sweeney, & Wondra, 2015). Distinct features of African American families that may impinge upon stepfamily life may include the importance of "fictive kin," who are people considered family but not related through biology or marriage (McLoyd, Hill, & Dodge, 2005). African Americans also display higher levels of involvement with extended family members than do Whites, and a stronger sense of financial and social obligation (Kim & McKenry, 1998). Some research suggests that the effect of stepfamilies on child well-being may be less negative among African Americans, whose culture is more likely to support multi-parental models (Taylor et al., 2013). African American stepfamilies are structurally diverse and more likely to be formed as a result of nonmarital childbearing and cohabitation as opposed to divorce, mainly due to low rates of marriage among low-income populations (Raley et al., 2015; Stewart, 1997). Bryant provides a comparison of the presence of step-relatives by race and ethnicity to show the prevalence of stepfamilies in this population, and finds that a substantially higher percentage of African Americans report having a step-relative (60%) versus Whites and Hispanics (39% and 46%, respectively), and a higher percentage of African American children reside in a stepfamily compared to Whites and Asians (17%, 15%, and 7%, respectively). This chapter provides the most up-to-date and comprehensive description of African American stepfamilies available.

Hispanic Stepfamilies

Chapter 4, on U.S. Hispanics, is by Steven Hoffman, Bethany Breck of the University of Texas at Austin, and Lauren Beasley of the University of Tennessee-Knoxville. Hispanics (also referred to as Latino/a/x) historically originated from Mexico, Central America, South America, Cuba, and Puerto Rico. This demographic is the fastest-growing population in the United States. Hispanics are also the largest racial and ethnic group of color in the United States, and demographers predict they will soon outnumber Whites in many states in the next decades. This is already the case in California and New Mexico (Bump, 2015). Nevertheless, Hispanic stepfamilies have not received much attention in the stepfamily literature. A potential problem recruiting Hispanics into studies is that "stepfamily" is not a recognized term in the Spanish language (Reck et al., 2012). This could also be related to their predominantly Catholic faith, conservative social values favoring marriage, and traditional gender roles allowing limited opportunities for women to participate in research. Yet, current rates of nonmarital childbearing, cohabitation, and divorce among Hispanics indicate that stepfamilies are prevalent in this population. Much like African Americans and American Indians, a main driver of low rates of marriage for Hispanics are their low incomes and high rate of poverty (Raley et al., 2015). Also similar to other people of color, strong intergenerational and extended family ties among Hispanics affect stepfamily dynamics in unique ways. Hispanics display higher levels of involvement with and obligation to extended family members than do Whites (Kim & McKenry, 1998). Hispanic families also traditionally include fictive kin who share childrearing responsibilities (Nelson, 2013). For instance, nonbiological parents and godparents often serve as co-parents, referred to as *compadrazgo*, and help facilitate the Catholic upbringing of children (Camacho, 2012; Lopez, 1999; Swartz, 2004). In another example, in a study of low-income married and cohabiting couples, Hispanic couples were more likely than other groups to modify their financial arrangements to move toward shared management (Addo & Sassler, 2010). In this chapter, Hoffman and colleagues present data showing the percentage of Hispanic children living with two biological parents, two adopted parents, and one biological/adopted parent and one stepparent. They found an interesting pattern in that a high number of Hispanic children with nonbiological parents are adopted (68%). This compares with 53% of White and 59% of African American children with nonbiological ties. They also found that Whites and Hispanics had a similar percentage of children in a married stepfamily (86%), compared with Blacks (78%). These findings show the danger of making assumptions about similarities across racial and ethnic minorities.

American Indian Stepfamilies

Ryan Turner and Gordon Limb from Brigham Young University, and Susan Stewart from Iowa State University, are the authors of Chapter 5. Studies of American Indian stepfamilies are virtually nonexistent. This is an unfortunate gap because the American Indian/Alaska Native population increased at twice the rate of the total U.S. population between 2000 and 2010 (Norris, Vines, & Hoeffel, 2012). There are also high rates of remarriage, cohabitation, and nonmarital childbearing within the American Indian communities (Elliot & Lewis, 2010). Although the precise number of American Indian stepfamilies is unknown, these figures suggest that stepfamilies are prevalent within this population. According to the 2009–2011 American Community Survey, there are more than 25,000 stepchildren in married or cohabiting American Indian/Alaska Native households. Although American Indians make up a small proportion of the United States population (roughly 2%), they remain an important racial and ethnic group both historically and also culturally (Kreider & Lofquist, 2014). Moreover, American Indians are not a monolithic group. Although they share many characteristics, there are more than 500 tribes, as noted previously (Bureau of Indian Affairs, 2014). But there are similarities. The inclusion of nonbiological family members is common in American Indian families. Data from the American Community Survey indicate that American Indian households contained a disproportionate number of adopted children relative to other racial and ethnic groups (Kreider & Lofquist, 2014). American Indian family life has long been characterized by collectivism, including interconnectedness, harmony, and community, and American Indian children are commonly cared for and reared by multiple parental figures beyond their immediate biological family context (Padilla, Ward, & Limb, 2013). Although stepfamilies are often perceived as detrimental to children's well-being from the dominant cultural perspective, stepparents can be a major support to children's well-being in American Indian communities (Caldwell et al., 2005). In addition to a review of the literature, Turner and colleagues present original data on American Indian stepfamilies based on the Stepfamily Experiences Project (STEP). A major finding is that compared with other racial and ethnic groups, American Indian children have less close and less positive relationships with their stepparents and assess their parents' and stepparents' relationships as being less positive. American Indian children also reported lower levels of social and emotional well-being than children of other racial and ethnic groups. These patterns are most likely associated, at least in part, with high rates of poverty, low levels of education, related social problems (e.g., alcohol abuse), and historical trauma.

East Asian Stepfamilies

Shinji Nozawa, from Meiji Gakuin University in China, is the author of Chapter 6. Asians are a culturally diverse minority group in the United States and worldwide. While a number of studies have examined Asian family structure generally, few studies have examined their distinctive features and cultural differences among Asian families, including step-families (Webber, 2003). Divorce, nonmarital childbearing, and cohabitation are historically low among Asians and Asian stepfamilies and are heavily stigmatized. In Korean culture, a divorce shames the entire family (Yang & Rosenblatt, 2001). But despite the stigma associated with divorce, cohabitation, and nonmarital childbearing, stepfamilies are becoming more common among Asians in the United States and in East Asia due to increasing divorce rates of late (Webber, 2003). Similar to the other groups cited previously, strong intergenerational and extended family ties and obligations among Asians affects stepfamily dynamics in unique ways (Kim & McKenry, 1998). In particular, Nozawa presents a new theory for understanding Asian stepfamily processes, which he refers to as "scrap and build," in which stepparents "replace" the child's nonresident biological parent as the main parental figure.

Religious Diversity in Stepfamilies

In Chapter 7, Todd M. Jensen, of the University of North Carolina at Chapel Hill, explores religion as it relates to stepfamilies. There are currently few studies of stepfamilies of different religious groups, such as Catholics, Fundamentalist Protestants, Mormons, and Muslims, and the role that religion plays in the stepfamily relationship, dynamics, and well-being. This is problematic due to the changing religious landscape of the population. More-over, some groups, namely Hispanics and African Americans, are more religious than other groups (i.e., Asians and Whites) (Pew Research Center, 2015). Remarried couples are more likely to come from different religious traditions than are first-married couples (Schramm et al., 2012), and the salience of religion and religious participation is lower among youth in stepfamilies than those raised in married, two-parent, biological/adopted families (Petts, 2015). In this chapter, Jensen, using the National Longitu-dinal Survey of Adolescent to Adult Health, compares religious affiliation, church attendance, religious salience, and religious homogamy among stepfamily members. He finds, for example, that parents in stepfamilies have lower church attendance than biological two-parent families: 24% of parents in stepfamilies reported attending religious meetings once a week or more, com-pared with 38% of parents in the latter group. Stepfamily members are also more likely to have non-matching religions and attachments to religion. How religion affects relationships between biological parents, stepparents, and stepchildren is complex.

Conclusion and Future Directions

Chapter 8 provides a comparison of theoretical perspectives, a summary of empirical findings, a discussion of similarities and differences in stepfamily life by race, ethnicity, and religion, and the implications of our findings for research, policy, and practice. The story that emerges is that racial, ethnic, and religious diversity in stepfamilies impinges on stepfamily life in both positive and negative ways. Additionally, we argue that stepfamilies of color and stepfamilies with different religious traditions have more in common with one another than they do with married, White, Christian stepfamilies, which remain privileged by scholars and are the family type against which all others are compared (i.e., the "deficit model"). Therefore, the historical and current focus of research on White stepfamilies severely limits our understanding of stepfamilies of all kinds.

The 21st century ushered in what Ganong and Coleman (2017a) refer to as the "new millennium era" in stepfamily scholarship. Stepfamily scholarship has advanced in the last decade to include diversity with respect to structure, race and ethnicity, and sexual identity (i.e., LGBTQ+ couples). It has also become much more international in Western countries and also in Asia, where union dissolution is becoming more common (Nozawa, 2015). As this book demonstrates, however, we have a long way to go in our understanding of stepfamilies in their full complexity. Our hope is to contribute to this scholarship and encourage others to conduct studies on these vibrant, constantly evolving, and fascinating family forms.

Questions for Discussion

1. What are some pitfalls of studying stepfamily diversity? How might categorizing stepfamilies into different racial, ethnic, and religious groups be problematic?
2. Define intersectionality. Why is this concept important for understanding stepfamily diversity?
3. List some challenges facing all stepfamilies, regardless of racial, ethnic, and religious differences and sexual identity.

Additional Resources

Ganong, L., & Coleman, M. (2017b). The cultural context of step-families. In *Stepfamily Relationships* (pp. 21–36). Boston, MA: Springer.

Papernow, P. (2013). *Surviving and thriving in stepfamily relationships*. New York, NY: Routledge.

Stewart, S. D. (2007). *Brave new stepfamilies: Diverse paths toward stepfamily living*. Thousand Oaks, CA: Sage.

The National Center for Marriage and Family Research at Bowling Green State University in Bowling Green, Ohio, has a "Family Profile Series" that provides continuously updated information (in the form of easy-to-read reports, charts, and graphs) on trends in family structure, complexity, and well-being over the life course.

References

Allan, G., Crow, G., & Hawker, S. (2011). *Stepfamilies*. New York, NY: Palgrave Macmillan.

Allman, D. (2013). The sociology of social inclusion. *Sage Open, 3*, 1–16.

Allred, C. A. (2018). *More than a century of change, 1900–2016*. Retrieved September 10, 2018, from https://www.bgsu.edu/ncfmr/resources/data/family-profiles/mahoney-lamidi-payne-religiosity-fp-15-06.html

Andersson, G. (2002). Children's experience of family disruption and family formation: Evidence from 16 FFS countries. *Demographic Research, 7*, 343–364.

Andersson, G., & Philipov, D. (2002). Life-table representations of family dynamics in Sweden, Hungary, and 14 other FFS countries: A project description of demographic behavior. *Demographic Research, 7*, 67–144.

Berger, R. (1998). *Stepfamilies: A multi-dimensional perspective*. New York, NY: Haworth Press.

Bump, P. (2015). *California is now the second state in which Hispanics outnumber Whites*. Retrieved September 6, 2016, from https://www.washingtonpost.com/news/the-fix/wp/2015/07/08/california-is-now-the-second-state-in-which-hispanics-outnumber-Whites/

Burdette, A. M., Haynes, S. H., & Ellison, C. G. (2011). Religion, race/ethnicity, and perceived barriers to marriage among working-age adults. *Sociology of Religion, 73*, 429–451.

Caldwell, J. Y., Davis, J. D., Bois, B. D., Echo-Hawk, H., Erickson, J. S., Golns, R. T., et al. (2005). Culturally competent research with American Indians and Alaska Natives: Findings and recommendations of the first symposium of the work group on American

Indian research and program evaluation methodology. *American Indian and Alaska Native Mental Health Research, 12,* 1–21.

Coltrane, S., Gutierrez, E., & Parke, R. D. (2008). Stepfathers in cultural context: Mexican American families in the United States. *The international handbook of stepfamilies: Policy and practice in legal, research, and clinical environments,* 100–121.

Camacho, M. (2012). La comay: An examination of the Puerto Rican *comadre* as a feminist icon, patriarchal stereotype, and television tabloid host. *Studies in Latin American Popular Culture, 30,* 124–137.

Coontz, S. (2015). Revolution in intimate life and relationships. *Journal of Family Theory & Review, 7* (March): 5–12.

Cornwall, M. (2013). Religion and family research in the twenty-first century. In *Handbook of Marriage and the Family* (pp. 637–655). New York, NY: Springer.

Cherlin, A. J. (2017). Introduction to the special collection on separation, divorce, repartnering, and remarriage around the world. *Demographic Research, 37,* 1275–1296.

Demos, J. (2000). *A little commonwealth: Family life in Plymouth Colony.* Oxford University.

Everett, C. (2014). *The stepfamily puzzle: Intergenerational influences.* New York, NY: Routledge.

Ganong, L., & Coleman, M. (2017a). *Stepfamily relationships.* Boston, MA: Springer.

Ganong, L., & Coleman, M. (2017b). The cultural context of stepfamilies. In *Stepfamily relationships* (pp. 21–36). Boston, MA: Springer.

Grady, B. (2009). A marriage blending family and race. *Social issues first hand: Blended families* (pp. 90–93), edited by S. Kiesbye. New York, NY: Greenhaven Press/Cengage Learning.

Guzzo, K. B. (2015). Twenty-five years of change in repartnering and stepfamily formation. *Center for Family and Demographic Research Working Paper,* no. 9.

Haskey, J. (2001). Demographics aspects of cohabitation in Great Britain. *International Journal of Policy and Family, 15,* 51–67.

Heuveline, P., Timberlake, J. M., & Furstenberg, F. F. (2003). Shifting childrearing to single mothers: Results from 17 western countries. *Population and Development Review, 29,* 47–71.

Jensen, T. M., Shafer, K., & Holmes, E. K. (2017). Transitioning to stepfamily life: The influence of closeness with biological parents and stepparents on children's stress. *Child & Family Social Work, 22,* 275–286.

Kalmijn, M. (2015). Family disruption and intergenerational reproduction: Comparing the influences of married parents, divorced parents, and stepparents. *Demography, 52,* 811–833.

Kennedy, S., & Fitch, C. A. (2012). Measuring cohabitation and family structure in the United States: Assessing the impact of new data from the Current Population Survey. *Demography, 49,* 1479–1498.

Kettlitz, R. E. (2016). Encouraging inclusiveness in doing sociology: Public and private, applied and clinical. *Journal of Applied Social Science, 10*, 87–89.

Kim, H. K., & McKenry, P. C. (1998). Social networks and support: A comparison of African Americans, Asian Americans, Caucasians, and Hispanics. *Journal of Comparative Family Studies*, 313–334.

Kreider, R., & Lofquist, D. A. (2014). *Adopted children and stepchildren: 2010* (P-20-572). Retrieved April 25, 2016, http://www.census.gov/prod/2014pubs/p20-572.pdf

Lamanna, M. A., Riedmann, A., & Stewart, S. D. (2018). *Marriages, families, and relationships: Making choices in a diverse society.* Cengage Learning.

Lewis, J. M., & Kreider, R. M. (2015). *Remarriage in the United States.* Report ACS-30. Retrieved April 11, 2016, https://www.census.gov/content/dam/Census/library/publications/2015/acs/acs-30.pdf

Livingston, G. (2014). *Four-in-ten couples are saying "I do," again.* Retrieved February 15, 2019, http://www.pewsocialtrends.org/2014/11/14/chapter-4-marriage-and-remarriage-among-newlywed-couples/

López, R. A. (1999). Las comadres as a social support system. *Affilia, 14*, 24–41.

Mahoney, A., Lamidi, E., & Payne, K. K. (2015). *Religiosity in U.S. families: Single, cohabiting, and married mothers.* Retrieved September 10, 2018, from https://www.bgsu.edu/ncfmr/resources/data/family-profiles/mahoney-lamidi-payne-religiosity-fp-15-06.html

Mandara, J., Rogers, S. Y., & Zinbarg, R. E. (2011). The effects of family structure on African American adolescents' marijuana use. *Journal of Marriage and Family, 73*, 557–569.

McLoyd, V. C., Hill, N. E., & Dodge, K. A. (2005). *African American family life: Ecological and cultural diversity.* New York, NY: Guilford.

Murry, V. M., Brown, P. A., Brody, G. H., Cutrona, C. E., & Simons, R. L. (2001). Racial discrimination as a moderator of the links among stress, material psychological functioning, and family relationships. *Journal of Marriage and Family, 63*, 915–926.

National Center for Family and Marriage Research. (2017). *Fast facts on American families.* Retrieved September 10, 2018, from https://www.bgsu.edu/content/dam/BGSU/college-of-arts-and-sciences/NCFMR/documents/Marketing/fast-facts-american-families.pdf

Norris, T., Vines, P. L., & Hoeffel, E. M. (2012). *The American Indian and Alaska Native population: 2010.* Retrieved June 15, 2016, from http://www.census.gov/prod/cen2010/briefs/c2010br-10.pdf

Nozawa, S. (2015). Remarriage and stepfamilies. In S. Quah (Ed.), *Handbook of families in Asia* (pp. 345–358). New York, NY: Routledge.

Nozawa, S. (2016). Remarriage and stepfamilies. *Routledge handbook of families in Asia*, 345.

Padilla, J., Ward, P., & Limb, G. E. (2013). Urban American Indians: A comparison of father involvement predictors across race. *Social Work Research, 37*, 207–217.

Papernow, P. L. (1993). *Becoming a stepfamily: Patterns of development in remarried families*. New York, NY: Routledge.

Papernow, P. (2013). *Surviving and thriving in stepfamily relationships*. New York, NY: Routledge.

Payne, K. K. (2018a). *First divorce rate in the U.S., 2016*. Retrieved September 10, 2018, from https://www.bgsu.edu/ncfmr/resources/data/family-profiles/payne-first-divorce-rate-fp-18-15.html

Payne, K. K. (2018b). *First marriage rate in the U.S., 2016*. Retrieved September 10, 2018, from https://www.bgsu.edu/ncfmr/resources/data/family-profiles/payne-first-marriage-rate-fp-18-14.html.

Petts, R. (2015). Parental religiosity and youth religiosity: Variations by family structure. *Sociology of Religion, 76*, 95–120.

Pew Research Center. (2011). *A portrait of stepfamilies*. Retrieved September 10, 2016, from http://www.pewsocialtrends.org/2011/01/13/a-portrait-of-stepfamilies/

Pew Research Center. (2015). *America's changing religious landscape*. Retrieved from http://www.pewforum.org/2015/05/12/americas-changing-religious-landscape/

Pryor, J. (2013). *Stepfamilies: A global perspective on research, policy, and practice*. New York, NY: Routledge.

Quah, S. R. (Ed.). (2015). *Handbook of families in Asia*. New York, NY: Routledge.

Raley, R. K., Sweeney, M. M., & Wondra, D. (2015). The growing racial and ethnic divide in US marriage patterns. *The Future of Children, 25*, 89.

Reck, K., Higginbotham, B., Skogrand, L., & Davis, P. (2012). Facilitating stepfamily education for Latinos. *Marriage & Family Review, 48*, 170–187.

Reid, M., & Andrew G. (2015). Vetting and letting: Cohabiting stepfamily formation processes in low-income Black families. *Journal of Marriage and Family, 77*, 1234–1249.

Shafer, K. (2013). Unique matching patterns in remarriage: Educational assortative mating among divorced men and women. *Journal of Family Issues, 34*, 1500–1535.

Smith, E. (2016). *What is the intersection theory in sociology?* Retrieved January 15, 2018, from https://www.quora.com/What-is-the-intersection-theory-in-sociology

Stewart, S. D. (2007). *Brave new stepfamilies: Diverse paths toward stepfamily living*. Thousand Oaks, CA: Sage.

Stewart. S. D. (2018). *Stepfamily laws and policies in the United States: Lessons from the west*. Paper presented at Old bonds, new ties: Understanding family transitions in re-partnerships, remarriages, and step-families in Asia. November 19–20, 2018. Asia Research Institute, National University of Singapore.

Stykes, B., & Guzzo K. B. (2015). *Remarriage and stepfamilies (FP-15-10)*. National Center for Family & Marriage Research. Retrieved April 11, 2016, from https://www.bgsu.edu/ncfmr/resources/data/family-profiles/stykes-guzzo-remarriage-stepfamilies-fp-15-10.html

Swartz, T. T. (2004). Mothering for the state: Foster parenting and the challenges of government-contracted carework. *Gender & Society, 18,* 567–587.

Taylor, R. J., Chatters, L. M., Woodward, A. T., & Brown, B. (2013). Racial and ethnic differences in extended family, friendship, fictive kin, and congregational informal support networks. *Family Relations, 62,* 609–624.

Thorsen, M. L., & King, V. (2016). My mother's husband: Factors associated with how adolescents label their stepfathers. *Journal of Social and Personal Relationships, 33,* 835–851.

U.S. Census Bureau. (2001). *The White population: 2000.* Retrieved August 10, 2016, from https://www.census.gov/prod/2001pubs/mso01-wp.pdf

U. S. Census Bureau. (2016). *Quick facts.* Retrieved August 10, 2016, from https://www.census.gov/quickfacts/table/PST045215/00

Weaver, S. E., Umaña-Taylor, A. J., Hans, J. D., & Malia, S. E. (2001). Challenges family scholars may face in studying family diversity: A focus on Latino families, stepfamilies, and reproductive technology. *Journal of Family Issues, 22,* 922–939.

Webber, R. (2003). Making stepfamilies work: Step-relationships in Singaporean stepfamilies. *Asia Pacific Journal of Social Work and Development, 13,* 90–112.

Wu, H. (2018). *Homogamy in U.S. marriages.* Retrieved September 10, 2018, from https://www.bgsu.edu/ncfmr/resources/data/family-profiles/wu-homogamy-marriages-fp-18-18.html

Yang, S., & Rosenblatt, P. C. (2001). Shame in Korean families. *Journal of Comparative Family Studies, 32,* 361–375.

CHAPTER TWO

What We *Really* Know About Stepfamilies

AN ELABORATION ON WHITE, MIDDLE-CLASS BIASES IN STEPFAMILY RESEARCH

J. Bart Stykes, PhD, Sam Houston State University

SINCE THE 1950S, families in the United States have become increasingly diverse (e.g., racial and ethnic status, religion) and also complex (e.g., cohabiting families, stepfamilies, single-parent families), though recent evidence suggests increases in family complexity plateaued in the mid-1990s (Manning, Brown, & Stykes, 2014). To describe contemporary families in the United States, one must first appropriately define the family. Adjusting our definitions of family behaviors, compositions, and dynamics is important given the steady divergence in family well-being by family structure that has accompanied deindustrialization since in the 1970s (Lundberg, Pollack, & Stearns, 2016). Taken together these factors suggest: (a) families in the United States have changed rapidly in the last half century; (b) inequalities in family and child outcomes have become increasingly pronounced; and (c) researchers must develop appropriate methodological tools to both define and measure contemporary families so that all family forms are identified and studied (Lundberg et al., 2016; Manning et al., 2014).

Stepfamilies provide a unique form of family diversity and complexity. Compared with other forms of family complexity that have garnered attention in recent decades—such as sibling complexity (Manning et al., 2014), same-sex couples/families (Biblarz & Stacy, 2010), and multipartner fertility (Guzzo & Furstenberg, 2007)—stepfamilies were identified and studied much earlier in history. Stepfamilies were identified as a nontraditional, alternative family form with a well-established body of scholarship before increases in diversity and complexity became a defining attribute of families in the United States. A well-established body of research has identified families formed through remarriage as a distinctive family form in comparison with families formed through a first marriage (Cherlin, 1978; Sweeney, 2010). Yet, prior work on stepfamilies, which has utilized a somewhat limited operational definition of stepfamilies, overlooks recent demographic trends that have implications for stepfamily living. For instance, (a) the emergence of cohabitation as a mainstay of family formation (Smock, 2000); (b) increasing attention to same-sex couples as parents (Manning, Fettro, & Lamidi, 2014); (c) the delayed transition to adulthood (Rindfuss, 1991); and, (d) diversity in custody arrangements (Cancian, Meyer, Brown, & Cook, 2014) all have implications for our understanding of contemporary stepfamilies. Drawing on Susan Stewart's classic book (2007), three factors remain crucial to a contemporary understanding of stepfamily living in the United States: (a) there is very likely as much variation *within* stepfamilies (and stepfamily dynamics) as there is between stepfamilies and other family forms; (b) there is not a clear consensus on conceptual and operational definitions of the stepfamily; and (c) due in part to a historical emphasis on remarried stepfamilies, most research and theory on stepfamilies is ill equipped to document diversity in stepfamily living and even today reflects a Christian, White, and middle-class bias.

In this chapter, I lay a foundation for the subsequent chapters by providing a critical literature review that places stepfamilies in historical context, details demographic changes and characteristics of contemporary stepfamilies, and discusses theoretical perspectives commonly used to explain stepfamily dynamics. In doing so, I frequently draw attention to the bias toward Christian, White, middle-class families based on the field's limited definition of stepfamilies. Then, drawing on the 2014 Survey of Income and Program Participation (SIPP), I consider the implications of stepfamily operational definitions by producing prevalence estimates of children's membership in stepfamilies when more versus less restrictive definitions are applied. These descriptive findings demonstrate that more restrictive definitions of stepfamilies (i.e., heterosexual, remarried couples with minor children) maintain an implicit bias in our understanding of stepfamilies. Moreover, this bias systematically excludes children living in stepfamilies that do not match this traditional definition, children who

America's iconic, outdated definition of the stepfamily.

are disproportionately non-White with less-educated parents. Lastly, I address key points for further consideration and practice by reviewing the legal standing of stepfamilies in the United States and providing recommendations for practitioners working with stepfamilies.

Stepfamily Living in the United States

As Stewart (2007) noted, stepfamilies in the United States are not a new family form. In the colonial Americas, remarriage was the main reason for stepfamily formation and it occurred in response to spousal loss. With increases in divorce rates through the 1980s, marital dissolution, rather than spousal loss, became the most common pathway into stepfamily living (Bumpass, Sweet, & Castro Martin, 1990; Cherlin & Furstenberg, 1994). Recently, scholars have noted that many stepfamilies are formed not through union dissolution, but through marital and cohabiting unions formed following a mothers' nonmarital birth (Bzostek, McLanahan, & Carlson, 2012; Stewart, 2007). In the contemporary United States, the pathways to stepfamily formation have become increasingly diverse and have come to include families formed after spousal loss, and through divorce and nonmarital childbearing. Moreover, the manner in which families transition into stepfamily status has unique implications for stepfamily living and interpersonal relationships within stepfamilies (Ganong & Coleman, 2017; Stewart, 2007).

Demographic Trends and Diversity in Contemporary Stepfamilies

A review of recent trends in union formation, dissolution, and childbearing is needed to better understand how structural inequalities on the basis of racial and ethnic identity and education are associated with the diversity in contemporary stepfamilies. Although the majority of adults in the United States desire (and are expected) to marry, steep economic requirements are now a necessity for entering into marriage—regardless of racial, ethnic, and class status (Cherlin, 2004; Edin & Kefalas, 2005). A wealth of evidence demonstrates that shared expectations and attachments to marriage do not translate to an equal propensity to marry. Based on analyses of first-marriage rates in the 1990s, Goldstein and Kenney (2001) asserted that marriage was becoming a luxury good exclusive to the college educated, and recent analyses of women's first-marriage rates note a similar pattern. Among college-educated women, 70 marriages occurred per 1,000 never-married women. Among less-educated women, there were between 27 and 39 marriages per 1,000 never-married women (Payne, 2018).

Given the broader social structure of the United States, institutional racism, and the legacy of slavery, income and wealth inequalities in the nation are often reflected in racial and ethnic inequalities. When viewed through the lens of marriage, these inequalities are apparent in the recent racial and ethnic divergences in Whites' versus non-Whites'—most notably Black and Hispanic—propensities to marry. White women (who occupy a position of relative privilege in comparison to their non-White counterparts) face fewer barriers to marriage. Not surprisingly then, White women experience higher rates of marriage (52 marriages per 1,000 never-married women) than their Black and native-born Hispanic counterparts, whose rates are 20 and 42 per 1,000 unmarried women, respectively (Payne, 2018). Recent efforts have sought to explain racial and ethnic differences in marriage rates by emphasizing the connection with class-based inequalities and differences in life changes. Marriage markets emphasize how racial and ethnic disparities in structural factors (e.g., precarious employment and unemployment, incarceration, active duty military status) make it more difficult for minority women to identify suitable suitors (see Lichter, McLaughlin, Kephart, & Landry, 1992). Yet, these efforts have not been able to fully explain racial and ethnic differences in marriage. Although substantial White-Black differences exist in marriage rates, Raley (1996) demonstrated the difference was greatly reduced once cohabitation was considered as a component of union formation. Others have also suggested that cohabitation might serve as an alternative to marriage among Black and Hispanic women (Smock, 2000). Collectively, these trends and findings suggest that both White and middle-class stepfamilies are more likely to be married, whereas non-White stepfamilies and those with less education most likely involve cohabiting unions.

Since the dissolution of a previous union (marriage or cohabitation) is now a primary entryway into stepfamilies, trends in dissolution are also important to understand stepfamily living. Research consistently demonstrates that non-White individuals (excluding Asians and foreign-born Hispanics) experience a greater risk of relationship instability than their White counterparts. Specifically, recent estimates of divorce rates by Payne (2018) show that among Black and native-born Hispanic women, 26 and 21 divorces occurred for every 1,000 married women, compared with 14 divorces for every 1,000 White married women. Both Asian and foreign-born Hispanic women reported lower divorce rates that White women. In terms of education, having some college experience is associated with an increased propensity to divorce. Divorce rates are highest among those having some college experience (20 divorces per 1,000 married women) whereas those having a college education, a high school diploma, or no degree reported similar divorce rates (ranging from 12–14 per 1,000 married women). Given costs associated with both divorce and marriage, it is most likely that remarried stepfamilies have higher levels of education than their cohabiting counterparts.

Lastly, I turn to trends in nonmarital childbearing, another important entryway into stepfamily living. Since the 1980s, researchers have observed a steady increase in women having children outside of a marital relationship (Wu, 2008). Black and Hispanic women and those having lower educational attainment are at an increased risk of experiencing both a nonmarital birth and also births with multiple partners (Guzzo & Furstenberg, 2007a, 2007b). Practically all the increase in nonmarital childbearing has occurred among cohabiting women (Raley, 2001) though a sizeable minority of nonmarital childbearing occurs among single women, who are more economically disadvantaged than their counterparts in cohabiting unions (Gibson-Davis & Rackin, 2014; Lichter, Sassler, & Turner, 2014). Nonmarital childbearing has implications for union formation and dissolution. Nonmarital childbearing can bolster entry into unions as nonmarital births are often a catalyst to enter into more serious relationships (Lichter et al., 2014), though these relationships are marked by high levels of instability (Carlson, McLanahan, & England, 2004). Recent discourse embraces the terminology of "fragile families" to refer to cohabiting families that are characterized by a shared nonmarital birth. Factors such as economic insecurity and gender mistrust, which are relatively common for many of these families, are linked with more rapid transitions into and out of romantic relationships (Carlson et al., 2004; McLanahan, 2009).

Existing research suggests two key points important for this chapter: (a) there are diverse pathways into stepfamily living, and (b) structural inequalities, especially with respect to racial and ethnic identity and education, are most likely associated with said pathways into stepfamily living. Traditional approaches to defining stepfamilies have focused on remarried stepfamilies that form after marital dissolution. Accordingly, this approach is ill equipped to identify stepfamilies that are not married and may be formed after nonmarital births rather than as a result of divorce. The first and most obvious shortcoming of the traditional approach is that it underestimates the prevalence of stepfamilies in the contemporary United States. Yet, this undercount is more problematic for some populations of families than others. Based on the trends in family formation discussed previously, this undercount is more problematic for non-White children, and those whose parents report lower levels of education (see Stewart, 2007). Specifically, high rates of dissolution and nonmarital childbearing (and multipartner fertility), coupled with barriers to marriage, suggest that disadvantaged individuals (e.g., non-White, lower levels of education) are more likely to experience stepfamily living in the context of relatively unstable, cohabiting unions. Thus, most of what is known about stepfamilies involve those who are White, and increasingly middle class. Based on my review of existing research, new theoretical approaches that might better account for diversity in stepfamily living are lacking.

Racial and ethnic diversity across contemporary families.

Gender, Sexuality, and Stepfamily Living

Lesbian, gay, bisexual, transgender, and queer/questioning individuals and others with a nonconforming gender or sexual identity (herein referred to as LGBTQ+) have historically been excluded from discussions of stepfamilies as well. Given the state's failure to recognize same-sex marriage prior to 2015 and the increasing public support that same-sex couples with and without children "count" as family (see Taylor, Morin, & Wang, 2011), scholars began critiquing definitions of stepfamilies that excluded same-sex stepfamilies as early as the 2000s (Berger, 2000; Stewart, 2007). Ganong and Coleman's (2017) recent review demonstrated that in many cases we still have more questions than answers when it comes to LGBTQ+ stepfamilies. The limited evidence we have suggests (a) LGBTQ+ stepfamilies are diverse, (b) we know little about stepfamily dynamics in LGBTQ+ stepfamilies, (c) experiences differ when contrasting planned LGBTQ+ families with LGBTQ+ stepfamilies, and (d) stepfamily experiences appear to differ for stepfamilies with gay versus lesbian parents (Ganong & Coleman, 2017).

The reluctance to document LGBTQ+ experiences in stepfamilies is particularly problematic for a couple of reasons. For starters, the majority of children raised by LGBTQ+ parents are from prior heterosexual and same-sex unions. This means that most childrearing in LGBTQ+ families occurs in the context of stepfamilies. Yet, a recent report on LGBTQ+-parent families, published by The William's Institute, illustrated that most recent work on LGBTQ+ parent families focused on planned childbearing in this context rather than the transition to LGBTQ+ stepfamilies after the dissolution of past relationships (Goldberg, Gartrell, & Gates, 2014). There are other issues beyond overlooking the most common pathway to stepfamily living within LGBTQ+ parent families. Most importantly, scholars have demonstrated that to more readily understand how the gender composition of parents is linked with children's outcomes, the field must grapple with the confounding effects of gender composition of parents and biological ties to children. Failure to do so runs the risk of attributing the "effects" of stepfamily dynamics to LGBTQ+ parenting and vice versa (see Biblarz & Stacey, 2010). Secondly, Berger (2000) provided compelling evidence that LGBTQ+ stepfamilies make up a group facing substantial stigma linked with sexual orientation, stepfamily living, and LGBTQ+ parenting, which has implications for future researchers and practitioners alike (see Papernow, 2013).

Reluctance to include LGBTQ+ stepfamilies and bring perspectives of sex- and gender-nonconforming individuals into stepfamily research prevents our ability to understand family dynamics in this unique context, though recent efforts show promise. For instance, recent endeavors have considered factors linked with power and decision making in lesbian stepfamilies (Moore, 2008), and also considered adult children's transitions into LGBTQ+ stepfamilies formed in response to dissolution of a former same-sex relationship (Goldberg & Allen, 2013). Separately, van Eeden-Moorefield and colleagues' (2012) findings suggested that LGBTQ+ stepfamilies report higher relationship quality than their counterparts who were in less complex family forms, such as first cohabiting partnerships or re-partnered without children present. Despite these efforts to embrace more inclusive definitions of stepfamilies, many researchers still fail to consider LGBTQ+ stepfamilies as a viable family form, and this greatly limits our ability to understand experiences within this type of family.

Theoretical Perspectives on Stepfamily Living and Stepfamily Dynamics

Efforts to better understand children's experiences in stepfamilies have focused on differences in child well-being. Consistently, and across a number of indicators of well-being, children living with one biological parent and one stepparent report more negative outcomes than their counterparts reared in traditional, two-biological/adopted-married parent families (see Brown, 2010, & Sweeney, 2010, for reviews). Taylor and colleagues (2012) provided a systematic review of 102 peer-reviewed, scholarly articles and found that the most widely cited perspectives to explain stepfamily dynamics, processes, and well-being were *family systems theory*, *social capital/exchange* perspectives, *evolutionary theory*, and *symbolic interactionism*. As I noted previously, such theoretical perspectives are relatively old and ill equipped to document and explain the contemporary U.S. stepfamily.

Family systems theory has been used to understand how multiple types of relationships in families contribute to stepfamily dynamics and functioning. Much of this work has focused on boundary ambiguity emphasizing who is counted as being part of the family (i.e., named as family members), and how challenges in determining "who counts" as family are associated with lower levels of closeness and family connectedness between parents and adolescent children (Brown & Manning, 2009) and lower relationship quality and stability among couples (Stewart, 2005). The vast majority of the studies reviewed by Taylor and colleagues were limited to *married* stepfamilies. This raises concerns as the challenges associated with family boundary ambiguity were more pronounced in cohabiting stepfamilies (Brown & Manning, 2009; Stewart, 2005). Others have applied a family systems approach to demonstrate that the perceived quality of relationships between both stepfather-adolescent and mother-adolescent ties were linked with an adolescent's sense of belonging in the family (King, Boyd, & Thorsen, 2015). The family systems perspective also illustrates that families extend beyond residential households, and stepfamilies provide an important lens to view such families—especially in order to study the mother-child relationship. For instance, King (2009) found that the introduction of a cohabiting stepfather was associated with lower levels of closeness between mothers and children but had little influence on nonresident fathers' ties with children. In addition, others have considered how stepfathers' relationships with their stepchildren differ according to involvement of the nonresident, biological father. Findings in this line of research are mixed as some work has suggested strong ties to nonresident, biological fathers present stressful relationships for stepfathers and their resident stepchildren (see MacDonald & Demaris, 2002). Others, however, reported that involved nonresident, biological fathers and resident stepfathers coparent and coexist, leading to better outcomes for children (King, 2006, 2009; Marsiglio & Hinojosa, 2007).

The *social capital perspective* has also contributed to our understanding of stepfamily living. Coleman (1988) defines social capital as the social relationships an individual can access to benefit from a friend's or a relative's human capital (i.e., acquired skills and knowledge). For example, this perspective has been used to better understand whether parents' lower social and emotional investment in their stepchildren than biological children leads to lower educational attainment of stepchildren (Devor, Stewart, & Dorius, 2018). Another key finding from research from this perspective suggests that stepchildren may not provide the same sources of social capital to parents and families as biological children, given the normative desire to have shared, biological children, resulting in higher fertility in stepfamilies (Holland & Thomson, 2011; Stewart, 2002). Apart from increasing fertility, this basic tenet from the social capital perspective has also been used to explain why parents are typically less involved with stepchildren compared with their biological children across a number of outcomes and indicators (see Hofferth, 2006; Ganong & Coleman, 2017).

The *evolutionary perspective* asserts that parents are strategic in distributing finite resources in a manner that prioritizes biological children over stepchildren (see Anderson, Kaplan, & Lancaster, 1999; Boyle, Jenkins, & Georgiades, 2004; Daly & Wilson, 1996; Popenoe 1994). Popenoe (1994) used this perspective to articulate why stepfathers were less vested in the day-to-day lives of their resident stepchildren than resident biological children. This logic has been further extended to explain sibling rivalry within stepfamilies. For example, differential treatment of step versus biological children has been found to be associated with poorer outcomes and more frequent conflict within stepfamilies (Boyle et al., 2004). The evolutionary perspective is also used to help explain stepchildren's increased risk of experiencing violence and abuse (e.g., Daly & Wilson, 1996). While many scholars have used this theory to *hypothesize* why stepfathers might invest less in step rather than biological children, direct tests of this perspective have found less evidence in support of biological or evolutionary perspectives (Hofferth & Anderson, 2003). As a result, applications of the evolutionary perspective in stepfamily research are increasingly less common in recent attempts to explain and understand stepfamily living.

The *symbolic interactionist perspective* emphasizes how the use of language, legal ties, and meanings attached to social interactions affect daily, lived experiences. When applied to stepfamilies this leads to a focus on how individual family members adapt to building stepfamilies and redefine their own personal roles in the context of a new family form (Taylor et al., 2012). Cherlin's (1978) classic piece on remarriage and stepfamilies as "an incomplete institution" draws heavily on this perspective. Cherlin argues that stepfamilies have more stress and have lower levels of well-being due, in part, to ambiguity in (a) language used to define relationships between stepparents and stepchildren (e.g., no normative title for stepparents), (b) legal rights of stepparents (e.g., visitation rights after dissolution), and (c) cultural norms for how stepparents are expected to interact with their stepchildren (e.g., stepparents as disciplinarians). Recent applications of this perspective have focused specifically on cohabiting stepfamilies. In this scenario (as illustrated in this chapter's vignette), the stepfamily's status as an incomplete institution is further compounded when legal ties between biological and stepparents are lacking (Brown & Manning, 2009; Guzzo, Stykes, & Burgoyne, 2015; Stewart, 2005).

Racial and ethnic diversity within contemporary families.

Although many have embraced and advocated for more inclusive operational definitions of stepfamilies (e.g., Ganong & Coleman, 2017; Stewart, 2007; Sweeney, 2010), steep data requirements and challenges to properly identifying stepfamilies across diverse contexts make this difficult to accomplish (Stewart, 2007). This leads us to ask, if the theoretical perspectives applied to stepfamily living are not *inherently limited to* married stepfamilies, why does the lingering bias toward White, middle-class, remarried stepfamilies persist? Historically, prior research on stepfamily dynamics has been limited to families that readily *identify as* stepfamilies by explicitly defining household members' relationships to one another as being between a stepparent/stepchild. This seems a reasonable assumption, but prior work on boundary ambiguity suggests such a stipulation reinforces a bias toward the limited definition of *married* stepfamilies (see Brown & Manning, 2009).

Peyton and Avery are two women who moved in together about eight months ago (two years after Peyton's divorce). Peyton now identifies as a lesbian and Avery is attracted to both men and women. They have two children who live in their home. Avery had Leah six years ago and has had minimal contact with Leah's father. Zoey is eight years old and is Peyton's biological child from a prior marriage. Zoey considers herself close to her dad (George) but does not see him as often as she'd like now that Peyton and Avery are living together. Consider the following scenario pertaining to this family:

After work, Peyton rushed quickly to pick up Zoey and Leah at school. Under normal circumstances, this wouldn't be a big deal. But today was especially rushed as Leah's piano recital was scheduled for 7:30 p.m., and it was an hour's drive from their home in rush-hour traffic. In addition, the girls attend different elementary schools about 20 minutes apart. Peyton and Avery thought it best to not have the children transfer schools to better cope with the new family transition.

To make the day even more stressful, Zoey was sent to the principal's office for fighting at school. The past few weeks haven't been too challenging for Leah, but Zoey was still having difficulty coping with her parents' recent divorce. While Avery and Zoey enjoyed shared activities such as making homemade ice cream together, Peyton and Avery thought it best that Avery refrain from any stern conversations with Zoey—at least during the transition to being one big family. Since a meeting with the teacher fell under "disciplinary action," Peyton wound up having to pick up both girls from school to get a report from Zoey's teacher.

Peyton was pleased to learn from the teacher that the altercation was really not so bad. Apparently some other children had been teasing Zoey about having two "mommies" and she'd retaliated by putting earthworms in one of the kid's lunch boxes. The teacher reassured Peyton that Zoey's response was not too problematic and did not escalate to a fight; however, she wanted to make Peyton aware that Zoey might be experiencing some bullying in light of recent events. In looking at her watch after the meeting, Peyton was pleased to see she still had plenty of time to pick up Leah at her after-school program, grab a bite to eat with both of the girls, and then meet Avery at the venue in time for the recital.

Fast-forward 45 minutes. Peyton anxiously glances at her watch while the after-school program worker tries calling Avery for a third time. Unbeknownst to Peyton and Avery, Leah's school had recently put into practice a more stringent parent pick-up system. Any adult who was not the biological parent, legal guardian, or legal spouse of the child's parent had to complete a background check and be "on file" to pick up children. Fortunately, the situation was resolved just in time for Peyton, Leah, and Zoey to *just* make it to Leah's recital.

Analyzing the scenario:

- This stepfamily provides a unique opportunity to *apply* key tenets of the theoretical perspectives referenced in this chapter. Drawing on a symbolic interactionist perspective, what specific actions has this family taken to adapt to new family members and relationships in the family?
- In what ways do Peyton's experiences demonstrate that stepfamilies today remain an incomplete institution? Does this family appear to face additional challenges by being an LGBTQ+ stepfamily?
- How do differences in Leah's and Zoey's pathways into a stepfamily seem to be shaping their experiences differently?

Redefining Stepfamilies: An Empirical Application

I have asserted that traditional operational definitions of step-families greatly impede our ability to document the diversity characteristic of contemporary stepfamilies. Moreover, I have revisited Stewart's (2007) claims and demonstrated how this methodological shortcoming has led to a heteronormative, White, middle-class bias inherent in much of our research on stepfam-ilies to date. To demonstrate the implications of using different working definitions of stepfamilies, I draw on a nationally rep-resentative dataset, the 2014 Survey of Income and Program Participation (SIPP). Although many children are part of non-resident stepfamilies (i.e., have a biological parent who lives with a spouse or partner in a different household) or live in a shared physical custody arrangement, the SIPP, as a household-based survey, does not identify these children. Despite this shortcom-ing, the 2014 SIPP provides a unique opportunity to identify the resident living arrangements of children by collecting both parent and also partner relationship pointers for *all* household members, regardless of the household member's age. Accordingly, these data can be used to impose more- versus less-restrictive definitions on stepfamily living. I make use of descriptive analytic techniques to (a) produce updated prevalence estimates of children living in stepfamilies, paying careful attention to changes in estimates when using different operational definitions; (b) demonstrate the incomplete picture that traditional approaches to stepfamilies provide; and (c) describe the sociodemographic composition of various types of stepfamilies.

Table 2.1 demonstrates that our definitions of stepfamilies have implications for the number of children estimated to live in stepfamilies. For instance, when the most restrictive definition of stepfamilies—one that requires the child to be under age 18 and that the child's biological parent be married to someone of the opposite sex—is applied, we see that approximately four million children, or 6% of all children under age 18, live in stepfamily households. When children whose biological parent is cohabiting with an opposite-sex partner are included, this estimate increases by approximately 75%, to just over seven million, or 10% of all children under age 18, which is consistent with other analyses of the 2009 SIPP panel (see Manning et al., 2014). Removing the restriction on same-sex couples has a less pronounced change on the number of children living in a stepfamily, which remained approximately 1 in 10. The final, least restrictive definition of stepchildren includes both minor and adult stepchildren living with a stepparent (i.e., stepchildren 18 and older). When adult

TABLE 2.1 *Children Living in Resident Stepfamilies, Based on Different Definitions of "Stepfamily"*

	NUMBER OF CHILDREN	PERCENTAGE
Married heterosexual parents	4,024,267	5.8
Including cohabiting parents	7,005,547	10.2
Including same-sex parents	7,161,392	10.4
Including children age 18 and over	10,555,619	3.4[1]

Source: 2014 SIPP.

1. The denominator for stepchildren that includes stepchildren age 18 and over is composed of all individuals in the survey as opposed to just minor children. Therefore, the percentage of children living with a stepparent drops markedly. Estimates are weighted to account for survey design.

stepchildren are included along with minor stepchildren, the number of "children" living in a stepfamily rises even more, to approximately 10.5 million. In the end, the number of children living in a stepfamily household increases by 163% when moving from the most to the least restrictive definition of stepfamily.

Supplemental analyses (available on request) indicated that two-thirds of children in stepfamilies were identified by linking the child to both a biological and also a stepparent living in the household; however, nearly 30% of children who lived in a stepfamily would be overlooked from approaches that only consider the child's ties to individuals explicitly identified as "parents." This undercount occurs when the respondent (a) only identifies one parent for the child but (b) identifies a live-in partner of the child's biological parent, a situation common in cohabiting stepfamilies. Although less common, it is also important to note that nearly 5% of children living in stepfamilies did not live with *any* biological or adoptive parents (i.e., they were living with a stepparent or stepparents alone).

Table 2.2 showcases the sociodemographic composition of children in three types of resident stepfamilies: (a) heterosexual, married couple stepfamilies with minor children; (b) unmarried heterosexual cohabiting couple stepfamilies with minor children; and (c) stepfamilies with no restrictions on the child's age (can be age 18 and older), legal marriage, or the sexual orientation

TABLE 2.2 *Sociodemographic Characteristics of Children Living in Residential Stepfamilies, by Definition of Stepfamily Living*

	TRADITIONAL STEPFAMILY (I.E., HETEROSEXUAL MARRIED WITH MINOR CHILDREN)	COHABITING STEPFAMILIES WITH MINOR CHILDREN	LEAST RESTRICTIVE DEFINITION (I.E., NO RESTRICTIONS ON AGE OF CHILDREN, MARITAL TIES, OR SEX COMPOSITION)
	% OR MEAN	% OR MEAN	% OR MEAN
Child Characteristics			
Racial and Ethnic Identity			
White	60	55	56
Black	12	10	13
Hispanic	21	27	23
Other	7	8	8
Age	11.6	9.8	15.2
Parental Characteristics			
Highest Parental Degree Earned			
No degree	12	17	13
High school (GED)	32	38	34
Some college	37	37	36
Bachelor's degree +	19	8	17
Younger parent's age	35.1	34.5	39.0
Household Poverty Status			
Below poverty	15	26	18
100–149% poverty	11	18	12
150–249% poverty	27	18	21
250%+poverty	47	38	49
N	1,906	807	2,733

Source: 2014 SIPP. Estimates are weighted to account for survey design.

of the parents. Results align with prior assertions. Specifically, compared with children in traditional stepfamilies, children in heterosexual cohabiting stepfamilies (column 2) are about two years younger, have less educated and slightly younger parents, have lower incomes, and are more likely to be non-White. Compared with children in traditional stepfamilies, the children in heterosexual or same-sex, married or cohabiting couple stepfamilies, with children of any age (column 3), are more than five years older, and have parents who are about four years older with a similar level of education. These children have similar household incomes, and a slightly higher percentage are non-White. These results are similar to Stewart's analysis of the National Survey of Families and Household nearly 20 years ago (Stewart, 2001).

Law and Policy

Research emphasizing stepfamilies as an incomplete institution continues to draw special attention to the precarious legal standing of married stepparents in the United States. Unlike many other Western societies, stepparents in the United States are considered "legal strangers" and are not typically granted legal rights (e.g., visitation after dissolution) nor are they financially obligated to their stepchildren (e.g., child support). This is problematic because many stepparents make meaningful contributions to their stepchildren's daily lives (e.g., schooling, healthcare, religion) and may be considered by the child's biological parent and the child to be a viable parent (see Mason et al., 2002). However, there is substantial variation in laws regarding stepfamilies across states with some states granting stepparents and stepchildren legal rights and some not (Pollet, 2010). There is also wide variation in how federal policies (e.g., military benefits) and social programs (e.g., social security) treat stepfamily relationships (Stewart, 2018). Most stepfamily advocates have lobbied for granting some legal status to stepparents aside from adoption, which requires the biological, nonresident parent to relinquish his/her legal rights. Yet, some proposals such as requiring stepparents to pay child support to stepchildren after marital disruption may be met with resistance from "former" stepparents (Malia, 2005).

Such ambiguity is very likely more prevalent in cohabiting and LGBTQ+ stepfamilies because they have only recently been recognized by the state. As early as the 1970s, the legal context of stepparents in remarried families was used to label stepfamilies as an "incomplete institution" (Cherlin, 1978). While progress has been made in some states to address the legal rights of stepparents in the United States, these changes are slight and not uniform. Accordingly, contemporary stepfamilies remain an incomplete institution today and there have been few legal challenges to existing laws.

Recommendations for Practice

This chapter has shown that contemporary stepfamilies in the United States are increasingly complex in both status (i.e., cohabiting, married LGBTQ+) and also their formation (e.g., dissolution followed by subsequent re-partnering, union formation following a nonmarital birth). These distinct pathways into stepfamily living have implications for stepfamily dynamics and daily experiences (Ganong & Coleman, 2017). Lastly, structural inequalities in the United States based on racial and ethnic identity, class, and gender/sexuality have continued to reinforce a White, middle-class, and heteronormative bias in our understanding of stepfamily living and dynamics. Based on these factors, I present three recommendations for family practitioners and those seeking to facilitate more positive stepfamily dynamics.

First, I urge practitioners to adopt a more inclusive definition of stepfamilies. Failure to acknowledge or legitimate stepparent-child relationships within more complex stepfamilies overlooks important family dynamics associated with both parents' and children's health and well-being. Second, I encourage practitioners to emphasize the pathway into stepfamily living to provide family-specific strategies for fostering more positive relationships. In addition, given substantial racial, ethnic, and religious diversity within stepfamilies, it is ill advised to take to a "one size fits all" approach to creating and maintaining positive family dynamics in stepfamilies. Third, I believe it is important to acknowledge the biases inherent in most research on stepfamily living and dynamics. Research has made recent progress in considering family dynamics among less traditional stepfamilies (cohabiting stepfamilies, LGBTQ+ stepfamilies, etc.), but there is still much that remains unanswered. Moreover, our understanding of how less traditional stepfamilies operate pales in comparison with our understanding of remarried stepfamilies formed after marital dissolution. Accordingly, practitioners should strive to acknowledge biases in prior research head-on and be sensitive to the fact that many components of stepfamily living among less traditional stepfamilies remain uncharted territory, as it is unwise to assume these families experience similar challenges and lived experiences as remarried stepfamilies formed after a marital dissolution.

Conclusion

The *Journal of Marriage and Family*'s most recent decade in review on stepfamilies applauded recent attempts to acknowledge diversity in stepfamily living by acknowledging cohabitating stepfamilies (Sweeney, 2010). Yet, substantial room for improvement remains, and much research on stepfamilies in the United States continues to perpetuate a White, middle-class bias by maintaining restrictive definitions of stepfamily. Many studies impose restrictions on operational definitions of stepfamilies that exclude a number of stepfamilies (e.g., same sex, cohabiting, stepfamilies with adult stepchildren). Specifically, Taylor and colleagues' (2012) meta-analyses of theoretical perspectives widely used in stepfamily research was disproportionately limited to *married* stepfamilies (notable exceptions include Hofferth and Anderson, 2003; Stewart, 2005). Indeed, two influential, peer-reviewed publications (Brown & Manning, 2009; Hofferth, 2006) that provided explicit tests of family systems and evolutionary perspectives *but were not limited to married stepfamilies* were excluded from the review.

Findings demonstrate that various definitions of what constitutes a stepfamily influence our understanding of their prevalence in society. In the analysis presented here, the number of children living in stepfamilies in the United States more than doubled when moving from the most restrictive definition of stepfamilies (i.e., different sex, married with minor children) to the least restrictive definition, in which stipulations concerning sex composition, marital status, and the age of children were removed. Three in ten stepchildren in the analysis were not actually linked with a "stepparent" based on the household roster. Rather, they were identified based on the presence of a biological parent's live-in partner. Finally, a more restrictive definition of stepfamilies does, in fact, produce a profile of stepfamilies that is disproportionately White and well educated in comparison with less restrictive definitions of stepfamilies.

Recent scholarship advocating for a more inclusive definition of stepfamilies has received substantial attention (Ganong

& Coleman, 2017; Stewart, 2007), and their recommendations have been well received. Thus, I expect the continued restriction on married stepfamilies is most likely due, in part, to data constraints. The original analyses presented in this chapter made use of one of the most sophisticated survey designs to document children's living arrangements in the United States, and even it encounters notable shortcomings in adequately identifying stepfamily living. These data can only identify *residential* stepfamily households. Other widely used secondary data sources (e.g., the National Longitudinal Study of Adolescent to Adult Health) are able to identify adolescents' exposure to nontraditional stepfamilies, such as cohabiting stepfamilies; however, questions pertaining to the quality of relationship ties with cohabiting stepparents are quite limited in current data collection efforts and have limited our ability to embrace more inclusive definitions.

Herein, I have focused on children's experiences in stepfamilies in the United States, but my approach is far from exhaustive. I expect that no single approach can effectively address all of the pressing methodological challenges associated with "counting" stepfamilies. For instance, an approach focusing on stepfamilies in later life that identifies another important context for stepfamily living (see Papernow, 2013), which falls beyond the scope of this chapter, would most likely have devoted more substantial efforts to Brown and Lin's (2012) recent work on the increase in gray divorce and its implications for stepfamilies or "living apart together" (LAT) relationships (van der Pas, van Tilberg, & Sivlerstein, 2013). Given the primary scope of this book, however, my approach has been to strategically draw attention to the White, middle-class biases that remain. Future research should continue to investigate changes in stepfamily living in other societies and stepfamilies in very different geographic, social, religious, and cultural contexts.

Questions for Discussion

1. Given the current diversity in stepfamilies, is it appropriate to retain stepfamilies as a singular "type" of family? What are potential ways we might redefine stepfamilies so that all forms of stepfamilies are included, and so that diversity within stepfamilies is recognized?
2. In this chapter, I considered children to be "living in stepfamily" if a stepparent was not clearly identified, but their resident, biological parent was identified as having

a spouse or cohabiting partner. How do these results demonstrate boundary ambiguity in stepfamilies?

3. I estimated the number of children who resided in a stepfamily. How would you define a "nonresident" stepfamily? What sorts of research questions do you think would be most compelling in the study of nonresident stepfamily dynamics?

Additional Resources

Ganong, L., & Coleman, C. (2017). *Stepfamily relationships: Development, dynamics, and interventions,* 2nd ed. New York, NY: Springer.

Stewart, S. D. (2007). *Brave new stepfamilies: Diverse paths toward stepfamily living.* Thousand Oaks, CA: Sage.

The National Stepfamily Resource Center (http://www.stepfamilies.info/) provides additional information on stepfamilies including educational materials, support services, and research-based answers to common questions about stepfamilies.

References

Anderson, K. G., Hillard, K., & Lancaster, J. (1999). Paternal care by genetic fathers and stepfathers: Reports from Albuquerque men. *Evolution and Human Behavior, 20,* 405–431.

Berger, R. (2005). Gay stepfamilies: A triple-stigmatized group. *Families in Society: The Journal of Contemporary Social Services, 81,* 504–516.

Biblarz, T. J., & Stacey, J. (2010). How does the gender of parents matter? *Journal of Marriage and Family, 72,* 3–22.

Boyle, M. H., Jenkins, J. M., Georgiades, K., Cairney, J., Duku, E., & Racine, Y. (2004). Differential-maternal parenting behavior: Estimating within- and between-family effects on children. *Child Development, 75,* 1457–1476.

Brown, S. L. (2010). Marriage and child well-being: Research and policy perspectives. *Journal of Marriage and Family, 72,* 1059–1077.

Brown, S. L., & Lin, I. (2012). The gray divorce revolution: Rising divorce among middle-aged and older adults, 1990–2010. *The Journals of Gerontology: Series B, 67,* 731–741.

Brown, S. L., & Manning, W. D. (2009). Family boundary ambiguity and the measurement of family structure: The significance of cohabitation. *Demography, 46,* 85–101.

Bumpass, L., Sweet, J., & Martin, T. C. (1990). Changing patterns of remarriage. *Journal of Marriage and Family, 52,* 747–756.

Bzostek, S. H., McLanahan, S. S., & Carlson, M. J. (2012). Mothers' repartnering after a nonmarital birth. *Social Forces, 90,* 817–841.

Cancian, M., Meyer, D. R., & Cook, S. T. (2011). The evolution of family complexity from the perspective of nonmarital children. *Demography, 48,* 957–982.

Cancian, M., Meyer, D. R., Brown, P. R., & Cook, S. T. (2014). Who gets custody now? Dramatic changes in children's living arrangements after divorce. *Demography, 51,* 1381–1396.

Carlson, M. J., McLanahan, S. S., & England, P. (2004). Union formation in fragile families. *Demography, 41,* 237–261.

Cherlin, A. J. (1978). Remarriage as an incomplete institution. *American Journal of Sociology, 84,* 634–650.

Cherlin, A. J. (2004). The deinstitutionalization of American marriage. *Journal of Marriage and Family, 66,* 848–861.

Cherlin, A. J., & Furstenberg, F. F. (1994). Stepfamilies in the United States: A reconsideration. *Annual Review of Sociology, 20,* 359–381.

Coleman, J. S. (1988). Social capital in the creation of human capital: Sociological analysis of economic institutions. *American Journal of Sociology, 94,* 95–120.

Daly, M., & Wilson, M. I. (1996). Violence against stepchildren. *Current Directions in Psychological Science, 5,* 77–81.

Edin, K., & Kefalas, M. (2005). *Promises I can keep: Why poor women put motherhood before marriage.* Los Angeles, CA: University of California Press.

Ganong, L., & Coleman, M. (2017). *Stepfamily relationships: Development, dynamics, and interventions,* 2nd ed. New York, NY: Springer.

Gibson-Davis, C., & Rackin, H. (2014). Marriage or carriage? Trends in union context and birth type by education. *Journal of Marriage and Family, 76,* 506–519.

Goldberg, A. E., & Allen, K. R. (2013). Same-sex relationship dissolution and LGB stepfamily formation: Perspectives of young adults with LGB parents. *Family Relations, 62,* 529–544.

Goldberg, A. E., Gartrell, N. K., & Gates, G. (2014). *Research report on LGB-parent families.* Retrieved from https://escholarship.org/uc/item/7gr4970w

Goldstein, J. R., & Kenney, C. T. (2001). Marriage delayed or marriage foregone? New cohort forecasts of first marriage for U.S. women. *American Sociological Review, 66,* 506–519.

Guzzo, K. G., & Dorius, C. (2016). Challenges in measuring and studying multipartnered fertility in American Survey Data. *Population Research and Policy Review, 35,* 553–579.

Guzzo, K. B., & Furstenberg, F. F. (2007a). Multipartnered fertility among American men. *Demography, 44,* 583–601.

Guzzo, K. B., & Furstenberg, F. F. (2007b). Multipartnered fertility among young women with a nonmarital first birth: Prevalence and risk factors. *Perspectives on Sexual and Reproductive Health, 39,* 29–38.

Guzzo, K. B., Stykes, J. B., & Burgoyne, S. (2015). The American family by the numbers. In E. Redmont (Ed.) *The economics of the family: How the household affects markets and economic growth* (pp. 27–58). Santa Barbara, CA: Praeger.

Hofferth, S. L., & Anderson, K. G. (2003). Are all dads equal? Biology versus marriage as a basis for paternal investment. *Journal of Marriage and Family, 65,* 212–232.

Hofferth, S. L. (2006). Residential father family type and child well-being: Investment versus selection. *Demography, 43,* 53–77.

King, V. (2006). The antecedents and consequences of adolescents' relationships with stepfathers and nonresident fathers. *Journal of Marriage and Family, 68,* 910–928.

King, V. (2009). Stepfamily formation: Implications for adolescent ties to mothers, nonresident fathers, and stepfathers. *Journal of Marriage and Family, 71,* 954–968.

King, V., Boyd, L. M., & Thorsen, M. L. (2015). Adolescents' perceptions of family belonging in stepfamilies. *Journal of Marriage and Family, 77,* 761–774.

Kreider, R. M., & Ellis, R. (2011). Living arrangements of children: 2009. Retrieved February 8, 2019, from https://www.census.gov/library/publications/2011/demo/p70-126.html

Lichter, D. T., McLaughlin, D. K., Kephart, G., & Landry, D. J. (1992). Race and the retreat from marriage: A shortage of marriageable men? *American Sociological Review, 57,* 781–799.

Lichter, D. T., Sassler, S., & Turner, R. N. (2014). Cohabitation, post-conception unions, and the rise in nonmarital fertility. *Social Science Research, 47,* 134–147.

Lundberg, S., Pollak, R. A., & Stearns, J. (2016). Family inequality: Diverging patterns in marriage, cohabitation, and childbearing. *The Journal of Economic Perspectives, 30,* 79–101.

MacDonald, W. L., & DeMaris, A. (2002). Stepfather-stepchild relationship quality: The stepfathers' demand for conformity and the biological father's involvement. *Journal of Family Issues, 23,* 121–137.

Malia, S. E. (2005). Balancing family members' interests regarding stepparent rights and obligations: A social policy challenge. *Family Relations, 54,* 298–319.

Manning, W. D., Brown, S. L., & Stykes, J. B. (2014). Family complexity among children in the United States. *Annals of the Academy of Political and Social Sciences, 654,* 48–65.

Manning, W. D., Fettro, M. F., & Lamidi, E. (2014). Child well-being in same-sex parent families: Review of research prepared for American Sociological Association Amicus Brief. *Population Research and Policy Review, 33,* 485–502.

Marsiglio, W., & Hinojosa, R. (2007). Managing the multifather family: Stepfathers as father allies. *Journal of Marriage and Family, 69,* 845–862.

Mason, M. A., Harrison-Jay, S., Svare, G. M., & Wolfinger, N. H. (2002). Stepparents: De facto parents or legal strangers? *Journal of Family Issues, 23,* 507–522.

McLanahan, S. S. (2004). Diverging destinies: How children are faring under the second demographic transition. *Demography, 41,* 607–27.

McLanahan, S. S. (2009). Fragile families and the reproduction of poverty. *Annals of the American Academy of Political and Social Science, 621,* 111–131.

Moore, M. R. (2008). Gendered power relations among women: A study of household decision making in Black, lesbian stepfamilies. *American Sociological Review, 73,* 335–356.

Papernow, P. L. (2013). *Surviving and thriving in stepfamily relationships.* New York, NY: Routledge.

Payne, K. K. (2018). *First divorce rate in the U.S., 2016.* Retrieved from https://doi.org/10.25035/ncfmr/fp-18-15.

Payne, K. K. (2018). *First marriage rate in the U.S., 2016.* Retrieved from https://doi.org/10.25035/ncfmr/fp-18-14.

Pollet, S. L. (2010). Still a patchwork quilt: A nationwide survey of state laws regarding stepparent rights and obligations. *Family Court Review, 48,* 528–540.

Popenoe, D. (1994). The evolution of marriage and the problem of stepfamilies: A biosocial perspective. In A. Booth & J. F. Dunn (Eds.) *Stepfamilies: Who benefits? Who does not?* (pp. 3–28). Hillsdale, NJ: Lawrence Erlbaum Associates.

Raley, R. K. (1996). A shortage of marriageable men? A note on the role of cohabitation in Black-White differences in marriage rates. *American Sociological Review, 61,* 973–983.

Rindfuss, R. R. (1991). The young adult years: Diversity, structural change, and fertility. *Demography, 28,* 493–512.

Sherkat, D. E., Powell-Williams, M., Maddox, G., & de Vries, K. M. (2011). Religion, politics, and support for same-sex marriage in the United States, 1988–2008. *Social Science Research, 40,* 167–180.

Smock, P. J. (2000). Cohabitation in the United States: An appraisal of research themes, findings, and implications. *Annual Review of Sociology, 26,* 1–20.

Stewart, S. D. (2001). Contemporary American stepparenthood: Integrating cohabiting and nonresident stepparents. *Population Research and Policy Review, 20,* 345–364.

Stewart, S. D. (2005). Boundary ambiguity in stepfamilies. *Journal of Family Issues, 26,* 1002–1029.

Stewart, S. D. (2007). *Brave new stepfamilies: Diverse paths toward stepfamily living.* Thousand Oaks, CA: Sage.

Stewart. S. D. (2018). *Stepfamily laws and policies in the United States: Lessons from the west.* Paper presented at Old bonds, new ties: Understanding family transitions in re-partnerships, remarriages, and step-families in Asia. November 19-20, 2018. Asia Research Institute, National University of Singapore.

Sweeney, M. M. (2010). Remarriage and stepfamilies: Strategic sites for family scholarship in the 21st century. *Journal of Marriage and Family, 72,* 667–84.

Taylor, P., Morin, R., & Wang, W. (2011). *The public renders a split verdict on changes in family structure.* Retrieved from http://www.pewsocialtrends.org/2011/02/16/the-public-renders-a-split-verdict-on-changes-in-family-structure/?src=family-interactive.

Taylor, A. C., Robila, M., & Fisackerly, B. (2012). Theory use in stepfamily research. In M. A. Fine and F. F. Fincchum (Eds.) *Handbook of family theories: A content-based approach* (pp. 280–295). New York, NY: Routledge.

Teachman, J. (2007). Race, military service, and marital timing: Evidence from the NLSY-79. *Demography, 44,* 389–404.

Tillman, K. H. (2008). Coresident sibling composition and the academic ability, expectations, and performance of youth. *Sociological Perspectives, 51,* 679–711.

van der Pas, S., van Tilburg, T. G., & Silverstein, M. (2013). Stepfamilies in later life. *Journal of Marriage and Family, 75,* 1065–1069.

van Eeden-Moorefield, B., Pasley, K., Crosbie-Burnett, M., & King, E. (2012). Explaining couple cohesion in different types of gay families. *Journal of Family Issues, 33,* 182–201.

Wu, L. (2008). Cohort estimates of nonmarital fertility for U.S. women. *Demography, 45,* 193–207.

CHAPTER THREE

African American Stepfamilies

Chalandra M. Bryant, PhD, University of Georgia

Introduction

Studies of stepfamilies rarely include race as a central component. Race is usually ignored or incorporated as a variable that is not of central interest. Consequently, very rarely do researchers focus solely on African American stepfamilies despite their history and unique experiences. Family scholar Francesca Adler-Baeder and her colleagues explain: "Shaped by their socio-historical context, African American families tend to operate as a 'pedi-focal' family system, centered on the children and are characterized by a communal-oriented philosophy, permeability of family boundaries, movement of children among households, and shared parenting among multiple parents" (Adler-Baeder et al., 2010, p. 396). Not only does this quote distinguish African American families from many other families, but it also suggests that parenting a child other than one's own offspring is common among African Americans. Despite that childrearing history, little is known about African American stepfamilies. This chapter will address conceptual frameworks guiding studies of families, stepfamilies, and African Americans; the sociohistorical context in which African Americans are situated; demographic characteristics of the group; and findings from recent research. Note that both the terms African American and Black are used in this chapter. The U.S. Census Bureau uses "Black," but Black and African American are generally used interchangeably in research. When history is discussed (e.g., movement from Africa), the term "African American" can be inaccurate.

Guiding Frameworks and Theories

Theories are ideas that help us understand and interpret research findings. Theories can be defined as "empirically testable interconnected ideas that explain some phenomenon" (Chibucos, Leite, & Weis, 2005, p. 6). Numerous theories, frameworks, and models can be used to guide studies of families in general, and stepfamilies in particular. Theories that are particularly useful for studying stepfamilies include family solidarity, family systems, family stress, and boundary ambiguity; because those theories are frequently mentioned in the stepfamily literature, they are explained in this chapter. These guiding frameworks have also been used in studies of African Americans more generally.

Family Solidarity Model

The Family Solidarity Model posits that a fundamental organizing feature of any given family is the bond between members of that family. Family dimensions such as affect, closeness, and support are highlighted. The model does not focus solely on financial support (giving or receiving money), as such exchanges can be constrained by poverty (Bengtson, Giarrusso, Mabry, & Silverstein, 2002; McChesney & Bengtson, 1988; Taylor, Chatters, Woodward, & Brown, 2013). Support can take many forms; for example, it can be financial, social, or even emotional. This model also acknowledges conflict in families, which is important because, even in healthy families, conflict is unavoidable (Bengtson, Giarrusso, Mabry, & Silverstein, 2002; Connidis & McMullin, 2002). A conflictual family interaction does not necessarily mean that a family lacks cohesion or that a family lacks positive sentiments about its members. This notion is reflected in the solidarity-conflict model, an extension of the family solidarity model. A study using indicators of family solidarity—such as frequency of contact, social support, and relationship quality—indicated that mothers who divorce and remarry and have custody of the offspring have greater parent-child solidarity than do single-mother families (White, 1994). Research has also indicated that for some stepchildren, family solidarity develops as a result of the birth of half-siblings (Ganong, Coleman, & Jamison, 2011).

Using a sample of African Americans from the 2001–2003 National Survey of American life, two studies assessed dimensions of solidarity such as association (behaviors between family members), affect (closeness between family members), and function (exchanges of social support between family members). The findings suggested that family-centered individuals experienced low levels of negative interaction with their relatives (Nguyen, Chatters, & Taylor, 2016; Taylor et al., 2013).

Another study based on this same survey, using the solidarity model as a guide, showed that African Americans who felt high levels of closeness to relatives (assessed with a single item asking *"How close do you feel toward your family members?"*) were more likely to receive various types of instrumental support such as transportation assistance, help with chores, financial assistance, and help during illnesses. Moreover, they were also more likely to offer three of the four forms of instrumental support examined in the study: transportation assistance, help with chores, and help during illness (Cross, Nguyen, Chatters, & Taylor, 2018). Thus, consistent with the family solidarity model, degree of family cohesion is linked to exchange of aid between family members (McChesney & Bengtson, 1988).

Family Systems

Studies of stepfamilies are often guided by family systems theory (Dupuis, 2010; Shapiro, 2014). This theory posits that families are defined by connections between family members and the family's unique roles, rules, and resources (Bowen, 1978; Minuchin, 1974; Satir, 1967). The formation of stepfamilies may generate imbalance in family roles, rules, resources, and other aspects of family life change. For example, James, a teenager, may have had a curfew of 10 p.m. but finds that in his new stepfamily home the rules are different; he must now abide by a curfew of 9 p.m. because his stepsiblings and stepparent have firmly established that as the appropriate time to return home. Another example may involve household chores. Perhaps in one household the children are responsible for taking out the

Among African Americans, family dynamics in cohabiting stepfamilies and married stepfamilies are more similar than different.

garbage each night after dinner, but in the stepfamily household there are no rules regarding chores. In newly merged families, strife might ensue if the set of children who are used to that chore must continue with no help from their stepsiblings. Clearly, a change must occur for after-dinner chores to operate smoothly.

If changes are balanced with a certain amount of stability and adaptability, then stepfamilies are more likely to be successful (Jensen & Shafer, 2013). In this particular situation, to maintain the stability of the rule regarding children doing chores, perhaps all of the children will be asked to take out the garbage. Adaptability can be reflected in the parents' decision to ensure that all the children share this particular chore, or perhaps create a list of various chores that rotate from child to child. Such actions may help generate a sense of fairness, which, in turn, may increase the stepfamily's likelihood of success.

Cooperation is valued in African American families; members expect others in the family to engage in decision making. Intergenerational interdependency is greater in African American families compared with other groups (for review, see Johnson-Garner & Meyers, 2002). A critical theme that emerged in a study of African American children centered around adaptability, defined as "the ability to adjust to family roles in response to change" (Johnson-Garner & Meyer, 2003, p. 264). African American children in that study were more resilient when the family system was able to adapt to environmental stressors.

Family systems acknowledges that various systems exist in a family, such as a parent-parent subsystem, a parent-child subsystem, and a sibling-sibling subsystem. A crisis in one subsystem (e.g., parent-parent) of the stepfamily can "spill over" into another family subsystem (e.g., parent-child). For example, parents may have an argument about money and that creates an argument with the child about something they want to buy.

Family Stress

Family stress suggests that stressful events in a family may interfere with a family's equilibrium and functioning (McCubbin & Figley, 1983). Stepparent-stepchild relationships can be more conflictual and stressful than biological family relationships, which can make family adjustment and stability challenging (Jensen & Shafer, 2013), which in turn may hinder the development of positive stepfamily relationships (Jensen & Shafer, 2013). Some examples of how family stress might affect stepparent-stepchild interactions include arguments about fair and equitable treatment of children from previous relationships merged into one household (as in the example about chores), or arguments regarding differences in parenting styles and discipline.

Not only can the concept of stress be used to study stepfamilies, but it can also be used to study African American families. This is because family stress can be viewed through a sociocultural lens; examples of sociocultural stressors include discrimination and oppression (Murry, Butler-Barnes, Mayo-Gamble, & Inniss-Thompson, 2018). Exposure to racism (a sociocultural stressor) can negatively affect family members by contributing to increased depressive symptoms, which in turn has been associated with family members exhibiting less supportive behaviors (Murry, Brown, Brody, Cutrona, & Simons, 2001). W. E. B. Du Bois (born 1868; died 1963), an African American sociologist, teacher, writer, and activist, noted that because race is a salient variable in studies of stress in African Americans, researchers need to assess the influence of financial and sociopolitical forces disproportionately impinging upon African American families (Murry et al., 2018). Similarly, Rand Conger and his colleagues (2002) found that psychological distress (stemming from financial hardship) experienced by Black parents impedes the use of effective stress-coping behaviors, which in turn negatively affects parenting. Given that such issues influence African American families in general, they also very likely influence African American stepfamilies.

Boundary Ambiguity

Boundary ambiguity is another theory that is particularly useful to guide studies of stepfamilies. The notion of boundary ambiguity, developed by Pauline Boss, grew out of family stress theory. Boundary ambiguity occurs when family members have unclear perceptions about who is *in* or *not in* the family (Boss, Bryant, & Mancini, 2017). For example, a wife may consider her cohabiting partner a member of the family whereas her children may not (Manning & Brown, 2006). In stepfamilies, differences in these perceptions are associated with lower quality relationships and greater risk of union dissolution (Stewart, 2005). African Americans are unique in that they have a history of accepting individuals referred to as "fictive kin." Fictive kin are people who are not related by marriage or blood, but nevertheless view one another as family or kin (Bryant, 2018; Sussman, 1976). These are important members of African American family networks as they are afforded status similar to that of family members (see Bryant, 2018; Taylor et al., 2013). Given the tradition of African

Americans accepting individuals into the family as fictive kin, it is surprising that relatively little is known about the roles that race and ethnicity play in boundary ambiguity (Stewart, 2005). This is an important avenue for further research. Sociologists Susan Brown and Wendy Manning examined family boundary ambiguity in reports of family structure obtained from mothers and their adolescent offspring. Their goal was to determine whether two family members agreed or differed in their reports of who was "in" or "not in" the family. Essentially, this was an assessment of shared versus divergent perceptions of family structure. Findings suggest that a high level of ambiguity existed in cohabiting stepfamilies (Brown & Manning, 2009). Only 30% of mother-adolescent pairs in which the adolescent, mother, or both reported being in a cohabiting family concurred that they lived in a cohabiting stepfamily, with the mother more likely to recognize the cohabiting partner than the child (Brown & Manning, 2009). Differences were most pronounced for Blacks. Three percent of Black adolescents reported residing in a cohabiting stepfamily versus 10% of their mothers, compared with overall figures of 3% and 5%, respectively. According to Brown and Manning, "Black adolescent-mother pairs were more likely to disagree about whether they reside in a cohabiting family" (2009, p. 95).

African American families typically have more permeable family boundaries, and have more flexible social roles than do White families. While "greater permeability of family boundaries among minorities may increase the odds that family members' definitions of family will clash," on the other hand "... less rigid family definitions may lower the likelihood of conflict" (Stewart, 2005, p. 1006). Definitions regarding who is in or not in the family are sociohistorically rooted.

Sociohistorical Overview of African American Families

Identifying unique features of African American families is a challenging task, "because of the alterable nature of culture and the demographic factors associated with Black history in the United States" (Roopnarine, 2015, p. 159). Typical references to African Americans can be traced to West and Central Africa or such references may, for example, focus on Blacks whose history was linked to enslavement. Enslaved Africans brought numerous beliefs and social practices to the United States that have not only been sustained over time, but that have also been mixed with beliefs and social practices of Native Americans, European cultures, and slaves from other African countries.

It was believed that practices such as unmarried childbearing and mother-headed households were a means by which some African Americans coped with the restrictions they had to bear during enslavement in the United States, including not being permitted to legally marry. Such practices were characterized as being unique to African Americans yet they have actually been observed in other parts of the world, including other places where Black slave trade was prominent, such as the Caribbean. This suggests that perhaps the practices are African traditions adapted as a result of enslavement experiences. (For review, see Roopnarine, 2015.)

Numerous journal articles compare African American family patterns with those of other racial and ethnic groups. The median age at first marriage among women in the United States is 27 years (Raley, Sweeney, & Wondra, 2015). Researchers typically point out that Black women tend to marry later in life compared with White women; among Black women the median age at first marriage is about four years higher than for White women (Raley et al., 2015). Moreover, Black women have higher rates of divorce and are less likely to marry compared with White women (McLanahan & Sawhill, 2015). Factors that have been attributed to lower marriage rates among African Americans have focused on "missing men" and a lopsided marriage market. Such factors include the availability of "marriageable" men (i.e., men with steady employment), higher mortality rates among Black men, and higher incarceration rates compared with other racial groups (Harknett & McLanahan, 2004; Pettit & Western, 2004; Wildeman, 2009; Wilson, 1987).

Much of the literature overlooks the fact that in the early 20th century, marital unions were common among Black families (Wilson, 1987). The patterns of declining marriage did not always exist. For example, Black women did not always marry at later ages than White women. There was a time in history (1890 through 1940) when Black women married at younger ages than White women (Elliott et al., 2012).

These diverging patterns began around the 1960s and since then have grown. Declining employment rates, increasing incarceration, and a history of enslavement do not fully explain the patterns observed. The patterns are partly explained by significant changes in ideas regarding family arrangements, which have essentially relegated marriage to something that is optional—not something that one must enter into to have a family. This phenomenon is widespread and not limited to African Americans. Although viewed as optional, marriage is still desirable (Raley, Sweeney, & Wondra,

2015). In addition, women's financial contributions to the household have increased relative to men's such that women can more easily support themselves and their children without a husband (Raley, Sweeney, & Wondra, 2015). The increase of women in the labor force contributed to changes in family and marriage patterns. It is important to note, though, that African American women historically have always had to contribute financially to their households (Benokraitis, 2008; Bryant, Wickrama, Bolland, Bryant, Cutrona, & Stanik, 2010; Durr & Hill, 2006; Haynes, 2000; Tucker, 2000). Financial circumstances have become an increasingly important factor for marriage, with marriage increasingly reserved for the middle class. Hence, the marriage gap between African Americans and Whites (and other racial and ethnic groups) has widened as financial circumstances have become increasingly germane to the decision to marry. Here is a story about how one family overcame challenges associated with childcare, support, and finances.

When Yvette and Koffi married, Yvette had one child and Koffi had nine. At the time of the interview, Koffi and Yvette had been married for 15 years, and their children ranged in age from 18 to 33. Despite not having primary custody of all the children, some of the children stayed with the couple for long periods. Some of the children joined Yvette and Koffi's at home for birthdays, weekends, holidays, and summers. Both sets of parents provided help with childcare. They even acquired the support of Koffi's former wives and Yvette's former partner for help with childcare. Money was an issue. Kofi was an author, amateur chef, and photojournalist, and Yvette was a marketing executive. Both quit their jobs and started a marketing firm together (using space in their home) in an attempt to improve their financial standing. The couple even changed how and where they shopped. They searched for bargains, used coupons, and avoided expensive stores. They focused on what they felt mattered for the family—not new clothes or new cars. These endeavors enabled them to pay for child support, family trips, summer camps, and even the first year of college for each child. The children knew that Yvette and Koffi cared for them. What mattered? What was important? Primarily, it was making the children "feel good about themselves" and exposing them to different experiences. With that in mind, if a child had a prom, that child went—even if it meant that Yvette or Koffi had to postpone getting something they wanted. (See article by Nance-Nash, 2004.)

- Analyzing the scenario: How does this stepfamily demonstrate the unique features and challenges of Black stepfamilies?
- In stepfamilies, especially when there are complicated child custody arrangements, financial and childcare responsibilities are often unclear. What were some strategies used by Yvette and Koffi to navigate this terrain?

Yvette and Koffi handled challenges by using support from extended family members. Extended family support (e.g., grandparents helping with childcare) is prevalent in African American families— including stepfamilies. Yvette and Koffi engaged in personal sacrifices and put their children's needs before their own. Because they treated all the children in the same manner— including paying for the first year of college for each child and for the children on family vacations— family solidarity appeared high and boundary ambiguity low. The cou-

Stepfamily relationships "spill over." Stepfathers who feel love and trust for their spouse tend to feel respected and loved by their stepchildren.

ple's strong parent-parent subsystem most likely engendered feelings of security among the children, which probably generated healthy parent-child relationships.

Structural Diversity of African American Families

Interpreting the data on family diversity can be overwhelming and figures come from different sources. There are numerous government-funded, nationally representative surveys of children and families, and the U.S. Census Bureau provides information in various forms. Data from multiple surveys indicate that African American stepfamilies are more structurally diverse than those of other racial and ethnic groups. First, they are more likely to be formed as a consequence of nonmarital childbearing rather than as a consequence of divorce. About 71% of children born to African Americans are nonmarital births (Hamilton, Martin, & Ventura, 2011). For this reason, marriage that involves children from prior unions among African Americans is typically a first marriage, instead of a remarriage (Adler-Baeder et al., 2010; Moore & Chase-Lansdale, 2001). Blacks experienced a 16% decline in married-couple households between 1995 and 2012 (Lamidi, 2014). Second, there are often unrelated male cohabiting partners living within "single-mother" families (Dunlap, Golub, & Benoit, 2010; Lichter, Turner, & Sassler, 2010). Overall, 40% of American children will for some period reside in a cohabiting home (Manning, 2015) before the age of 12 years. The percentage of cohabiting households among all households is relatively similar across racial and ethnic groups, at 6% among African Americans, 6% among Whites, 4% among Asians, and 9% among Hispanics in 2012 (Lamidi, 2014).

The decrease in marriage rates among African Americans is not a reflection of a decline in the value of marriage or family. When examining the country as a whole, census reports suggest that married couples are the most common group among family households in the United States but there are vast racial and ethnic differences in marriage rates. Based on data from the U.S. Census Bureau, nearly 80% of non-Hispanic Whites and Asians are in married family groups compared with 60% of Hispanics and 43% of Blacks (Vespa, Lewis, & Kreider, 2013). Again, it is important to point out that just because a group's marriage rates are low does not mean that marriage is viewed as unimportant by that group. Kathryn Edin, a sociologist, has written extensively about this topic. She and her colleague, Joanna Reed, stated that "... Black Americans [women] have the same marital aspirations as other women ..." (Edin & Reed, 2005, p. 119). Their study of families in low-income neighborhoods in Philadelphia revealed that both Black and White single mothers had complex attitudes about children and marriage:

... these mothers generally believe that having children before marriage is not the ideal way of doing things, they must calculate the risks and rewards of the partnerships available to them and balance their marital aspirations with their strong moral views about the conditions under which it is right and proper to marry ... (Edin & Reed, 2005, p. 124).

Further evidence of the structural diversity of families can be found in the proportion of mother-only family groups. Single-mother households are found across racial and ethnic categories, but there is a large variation across racial and ethnic groups—about 29% of Blacks, 8% of non-Hispanic Whites, 18% of Hispanics, and 6% of Asians are in mother-only family groups. Structural barriers to marriage (such as the availability of marriageable men) have been cited as a reason for these marriage gaps (Cohen & Pepin, 2018). William Julius Wilson underscored the importance of local availability of marriageable men for women, and he defined unmarriageable in terms of being unemployed, incarcerated, deceased, or already married (Wilson, 1987; Wilson, Neckerman, & Rainwater, 1985). Even for established couples who have children, economic instability can be a barrier to marriage (Gibson-Davis,

Edin, & McLanahan, 2005). In addition to barriers, attitudes have also played a role. Lack of availability of marriageable men has been linked to more negative attitudes about marriage (Harknett & McClanahan, 2004). The likelihood of marriage decreases for those women who delay marriage to focus on education and careers. A reason highlighted in the literature is that men tend to marry younger women, and women tend not to marry rather than marry "down" to a man with a lower level of education and income than themselves (England & McClintock, 2009). There is far less racial variation in single-father family groups, which are much less common than single-mother families regardless of race. For example, less than 5% of families are single fathers with their children, because mothers get custody of the children the majority of the time.

Other census data quantify the number of children living with one or both of their biological parents. Seventy percent of non-Hispanic White children under 18 resided with both of their biological parents in 2014, as did 59% of Hispanic children. But only slightly more than one-third of Black children lived with both biological parents during that period (U.S. Census Bureau, 2014). For all children, poorer child outcomes (e.g., teen pregnancy, lower educational achievement) have been linked to single-parent families; however, many children raised in such homes have, indeed, thrived and achieved great success (Cavanaugh & Fomby, 2012; Cherlin, 1999). While the notion that single-parent families are directly linked to negative outcomes for children is pervasive, the preponderance of evidence indicates that it is not family structure itself but, instead, economic distress—more common in single-parent homes—that is primarily responsible for negative outcomes for children (Fomby & Cherlin, 2007). Remarriage may alleviate some of the economic stress single-parent households experience, but parents tend to provide less economic support to stepchildren compared with their biological children (Pruett, Calsyn, & Jensen, 1993; White, 1994). Children living with a stepparent tend to be better off economically compared with children in single-parent households, but their standard of living tends to be lower compared with those children living with both of their biological parents (Kreider & Fields, 2005; Thomson, 1994). Some researchers suggest there is little difference in socioemotional outcomes between children raised in single-parent homes and those raised in stepfamilies once income is controlled (Stewart, 2007).

Studies have shown that the effect of family structure on children's outcomes varies by the child's age. For instance, family structure at birth influences the health outcomes of young children. Sociologist Wendy Manning (2015) summarized differences in outcomes by age. Children born into families with cohabiting parents tend to have low birth weight compared with those born into families with married parents, with their lower weight continuing through five years of age. Children born into families with cohabiting parents are also more likely to experience asthma and obesity compared with those born into families with married parents. Yet, these two groups of children have similar levels of health (obesity, asthma) when family structure is assessed at older ages. Family stability is the factor that consistently has a negative influence on child health whether the parents are married or cohabiting. Young children residing in homes with married stepparents tend to experience more positive outcomes than those children residing in homes with cohabiting stepparents. At age five, children residing in families with married stepparents tend to have higher literacy scores and better academic outcomes compared with children residing in families with cohabiting stepparents. Likewise, children from birth to 12 years of age also tend to exhibit better academic outcomes if they are residing in families with married stepparents (Manning, 2015). Findings for adolescents are different. When comparing adolescents residing in families with cohabiting stepparents to those residing in families with married stepparents (after controlling for sociodemographic factors and parents' health), no significant differences were found in terms of academic achievement and physical and emotional well-being (Manning, 2015).

Similar levels of depressive symptoms have been observed in teens when they move into married and cohabiting stepparent families, but adolescents living in cohabiting stepfamily households exhibit more depressive symptoms than do those adolescents living in married stepfamily households (Langton & Berger, 2011, as reported by Manning, 2015).

Following overall racial and ethnic differences in marriage rates, Whites are more likely than other groups to remarry after divorce or the death of a spouse. Asians, Blacks, and Hispanics are less likely to remarry (Livingston, Parker, & Rohal, 2014). Asians have higher rates of marriage, but they have lower rates of remarriage, as they are less likely to divorce. Nevertheless, the difference is greatest between Whites and Blacks. As shown in Figure 3.1, in 2012, 60% of Whites remarried compared with only 48% of Blacks. Most remarriages involve children from previous relationships and four in ten families in the United States are stepfamilies (Livingston et al., 2014; Parker, 2011). More than 60% of women who remarried have children from previous marriages in the household (Pew Research Center, 2015).

Remarriage, however, is just one way in which stepfamilies are formed. Stepfamilies can arise through nonmarital childbearing and cohabitation. Cohabiting unions with children have increased significantly over the decades; in the 2000s, children were present in 40% of cohabiting unions compared with 20% in the early 1980s. Cohabitation is typically more likely to occur among women who have low levels of education (Manning, 2015). The structure of cohabiting stepfamily households is often more complex than married stepfamily households. Compared with married parent families, cohabiting

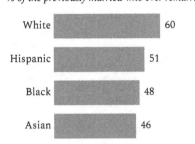

Whites Most Likely to Remarry
% of the previously married who ever remarried

White	60
Hispanic	51
Black	48
Asian	46

Note: Blacks, Asians and Whites include only non-Hispanics. Hispanics are of any race. Previously married are those eligible for remarriage. Based on people ages 18 and older.
Source: Pew Research Center analysis of 2012 American Community Survey (1% IPUMS)

FIGURE 3.1   Percent Remarried Among Previously Married by Race and Ethnicity

Source: http://assets.pewresearch.org/wp-content/uploads/sites/3/2014/11/2014-11-14_remarriage-final.pdf

households are more likely to include stepsiblings or half-siblings. About 37% of children in cohabiting households reside with stepsiblings or half-siblings (Manning, 2015). Statistics vary by race and ethnicity. In 2016, 16% of children in cohabiting stepfamilies were Black, compared with 11% in married stepparent families. Twenty-five percent of children in cohabiting stepparent families were Hispanic compared with 22% in married stepparent families. The same percentage of children in cohabiting and married stepparent families were Asian, at 3%. More than half (51%) of children in cohabiting stepparent families were White, compared with 58% who were in married stepparent families (Eickmeyer, 2017).

Having step-relatives is common for people in the United States. According to data provided by the Pew Research Center (2011), three groups are significantly more likely to have step-relatives—Blacks, individuals lacking a college degree, and young people (see Table 3.1). Blacks (60%) are more likely than Whites (39%) or Hispanics (46%) to have step-relatives. The percentage of Black, White, and Hispanic children who *reside* in a stepfamily is relatively similar. Data based on the 2009 Survey of Income and Program Participation (SIPP) indicate that about 15% of White children, 17% of Black children, and 17% of Hispanic children live in a "blended" family, that is, with a stepparent, stepsibling, or half-sibling (see Figure 3.2). This measure, however, only captures stepfamily members related by marriage and

---

Demographics of Stepfamilies

% who have ...

	Any step relative	Step or half sibling	Step-parent	Step-child
Men	40	27	17	15
Women	44	33	19	12
18–29	52	44	33	2
30–49	45	35	23	14
50–64	39	23	10	18
65+	34	16	2	22
White	39	26	18	14
Black	60	45	21	19
Hispanic	46	38	18	8
College	33	21	15	11
Some College	45	34	21	12
HS or less	47	34	19	16
East	39	27	13	11
Midwest	39	28	19	12
South	44	32	19	15
West	45	32	20	13

Note: Hispanics are of any race, Whites and Blacks include only non-Hispanics. Only those who have ever been married were asked if they have stepchildren; however, the percentages reported in the table are based on all respondents.
Source: Pew Social & Demographic Trends survey
(Oct 1–21, 2010; n = 2,691)

PEW RESEARCH CENTER

TABLE 3.1 Demographics of Stepfamilies and Percent Who Have Step-Relatives

Source: http://www.pewsocialtrends.org/2011/01/13/a-portrait-of-stepfamilies/

does not include unmarried partners and their children.

Quantifying stepfamilies among African Americans is particularly challenging, because African Americans may interpret the terms stepsibling, stepparent, and half-sibling differently, given their more permeable family boundaries. For example, Table 3.1 delineates four categories of steps: (a) any step-relative; (b) step- or half-sibling; (c) stepparent; and (d) stepchild. "Any step-relative" is an extremely broad category and vague, because some individuals may count a step-aunt or step-cousin when responding to that category whereas others may not. The use of the category "step or half-sibling" is also broad and vague because, for example, some individuals may instead identify a "half brother" as simply "brother," given the blood tie and cultural norms. In contrast with Table 3.1, Figure 3.2 focuses specifically on residing with step-relatives. (See Box 3.1 and 3.2 for discussions of the difficulties of defining stepfamily members.) Decennial census reports are used to count the number of U.S. residents. The U.S. Census Bureau question posed to collect those data can be found in Figure 3.3. The census asks how the "householder" is related to each member of the household. The census considers a householder to be the person whose name appears on the mortgage or lease as long as that person is 15 years of age or older.

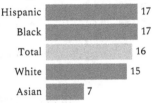

One-in-six kids is living in a blended family

% of children living with a stepparent, stepsibling or half-sibling

Hispanic	17
Black	17
Total	16
White	15
Asian	7

Note: Whites, Blacks and Asians include only single-race non-Hispanics. Hispanics are of any race.
Source: U.S. Census Bureau, Survey of Income and Program Participation (SIPP) 2009 estimates

FIGURE 3.2   Percent of Children Living in a Stepfamily
Source: http://assets.pewresearch.org/wp-content/uploads/sites/3/2015/12/2015-12-17_parenting-in-america_FINAL.pdf.

How is this person related to Person 1? *Mark (X) ONE box.*

☐ Husband or wife

☐ Biological son or daughter

☐ Adopted son or daughter

☐ Stepson or stepdaughter

☐ Brother or sister

☐ Father or mother

☐ Grandchild

☐ Parent-in-law

☐ Son-in-law or daughter-in-law

☐ Other relative

☐ Roomer or boarder

☐ Housemate or roommate

☐ Unmarried partner

☐ Foster child

☐ Other nonrelative

FIGURE 3.3   Relationship to Householder From the American Community Survey
Source: https://www.census.gov/prod/2014pubs/p20-572.pdf.

Such data may yield inaccurate counts of stepparents and stepchildren, because if a child resided with two parents, the questions posed do not help determine whether the second parent is the child's step, adoptive, or biological parent (Kreider & Lofquist, 2014). In addition, the report does not include the stepchildren of other adults in the household.

BOX 3.1 HOUSEHOLDERS, STEPCHILDREN, AND ADOPTED CHILDREN AS DEFINED BY THE U.S. CENSUS

WHO IS INCLUDED IN "STEPCHILDREN OF THE HOUSEHOLDER?"

Traditionally, a stepchild was the biological child of an individual's spouse who was not also the individual's biological child. Earlier data, however, show that the usage of the term has shifted and adults who are not currently married, and in some cases have never been married, report living with stepchildren. Often, these adults have an unmarried partner in the household, who is presumably the child's biological parent.[1] Since the English language does not have a more precise word to describe this type of relationship, some respondents may decide to report their partner's child as their stepchild, even though they are not married to the child's biological parent.

It is important to keep in mind that, as is the case for adopted children, estimates of stepchildren from decennial and American Community Survey data do not capture all children who are living with a stepparent. This is because these surveys only ask for the relationship to the householder. If the child has a second parent in the household, the type of relationship between that second parent and the child will not be captured in the data. In addition, many children may have stepparents who live in other households. Since the U.S. Census Bureau surveys sample addresses, and then determines who lives in the housing unit at that address, the data do not reflect relationships that cross household boundaries.

Similarly, there is some potential overlap between children who are reported as adopted and those reported as stepchildren, since stepchildren may be adopted by their stepparents. As noted previously, respondents report the relationship between the householder and their child as they choose, so we do not know how often stepparents who have adopted their stepchildren might report the child as a stepchild rather than an adopted child. The demographics of stepchildren adopted by a stepparent have been found to be more similar to other stepchildren than to other adopted children.[2]

1 From "Adopted children and stepchildren: 2000," by Rose M. Kreider, *Census 2000 Special Reports*, CENSR6-RV, 2003, U.S. Census Bureau, Washington, DC, available online at www.census.gov/prod/2003pubs/censr-6.pdf

2 From "When stepparents adopt: Demographic, health and health care characteristics of adopted children, stepchildren, and adopted stepchildren," by Matthew D. Bramlett, *Adoption Quarterly*, 2010, Vol. 13, pp. 248–267.

Source: United States Census Bureau, Rose M. Kreider, and Daphne A. Lofquist, "Householders, Stepchildren, and Adopted Children as Defined by the U.S. Census," Adopted Children and Stepchildren: 2010, pp. 3, U.S. Department of Commerce, 2014.

Given the greater permeability in family boundaries among Blacks, they may use the term stepchild more broadly than other racial groups. For example, stepchildren might be reported as adopted. The most common form of adoption in the United States is the adoption of a stepchild, and stepchild adoption is more common among African Americans than other racial and ethnic groups (Stewart, 2010). Although the degree to which stepparents who have adopted their stepchildren report those children as steps versus adopted is not clear, informal adoptions are thought to be more common among Blacks.

BOX 3.2 HOUSEHOLDERS, STEPCHILDREN, AND ADOPTED CHILDREN AS DEFINED BY THE U.S. CENSUS

WHO IS INCLUDED IN "ADOPTED CHILDREN OF THE HOUSEHOLDER?"

The type of relationship between parents and children is reported by respondents, and includes all variations of individuals they may view as their adopted child. Estimates of adopted children from decennial and American Community Survey (ACS) data do not capture all children who are living with a stepparent. This is because these surveys only ask for the relationship to the householder. The category includes various types of adoption, such as adoption of biologically related and unrelated children, adoption of stepchildren, adoption through private and public agencies, domestic and international adoptions, and independent and informal adoptions. Informal adoptions are more common among some cultural groups, as people differ widely in the way they view family relationships and the process of adoption. A qualitative study prepared for the U.S. Census Bureau found that informal adoption of biological grandchildren was common in Inupiaq communities in Alaska.[1] Informal adoptions may also be more common among Hispanics and Blacks than other race and ethnic groups.[2] In Census 2000 data, a substantial proportion of foreign-born Latin American children reported as adopted had not come into the United States on visas that would indicate they had been legally adopted.[3] Other studies have found that some parents who have legally adopted children related to them may not report the child as adopted.[4] We cannot distinguish among children who were adopted by their stepparents, children adopted by their biological grandparents or other relatives, and children adopted by people to whom they were not biologically related.[5]

1 From "Complex Inupiaq Eskimo households and relationships in two northwest Alaska rural communities," by Amy Craver, Alaska Native Science Commission, 2001, University of Alaska, Anchorage, AK.

2 From "Latino adoption issues," by Maria Suarez Hamm, *Adoption Factbook III*, 1999, National Council for Adoption, Washington, DC, pp. 257–260.

From "The well-being of African American adolescents within formal and informal adoption arrangements," by Priscilla A. Gibson, Justine Nelson-Christinedaughter, Harold D. Grotevant, and Hee-Kyung Kwon, *Adoption Quarterly*, 2005, Volume 9:1.

3 From "Foreign-born adopted children in the U.S., 2000," by Rose M. Kreider. In Thomas Atwood, Lee Allen, and Virginia Ravenel, eds., *Adoption Factbook IV*, National Council for Adoption, Washington, DC, 2007, pp. 133–153.

4 From "Legal and informal adoption by relatives in the U.S.: Comparative characteristics and well-being from a nationally representative sample," by Laura F. Radel, Matthew D. Bramlett, and Annette Waters, *Adoption Quarterly*, 2010, Volume 13, pp. 268–291.

5 An estimate for 1992, derived from court records, found that about 42% of all adoptions were by stepparents or a relative. From "How many children were adopted in 1992," by Victor Flango and Carol Flango, *Child Welfare*, 1995, Volume LXXIV, No. 5, pp. 1018–1024.

Source: United States Census Bureau, Rose M. Kreider, and Daphne A. Lofquist, "Householders, Stepchildren, and Adopted Children as Defined by the U.S. Census," Adopted Children and Stepchildren: 2010, pp. 2, U.S. Department of Commerce, 2014.

Because it is informal, it is not clear whether those parents refer to those children as their biological, step, or adopted children. Informal adoptions and permeable boundaries contribute to the structural diversity and complexity in relationships among African American families. Given the permeability of those boundaries, special consideration of well-being in African American families is warranted.

Relationship Quality in African American Stepfamilies

The paucity of research specifically focused on African American stepfamilies has contributed to the dearth of information on the topic. Much more is known about the well-being of White step-families. In addition, when race is examined as a salient variable, the studies tend to focus on co-parenting among the partners who are no longer together rather than on the stepfamily. For example, in one study examining Black and White couples who had been divorced for about seven years, no race differences in emotional involvement of parents was found—assessed by asking questions such as *How often do you still get your former spouse's advice about important personal decisions?* and *How close do you feel to your former spouse's family?* The researchers also found no race differences in perceptions of the quality of co-parenting—assessed by asking *How satisfied are you with the relationship your child/children has/have with your former spouse and How satisfied are you with the relationship you have with your former spouse?* (Gurmen, Huff, Brown, Orbuch, & Birditt, 2017.) As stated earlier, although that study included race as a salient variable, it focused on relationship quality among couples in the dissolved relationship, rather than among couples in the new stepfamily relationship. Data sets that can address African American stepfamilies do exist. The National Longitudinal Study of Adolescent to Adult Health (referred to as Add Health) is a nationally representative sample of adolescents followed from 1994/1995 (when they were in grades seven to 12) through young adulthood in 2016/2018. Sociologists Valerie King and her colleagues (King, Amato, & Lindstrom, 2015) used a part of the Add Health data and a sample of adolescents who were residing with their unmarried biological mothers who did not have a partner in the home at Wave 1 of the study, and who, by Wave 2, had transitioned to married-stepfather families. Stepfather-stepchild relationship quality was assessed by asking the adolescents how satisfied they were overall with the relationship and communication. Findings revealed that Black adolescents reported less positive relationships with their stepfathers than did the White adolescents. That finding, however, was not consistent with other studies that found no racial differences between Black and White adolescents' reports about their relationships with their stepfathers (King Thorsen, & Amato, 2014).

King surmises that perhaps that study indicated no racial differences between Black and White adolescents' reports about their relationships with their stepfathers because it differed in one key manner: the 2014 study included stepfamilies of all durations, and those durations varied widely from less than two years as a stepfamily to more than 10 years. Perhaps, for Black adolescents, developing positive relationships with their stepfathers is only challenging during the initial transition into the stepfamily, or perhaps it is only challenging for Black youth during that adolescent phase. Perhaps there are other factors involved that were not identified. There is clearly a need for additional research.

Using a sample of 149 newly married African American stepfathers, colleagues (Bryant, Futris, Hicks, Lee, & Oshri, 2016) and I examined links between stepparent-stepchild relationship quality and aspects of the stepfathers' marriage—specifically marital quality and marital interactions. We used a dataset focusing specifically on African American families. Stepfather-stepchild relationship quality was measured by assessing the degree to which the stepfathers indicated they felt respected, loved, and liked by their stepchildren. Marital quality was measured by assessing commitment, trust, passionate love, friendship-based love, and happiness. Marital interactions were measured by assessing intimacy, shared activities, and verbal communication. Our findings indicated that positive stepfather-stepchild relationship quality was strongly associated with positive marital quality. These findings illustrate how a situation in one subsystem (e.g., parent-child) of the stepfamily can "spill over" into another family subsystem (e.g., parent-parent). In this case, stepfathers' feeling respected, loved, and liked by their stepchildren was associated with stepfathers' positive reports of commitment to, trust of, love for, and happiness with their spouses. Future research (discussed later) should involve replicating this study (including its distinction between marital quality and marital interactions) not only with other racial groups but also with a sample in which the couple has been married for a longer period. That study focused on married fathers and not cohabiting stepfathers who were not married to the mother of the children, often known as "social fathers."

African American stepchildren often receive substantial social and emotional support from grandparents.

There are contradictory notions about the roles of social fathers in African American families. Some literature indicates that while it is possible for male cohabiting partners to function as stepfathers (Bzostek, 2008), cohabiting stepfathers are less involved with stepchildren than married stepfathers or cohabiting biological fathers (Carlson & Berger, 2013). Although Black men are more likely to be cohabiting stepfathers than men in other groups, research debunks the notion that Black men are not involved fathers. Using a sample of low-income, African American urban cohabiting couples who had adolescent children from prior relationships, Forehand, Parent, Golub, and Reid (2014) found that male cohabiting partners were involved in daily child-related tasks and setting limits. In most of the stepfamilies in the study, the male cohabiting partners were viewed as co-parents by the mothers and also the adolescents. The mother can help facilitate stepfather-stepchild relationships. A male cohabiting partner was more likely to be involved in parenting when a mother actively communicated with him about her child and sought his involvement.

Recommendations for Future Research

Additional research on Black stepfamilies is greatly needed. Relative to the literature on stepfamilies in general, the literature on this specific topic is woefully lacking. In addition to shedding light on contradictory findings, there are many issues on which future research should focus. Three issues in particular have been typically ignored: the first involves acknowledging heterogeneity, the second involves the notion of intersectionality, and the third involves the length of relationship. Heterogeneity involves acknowledging that there is great diversity among the Black (and African American) population. Intersectionality refers to examining multiple factors simultaneously and trying to understand how those factors are intertwined. Such an approach provides better information about how or why a family functions the way it does rather than examining one variable at a time. The length of stepfamily relationships plays a role in the interactions of all families. This variable may be particularly salient in studies of African American families because studies of longtime-married African American couples (especially longtime-married stepfamily couples) are conspicuously missing from the scientific literature.

Regarding heterogeneity in this population, it important to note that not all Blacks identify as "African American." Some Blacks identify as mixed race and others "Black." For example, not all African Americans are descendants of slaves brought to this nation from Africa. Some are descendants of immigrants from many nations of Africa, the Caribbean Islands, or South America. Others are recent immigrants from Africa and identify with their home countries. Thus, the labels "African American" and "Black" are typically used as a means of grouping together a population of people who are quite different socially and culturally. Originating from different regions of the world may shape parenting practices and family interactions. Future research should explore issues of heterogeneity among African American stepparents including education level, financial status, neighborhood context, and even parenting styles.

Second, relatively little is known about the intersectionality of race, socioeconomic status, and stepparenting. This is also an opportunity to creatively link two or more theories and contextual variables (e.g., race, financial circumstances, stressors) to multiple aspects of family functioning. For African American stepfamilies there is an additional level of nuance because family boundaries tend to be more permeable among African American families.

Third, the length of couple relationship (length of marriage, cohabiting union, or monogamous relationship) needs to be more clearly acknowledged in studies of African American stepfamilies. Parent-stepparent and parent-stepchild relationships do not remain static. These relationships, much like individuals, develop and change over time. Biological parent-child, stepparent-stepchild, and stepparent-biological parent relationships change as the stepchild ages. This affects stepfamily dynamics, roles, and rules. Interactions that may have been cordial when the stepchildren were younger may deteriorate years later. For example, after the death of a spouse, stepparents and stepchildren are faced with inadequate, ambiguous inheritance laws, and in the absence of a will, "who gets what" can be unclear, leading to conflict (Papernow, 2013). Also, generally speaking, compared with biological parents, many stepparents are more likely to want their stepchildren "launched" from the home. Indeed, stepchildren leave the home at younger ages than do biological children (Crosbie-Burnett et al., 2005). This is particularly salient for older remarried couples. "A partner's unlaunched adult child can feel especially burdensome to a stepparent who is 'done' with parenting" (Papernow, 2013, p. 149). Although that is generally the sentiment across families, little is known about the sentiments and relational dynamics in African American stepfamilies. Keep in mind that African American children are more accustomed to being parented and disciplined not only by their biological parents, but also by grandparents, other family members, and even by family friends. Thus, being parented by someone other than their biological mother or father is not a foreign experience. In addition, stepfamily relationships garner more support among African Americans. This may explain why African American stepchildren have more positive outcomes (e.g., self-esteem and broader well-being) than do White stepchildren

(Papernow, 2013). We know relatively little about how African American family relationships unfold because there are so few studies of longtime-married African American couples who have been followed over time. The vast majority of the literature continues to focus on unmarried African American couples of unstable African American households. These are internal changes occurring inside the family; however, external factors, such as federal and state level family policies, can also influence stepfamily life.

Policy issues regarding stepfamilies are complex and fraught with dilemmas. Much of this stems from the fact that in the United States stepparents are not granted legal rights over their stepchildren, even when the stepparents are legally married to the biological parent of their stepchildren (Hans, 2002; Mason, Harrison-Jay, Svare, & Wolfinger, 2002). Thus, issues regarding physical custody or the right to make major medical treatment decisions are typically out of their purview despite the daily caregiving tasks they perform or the financial support they provide. Rights are conferred only upon adoption. This is problematic, however, because for a stepparent to legally adopt a stepchild the noncustodial biological parent must agree to relinquish his or her parental rights. Given the informal adoptions and permeable family boundaries characterizing many Black families, the strict enforcement of policies may do more harm than good because it may be divisive and create barriers that need not be highlighted between noncustodial biological parents and stepparents. Moreover, if rights are granted, stepparents could potentially be required to pay child support for their stepchild if the marriage to their stepchild's biological parent ended.

Policies regarding stepparents' rights and obligations are not the same in every state (Hans, 2002; Mason, Harrison-Jay, Svare, & Wolfinger, 2002). In some states, stepparents are permitted to petition for visitation rights if the marriage to the child's biological parent ends. In other states such petitions are not permissible or are considered on a case-by-case basis. Some states allow such petitions only if the biological parent has died. Studies of the implications of policies such as these warrant attention for all stepfamilies, especially for African Americans.

Recommendations for Practice

A few recommendations regarding practice are noted. First, given the extent of cohabitation among Blacks, therapists and clinicians need to learn how to better identify and address the needs of stepfamilies that consist of cohabiting partners. Perhaps family intervention and prevention programs should consider involving cohabiting partners. Positive relationships between a parent's cohabiting partner and children will very likely lead to the cohabiting partner's increased involvement with childrearing. Second, given the importance of extended family members who provide support and affect family dynamics, therapists should consider including them in family therapy sessions. Third, the development of culturally sensitive programs is needed, especially since for Blacks definitions regarding who is *in* or *not* in the family are sociohistorically rooted. Fourth, given that Blacks tend not to seek help from therapists, the profession needs to explore ways of reaching out to this population. Perhaps the development of culturally sensitive programs is one way that this can be achieved. Those culturally sensitive programs should consider addressing external stressors that are particularly salient for Blacks, such as racial discrimination and racial profiling and how those issues can influence family dynamics.

Conclusion

Many frameworks can be used to guide studies of stepfamilies, such as the ones covered here—the family solidarity model, family systems theory, family stress theory, and boundary ambiguity. Studies should be well-grounded in a specific framework or theory and researchers may incorporate more than one theory into their analyses. For example, both boundary ambiguity and family solidarity could be used jointly, because families having trouble agreeing who is in or not in the family may feel low levels of cohesion. Keep in mind that Black families may not perceive or interpret issues as burdensome or problematic. Consequently, their family interactions may differ from other groups. According to Patricia Papernow:

Unlike some of the Anglo nonresidential fathers ... levels of direct interaction and play between children and African American stepfathers equals that of never-divorced biological fathers. Black stepfathers also participated more actively in activities such as religious and oral education than White stepfathers ... (Papernow, 2013, p. 137)

This means that when choosing a theory, one should think very carefully because the theory must be able to help explain *how* or why—such as *why* some stepfamilies have high levels of relationship quality whereas others do not, or *how* unclear perceptions about who is in or not in a family can generate stress. Again, keep in mind that Black families more readily allow others to permeate their family boundaries.

Indeed, the history of African Americans (e.g., needing to take care of the children of others; being unable to legally marry) may explain their current willingness to allow their family boundaries to be more easily permeated. This does not necessarily mean that stepparent-stepchild relationships in African American families run smoothly all the time. Negative spillover can occur between their stepparent-child and stepparent-biological parent subsystems. Their history and the traditions that grew out of their history may mean the implementation of policies that could hinder a fluid exchange of child-care responsibilities between biological and stepparents may have more negative effects on Black stepfamilies than other racial and ethnic groups, because as pointed out on the first page of this chapter, "Shaped by their sociohistorical context, African American families tend to operate as a 'pedi-focal' family system, centered on the children and are characterized by a communal-oriented philosophy, permeability of family boundaries, movement of children among households, and shared parenting among multiple parents" (Adler-Baeder et al., 2010, p. 396).

Questions for Discussion

1. How is stepfamily formation among African Americans different from that of other racial and ethnic groups? How might the structure of African American families affect relationships between family members?
2. Identify two theories that may explain marriage rates among African Americans and explain why the theories are especially applicable to African Americans.
3. If you were a family therapist working with stepfamilies such as Yvette and Kofi's, what kind of guidance would you provide?

Additional Resources

Bryant, C. M., Futris, T. G., Hicks, M. R., Lee, T., & Oshri, A. (2016). African American stepfather-stepchild relationships, marital quality, and mental health. *Journal of Divorce and Remarriage, 57,* 375–388.

Coles, R. L., & Green, C. (Eds). (2010). *The myth of the missing Black father.* New York, NY: Columbia University Press.

Cutrona, C. E., Clavel, F. D., & Johnson, M. A. (2016). African American couples in rural contexts. In Lisa J. Crockett & Gustavo Carlo (Eds.) *Rural ethnic minority youth and families in the United States: Theory, research, and applications,* p. 127–142. Switzerland: Springer International.

Leite, R., & McKenry, P. (2006). A role theory perspective on patterns of separated and divorced African American nonresidential father involvement with children. *Fathering, 4,* p. 1–21.

Vaterlaus, J. M., Skogrand, L., Chaney, C. M., & Gahagan, K. (2016). Marital expectations in strong African American marriages. *Family Process, 17.* Retrieved February 9, 2019, from http://onlinelibrary.wiley.com/doi/10.1111/famp.12263/abstract

References

Adler-Baeder, F., Russell, C., Kerpleman, J., Pittman, J. L., Ketrink, S., Smith, T., Lucier-Greer, M., Bradford, A., & Stringer, K. (2010). Thriving in stepfamilies: Exploring competence and well-being among African American youth. *Journal of Adolescent Health, 46,* 396–398.

Adler-Baeder, F., & Schramm, D. (2006). *Examining the experiences of ethnic minority stepfamilies.* Minneapolis, MN: National Council on Family Relations Conference.

Bengtson, V., Giarrusso R., Mabry, J. B., & Silverstein, M. (2002). Solidarity, conflict, and ambivalence: Complementary or competing perspectives on intergenerational relationships? *Journal of Marriage and Family, 64,* 568–576.

Benokraitis, N. (2008). *Marriages and families: Changes, choices, and constraints* (6th ed.) Upper Saddle River, NJ: Pearson/Prentice Hall.

Boss, P., Bryant, C. M., & Mancini, J. A. (2017). *Family stress management* (3rd ed.). Thousand Oak, CA: Sage.

Bowen, M. (1978). *Family therapy in clinical practice.* New York, NY: Jason Aronson.

Brown, S. L., & Manning, W. D. (2009). Family boundary ambiguity and the measurement of family structure: The significance of cohabitation. *Demography, 46,* 85–101.

Bryant, C. M. (2018). African American fictive kin: Historical and contemporary notions. *Family Focus,* Issue FF75, F10–F11.

Bryant, C. M., Futris, T., Hicks, M. R., Lee, T-K., & Oshri, A. (2016). African American stepfather-stepchild relationships, marital quality, and mental health. *Journal of Divorce & Remarriage, 57,* 375–388.

Bryant, C. M., Wickrama, K. A. S., Bolland, J. M., Bryant, B. M., Cutrona, C. E., & Stanik, C. E. (2010). Race matters, even in marriage: Identifying factors linked to marital outcomes for African Americans. *Journal of Family Theory and Review, 2*, 157–174.

Bzostek, S. H. (2008). Social fathers and child well-being. *Journal of Marriage and Family, 70*, 950–961.

Carlson, M. J., & Berger, L. M. (2013). What kids get from parents: Packages of parental involvement across complex family forms. *Social Service Review, 87*, 213–249.

Cavanaugh, S. E., & Fomby, P. (2012). Family instability, school context, and the academic careers of adolescents. *Sociology of Education, 85*, 81–97.

Cherlin, A. (1999). Going to extremes: Family structure, children's well-being, and social science. *Demography, 36*, 421–428.

Chibucos, T. R., Leite, R. W., & Weis, D. L. (2005). *Readings in family theory*. Thousand Oaks, CA: Sage.

Cohen, P. N., & Pepin, J. R. (2018). Unequal marriage markets: Sex rations and first marriage among Black and White women. *Socius: Sociological Research for a Dynamic World, 4*, 1–10.

Conger, R. D., Wallace, L. E., Sun, Y., Simons, R. L., McLoyd, V. C., & Brody, G. H. (2002). Economic pressure in African American families: A replication and extension of the family stress model. *Developmental Psychology, 38*, 179–193.

Connidis, I., & McMullin, J. A. (2002). Ambivalence, family ties, and doing sociology. (2002). *Journal of Marriage and the Family, 64*, 594–601.

Crosbie-Burnett, M. et al. (2005). Advancing theory through research: The case of extrusion in stepfamilies. In V. L. Bengston, A. C. Acock, K. R. Allen, P. Dilworth-Anderson, & D. M. Klein (Eds.) *Sourcebook of family theory and research* (p. 213–230). Thousand Oaks, CA: Sage.

Cross, C. J., Nguyen, A. W., Chatters, L. M., & Taylor, R. J. (2018). Instrumental social support exchanges in African American extended families. *Journal of Family Issues, 39*, 3535–3563.

Dunlap, E., Golub, A., & Benoit, E. (2010). The invisible partners: Cohabiting males as "caring daddies" in inner-city "mother only" households. In F. Columbus (Ed.) *Family life: Roles, bonds and impact* (pp. 33–54). Hauppage, NY: Nova Science.

Dupuis, S. (2010). Examining the blended family: The application of systems theory toward an understanding of the blended family system. *Journal of Couple & Relationship Therapy, 9*, 239–251.

Durr, M., & Hill, S. A. (2006). The family-work interface in African American households. In M. Durr & S. A. Hill (Eds.) *Race, work, and family in the lives of African Americans* (pp. 73–85). Lanham, MD: Rowman & Littlefield.

Edin, K., & Reed, J. M. (2005). Why don't they just get married? Barriers to marriage among the disadvantaged. *The Future of Children, 15*, 117–137.

Eickmeyer, K. J. (2017). American children's family structure: Stepparent families. Family Profiles, FP-17-16. Bowling Green, OH: National Center for Family & Marriage Research.

Elliot, D. B. et al. (2012) *Historical marriage trends from 1890–2010: A focus on race differences.* SEHSD Working Paper No. 2012-12 presented at the annual meeting of the Population Association of America. San Francisco, CA, May 2012. http://www.census.gov/hhes/socdemo/marriage/data/acs/ElliottetalPAA2012paper.pdf

England, P., & McClintock, E. A. (2009). The gendered double standard of aging in US marriage markets. *Population and Development Review, 35,* 797–816.

Fagan, J., & Cabrera, N. (2012). Longitudinal and reciprocal associations between coparenting conflict and father engagement. *Journal of Family Psychology, 26,* 1004–1011.

Fomby, P., & Cherlin, A. (2007) Family instability and child well-being. *American Sociological Review, 72,* 181–204.

Forehand, R., Parent, J., Golub, A., & Reid, M. (2014). Correlates of male cohabiting partners' involvement in child-rearing tasks in low-income urban Black stepfamilies. *Journal of Family Psychology, 28,* 336–345.

Ganong, L. H., Coleman M., & Jamison, T. (2011). Patterns of stepchild-stepparent relationship development. *Journal of Marriage and Family, 73,* 396–413.

Gibson-Davis, C. M., Edin, K., & McLanahan, S. (2005). High hopes but even higher expectations: The retreat from marriage among low-income couples. *Journal of Marriage and Family, 67,* 1301–1312.

Gurmen, M. S., Huff, S. C., Brown, E., Orbuch, T. L, & Birditt, K. S. (2017). Divorced yet still together: Ongoing personal relationships and coparenting among divorced parents. *Journal of Divorce & Remarriage, 58,* 645–660.

Hamilton, B. E., Martin, J. A., & Ventura, S. J. (2011). Births: Preliminary data for 2010. *National Vital Statistics Reports, 60,* 1–25.

Harknett, K., & McLanahan, S. S. (2004). Racial and ethnic differences in marriage after the birth of a child. *American Sociological Review, 69,* 790–811.

Hans, J. D. (2002). Stepparenting after divorce: Stepparents' legal position regarding custody, access and support. *Family Relations, 51,* 301–307.

Haynes, F. E. (2000). Gender and family ideals: An exploratory study of Black middle-class Americans. *Journal of Family Issues, 21,* 811–837.

Jia, R., & Schoppe-Sullivan, S. J. (2011). Relations between coparenting and father involvement in families with preschool-age children. *Developmental Psychology, 47,* 106–118.

Jensen, T. M., & Shafer, K. (2013). Stepfamily functioning and closeness: Children's views on second marriages and stepfather relationships. *Social Work, 58,* 127–136.

Johnson-Garner, M., & Meyers, S. A. (2003). What factors contribute to the resilience of African American children within kinship care. *Child & Youth Care Forum, 32*, 255–269.

King, V., Amato, P. R., & Lindstrom, R. (2015). Stepfather-adolescent relationship quality during the first year of transitioning to a stepfamily. *Journal of Marriage and Family, 77*, 1179–1189.

King, V., Thorsen, M., & Amato, P. R. (2014). Factors associated with positive relationships between stepfathers and adolescent stepchildren. *Social Science Research, 47*, 16–29.

Kreider, R. M. (2007). Current population reports. Washington, DC: U.S. Census Bureau. *Living Arrangements of Children: 2004*, 70–104.

Kreider, R. M., & Fields, J. (2005). *Living arrangements of children: 2001*. Current Populations Reports, P70–104, Washington, DC: U.S. Census Bureau.

Kreider, R. M., & Lofquist, D. A. (2014). *Adopted children and stepchildren: 2010 population characteristics*. Retrieved November 5, 2017, from https://www.census.gov/prod/2014pubs/p20-572.pdf

Lamidi, E. (2014). *Single, cohabiting, and married households, 1995–2012*. (FP-14-1). National Center for Family & Marriage Research. Retrieved February 9, 2019, from https://www.bgsu.edu/content/dam/BGSU/college-of-arts-and-sciences/NCFMR/documents/FP/FP-14-01.pdf

Langton, C. E., & Berger, L. M. (2011). Family structure and adolescent physical health, behavior, and emotional well-being. *Social Service Review, 85*, 323–357.

Lichter, D. T., Turner, R. N., & Sassler, S. (2010). National estimates of the rise in serial cohabitation. *Social Science Research, 39*, 754–755.

Livingston, G., Parker, G., & Rohal, M. (2014). *Four-in-ten couples are saying "I do," again: Growing number of adults have remarried*. Retrieved June 7, 2017, from http://assets.pewresearch.org/wp-content/uploads/sites/3/2014/11/2014-11-14_remarriage-final.pdf

Mandara, J., Rogers, S. Y., & Zinbarg, R. E. (2011). The effects of family structure on African American adolescents' marijuana use. *Journal of Marriage and Family, 73*, 557–569.

Manning, W. D. (2015). Cohabitation and child wellbeing. *Future of Children, 25*, 51–66.

Mason, M. A., Harrison-Jay, S., Svare, G. M., & Wolfinger, N. H. (2002). Stepparents: De facto parents or legal strangers? *Journal of Family Issues, 23*, 507–522.

McChesney, K. Y., & Bengtson, V. L. (1988). Solidarity, integration, and cohesion in families: Concepts and theories. In D. J. Mangen, V. L. Bengtson, & P. H. Landry Jr. (Eds.) *Measurement of intergenerational relations* (pp. 15–30). Newbury Park, CA: Sage.

McCubbin, H. I., & Figley, C. R. (Eds). (1983). *Stress and the family: Coping with normative transitions* (Volume 1). New York, NY: Routledge.

McLanahan, S., & Sawhill, I. (2015). Marriage and child wellbeing revisited: Introducing the issue. *The Future of Children, 25*(2), 3–9. Retrieved November 7, 2017, from http://files.eric.ed.gov/fulltext/EJ1079423.pdf

McLoyd, V. C., Cauce, A. M., Takeuchi, D., & Wayne, L. W. (2000). Marital processes and parental socialization in families of color: A decade review of research. *Journal of Marriage and Family, 62*, 1070–1093.

Minuchin, S. (1974). *Families and family therapy.* Cambridge, MA: Harvard University Press.

Moore, M. R., & Chase-Lansdale, P. L. (2001). Sexual intercourse and pregnancy among African American girls in high poverty neighborhoods: The role of family and perceived community environment. *Journal of Marriage and Family, 63*, 1146–1157.

Murry, V. M., Brown, P. A., Brody, G. H., Cutrona, C. E., & Simons, R. L. (2001). Racial discrimination as a moderator of the links among stress, maternal psychological functioning, and family relationships. *Journal of Marriage and Family, 63*, 915–926.

Murray, V. M, Butler-Barnes, S. T., Mayo-Gamble, T. L, & Inniss-Thompson, M. N. (2018). Excavating new constructs for family stress theories in the context of everyday life experiences of Black American families. *Journal of Family Theory and Review, 10*, 384–405.

Nance-Nash, S. (2004), Managing a blended family. *Black Enterprise, 34*, 87–92.

Nguyen, A. W., Chatters, L. M., & Taylor, R. T. (2016). African American extended family and church-based social network typologies. *Family Relations, 65*, 701–715.

Papernow, P. L. (2013). Surviving and thriving in stepfamily relationships: What works and what doesn't. London, UK: Routledge.

Parker, K. (2011). A portrait of stepfamilies. Pew Research Centers Social Demographic Trends Project RSS. Retrieved June 7, 2017, from http://www.pewsocialtrends.org/2011/01/13/a-portrait-of-stepfamilies/

Pettit, B., & Western, B. (2004). Mass imprisonment and the life course: Race and class inequality in U.S. incarceration. *American Sociological Review, 69*, 151–169

Pew Research Center (2011). *A portrait of stepfamilies.* Retrieved June 7, 2017, from http://www.pewsocialtrends.org/2011/01/13/a-portrait-of-stepfamilies/

Pew Research Center (2015). *Parenting in America: Outlook, worries, aspirations are strongly linked to financial situation.* Retrieved June 7, 2017, from http://www.pewsocialtrends.org/2015/12/17/1-the-american-family-today/

Pruett, C. L., Calsyn, R. J., & Jensen, F. M. (1993). Social support received by children in stepmother, stepfather, and intact families. *Journal of Divorce & Remarriage, 19*, 165–179.

Raley, R. K., Sweeney, M. M., & Wondra, D. (2015). The growing racial and ethnic divide in US marriage patterns. *The Future of Children, 25*, 89.

Roopnarine, J. L. (2015). *Fathers across cultures: The importance, roles, and diverse practices of dads.* Santa Barbara, CA: Praeger/ ABC-CLIO.

Satir, V. (1967). *Conjoint family therapy.* Palo Alto, CA: Science and Behavior.

Shapiro, D. (2014). Stepparents and parenting stress: The roles of gender, marital quality, and views about gender roles. *Family Process, 53,* 97–108.

Stewart, S. D. (2005). Boundary ambiguity in stepfamilies. *Journal of Family Issues, 26,* 1002–1029.

Stewart, S. D. (2007). *Brave new stepfamilies: Diverse paths toward stepfamily living.* Thousand Oaks, CA: Sage.

Styles, B., & Guzzo, K. B. (2015). Remarriage & stepfamilies (FP15-10). National Center for Family & Marriage Research. Retrieved February 9, 2019, from www.bgsu.edu/ncfmr/recources/data/famiy-profiles/ stykes-guzzo-remarriage-stepfamilies-fp-15-10.html

Sussman, M. B. (1976). The family life of old people. In R. Binstock & E. Shanas (Eds.) *Handbook of aging and the social sciences* (pp. 218– 243). New York, NY: Van Norstrand Reinhold.

Taylor, R. J., Chatters, L. M., Woodward, A. T., & Brown, B. (2013). Racial and ethnic differences in extended family, friendship, fictive kin, and congregational informal support networks. *Family Relations, 62,* 609–624.

Thomson, E. (1994). "Setting" and "development" from a demographic point of view. In A. Booth & J. Dunn (Eds.) *Stepfamilies: Who benefits? Who does not?* (pp. 89–96). Hillsdale, NJ: Lawrence Erlbaum.

Tucker, M. B (2000). Marital values and expectations in context: Results from a 21-city survey. In L. J. Waite, C. Bachrach, M. J. Hindin, E. Thomson, & A. Thornton (Eds.) *The ties that bind: Perspectives on marriage and cohabitation.* Hawthorne, NY: Aldine de Gruyter.

U.S. Census Bureau. (2014). *America's families and living arrangements: 2014 children* (C Table Series). Retrieved February 9, 2019, from https://www.census.gov/hhes/families/data/cps2014.html

Vespa, J., Lewis, J. M., & Kreider, R. M. (2013). America's families and living arrangements: 2012. Issued August 2013, P20-570.

Wildeman, C. (2009). Parental imprisonment, the prison boom, and the concentration of childhood disadvantage. *Demography, 46,* 265–280.

White, L. (1994). Growing up with single parents and stepparents: Long-term effects on family solidarity. *Journal of Marriage and Family, 56,* 935–948.

Wilson, W. J. (1987). *The truly disadvantaged: The inner city, the underclass, and public policy.* Chicago: University of Chicago Press.

CHAPTER FOUR

Hispanic Stepfamilies

Steven Hoffman, PhD, MSW
Bethany Breck, MSW, University of Texas at Austin
Lauren Beasley, MSW, University of Tennessee-Knoxville

Introduction

Today, the Hispanic population represents the largest racial and ethnic minority group in the United States. Estimates from the 2015 American Community Survey (ACS) indicate that approximately 18% of the U.S. population identifies as Hispanic, regardless of other racial identification. By comparison, both Blacks and Asians constitute relatively smaller proportions of the population, at 12% and 6%, respectively (U.S. Census Bureau, 2012–2016). Significantly, the number of Hispanics in the United States continues to increase. For example, from 2000 to 2010 there was a 43% increase in the Hispanic population, accounting for half of all U.S. population growth (U.S. Census Bureau, 2011). Population growth among individuals of Hispanic ethnicity is rooted in two demographic trends. First, Hispanics in the United States have higher birth rates than other racial and ethnic groups. Second, strong migration streams from Mexico, Central America, South America, and the Caribbean help account for substantial population growth in the United States (Colby & Ortman, 2017; Cauce & Domenech-Rodriguez, 2002; Knight, Roosa, & Umaña-Taylor, 2009). Given these trends, it is expected that one-third to one-fourth of the U.S. population will be of Hispanic descent by 2060 (U.S. Census Bureau, 2010; see Figure 4.1).

Although the Hispanic population is often subsumed together in a seemingly homogenous group, the reality is that the Hispanic

Nearly all Latinos lived in half of the nation's more than 3,000 counties in 2014
The number of Latinos residing in counties with at least 1,000 Latinos

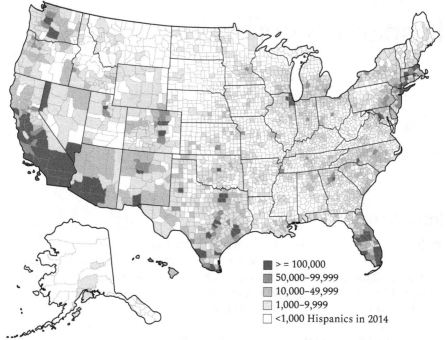

Legend:
- ■ > = 100,000
- ■ 50,000–99,999
- ■ 10,000–49,999
- □ 1,000–9,999
- □ <1,000 Hispanics in 2014

Source: Pew Research Center tabulations of U.S. Census Bureau population estimates.
'U.S. Latino Population Growth and Dispersion Has Slowed Since Onset of the
Great Recession'
PEW RESEARCH CENTER

FIGURE 4.1 Although the Hispanic population growth slowed during the Great Recession, Hispanics still represent the fastest-growing minority in the United States.

Source: http://www.pewhispanic.org/2016/09/08/latino-population-growth-and-dispersion-has-slowed-since-the-onset-of-the-great-recession/ph_2016-09-08_geography-03/.

population is composed of a rich, diverse, and vibrant set of people with varying cultures, experiences, and histories. The cultural values of various groups of Hispanics are shaped by country of origin, generational status, and nativity. In this chapter we use those terms as they are defined by the U.S. Census Bureau (2010): *Country of Origin*—the country from which an individual originally comes; *Generational Status*—the place of birth of an individual or of an individual's parents; and *Nativity*—where an individual was born. Although there is wide variation in the literature regarding how to refer to people in the United States who are of Latin descent (e.g., Hispanic, Latino/a, Latinx), the U.S. Census Bureau (2018) uses the term "Hispanic" to describe any individual of Cuban, Mexican, Puerto Rican, South or Central American, or other Spanish cultural origin. As we have throughout our introductory remarks, this chapter will follow census terminology and use the term "Hispanic" to describe our population of interest.

Given the increasing size of the Hispanic population and its visibility within American culture, scholars have become increasingly interested in their experiences in the United States. Such scholarly attention includes an empirical examination of Hispanic family life—including parenting, marriage patterns, and the influence of culture on family life and family-related outcomes. Yet, much of this research is in its infancy and tends to emphasize similarities and differences between Hispanics and other racial/ethnic groups, particularly Whites. With comparatively few studies addressing Hispanic family life in the United States, it is perhaps unsurprising that Hispanic stepfamilies are a significantly understudied group.

Due to the lack of research on Hispanic stepfamilies, we approach this chapter by first providing a demographic profile of Hispanic stepfamilies in the United States. Next, we follow up this demographic analysis with a discussion of how Hispanic stepfamily functioning is similar and different from other racial and ethnic groups in the United States. Next, we discuss how cultural and structural issues may uniquely affect Hispanic stepfamilies. Finally, we provide several future directions for research, practice, and policies specific to Hispanic stepfamilies. Our goal in this chapter is to provide both a current portrait of Hispanic stepfamily life and also a groundwork for future research.

A Demographic Profile of Hispanic Stepfamilies

Due to the early state of the research on Hispanic families in the United States generally, few studies have provided a demographic portrait of stepfamilies in the Hispanic population. For example, we know little about how many stepfamilies exist of Hispanic origin, the structure of these stepfamilies, or how Hispanic families are similar to or different from stepfamilies of other racial/ethnic origins. Data from the 2009 ACS showed no difference in in the marriage and divorce rates of Hispanic men and women: about 16% were married and 13% were divorced. When looking at marriage among the entire U.S. population, the 2009 data showed that 16% of women and men married in the last 12 months were of Hispanic origin, which is slightly higher than the 14% of the total population that was in this group (Elliot & Simmons, 2011). These data are applicable when working with adults as individual units; however, a gap in the literature still exists for stepfamilies as a unit, and more recent data provides more relevant information.

Notable are the 2016 divorce rates provided by the National Center for Family & Marriage Research (Payne, 2018b). For all racial and ethnic groups, divorce rates plateaued from 2009–2012 at approximately 17%, and the rate of first-time divorce has decreased somewhat since 2008. As far as general population remarriage, the rates of remarriages were at 27%, down from 2008's 31% rate of remarriage. When specifically looking at trends of divorce by race and ethnicity, it was notable that among Hispanic divorcees, foreign-born Hispanics had a lower divorce rate than native-born Hispanics. As far as remarriage, Hispanic men had the greatest decline in remarriage rates, dropping from 54% to 42% (Payne, 2018a).

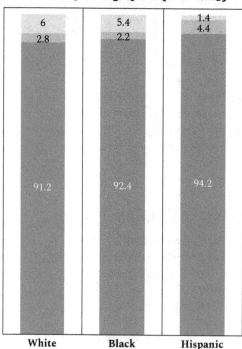

U.S. Family Demographics (2011–2015)

White: 6, 2.8, 91.2
Black: 5.4, 2.2, 92.4
Hispanic: 1.4, 4.4, 94.2

■ Biological ■ Adopted ■ Stepchild

FIGURE 4.2 According to the American Community Survey, the proportion of Hispanic children living with two biological parents was roughly equal to that of Black and White children.

To understand more of the complexities faced by Hispanic stepfamilies, we analyzed data from the 2011–2015 ACS) to create basic demographic information about Hispanic stepfamilies in the United States. Figure 4.2 shows the proportion of children under 18 living with two biological parents, two adopted parents, and one biological parent and one stepparent by race and ethnicity. While these are snapshot measures and do not provide an estimate of the lifetime likelihood of ever living in a stepfamily, the results show that Hispanic children had a similar chance of living in a stepfamily as did White and Black children. For all the groups, the vast majority of children living with two parents were living with two biological parents; however, the results showed variation by race and ethnicity in living with adoptive parents and stepparents. About 4% of Hispanic children living with two parents were adopted compared with 3% of white children and 2% of Black children. A substantially lower percentage of Hispanic children were stepchildren than were White and Black children, at 1%, 6%, and 5%, respectively. These findings may be attributed to cultural and familial values, which will be elaborated upon in the following sections.

Using the same 2011–2015 ACS data, we looked at three of the most common stepfamily households in the United States: married biological mother-stepfather families, married biological father-stepmother families, and cohabiting stepfamilies. Significantly, nearly all cohabiting stepfamilies, also known as *fragile families* in ACS, consisted of a biological mother and her cohabiting partner. As a result, we combined mother-cohabiting stepfamilies and father-cohabiting stepfamilies.

Figure 4.3 indicates substantial racial and ethnic differences in stepfamily type. For Hispanics, nearly 67% of stepchildren were living in a married couple household with a biological mother and stepfather. In comparison, 70% of White children lived in a married mother-stepfather household. A substantially lower

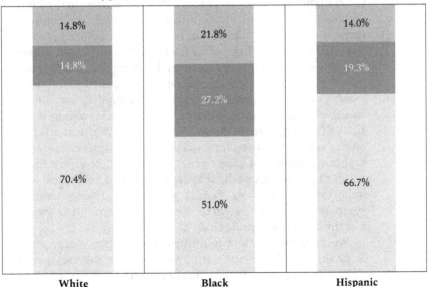

Types of Stepfamilies in the U.S. (2011–2015)

FIGURE 4.3   A substantially lower proportion of Hispanic and White children lived in a cohabiting stepfamily compared with Black children.

percentage of Black children lived in a married mother-stepfather household, at 51%. Compared with Whites, a higher percentage of Hispanic stepchildren lived with a biological father and a stepmother (19% vs. 15%). A substantially higher percentage of Black children resided with a biological father and stepmother than the other groups, at 27%. Meanwhile, a substantially lower proportion of Hispanic (14%) and White (15%) children lived in a cohabiting stepfamily compared with Black children (22%).

Thus, the circumstances of stepchildren's living arrangements varies substantially by race and ethnicity. In sum, these data suggest that about two-thirds of Hispanic children in stepfamily households reside in a married stepfamily with a biological mother and stepfather, one in five reside in a married stepfamily with a biological father and stepmother, and 14% reside with a cohabiting stepfamily, the majority of which consist of a mother and her cohabiting partner. Our analysis indicates that Hispanic stepchildren's living arrangements were more similar to those experienced by White children than those of Black children.

Several studies have identified key racial differences and similarities between racial minority stepfamilies in the United States. Many minority stepfamilies face some type of racial marginalization or discrimination. One study found that minority families faced higher levels of stress caused by racial marginalization as compared with White stepfamilies. Due to this discrimination, there is a higher likelihood that racial/ethnic minority stepfamilies will have less feelings of family belonging (Coleman, Ganong, & Rothrauff, 2006). More recent studies have focused on growth following stressful experiences, sometimes called *post traumatic growth*, and have found that minority stepfamilies actually have stronger bonds with stepfathers and higher levels of family cohesion (King, Thorsen, & Amato, 2014). Still, White stepfamilies do not experience the same racial prejudice, thus resulting in a higher likelihood of cohesiveness. These findings are important because the strengths that stepfamilies of color have are an important part of their identity, and their outcomes cannot be compared with White stepfamilies without accounting for racial discrimination and prejudices.

As mentioned at the beginning of this chapter, because of the large amount of diversity within the Hispanic culture, there is a corresponding amount of cultural values and norms within these groups. We will focus on some of the broad cultural values found within Hispanic families such as familism, traditional gender roles, and religiosity (typically defined as religious salience and religious behavior). Each of the findings will also be related to the ethnic and racial cultures found within the stepfamily literature in the United States as a theoretical way to bridge the lack of research specific to Hispanic stepfamilies. The following vignette details a few unique complexities of Hispanic stepfamilies. This family will also be referenced later in the chapter to help illustrate some of these cultural values and topics.

Juan is a 34-year-old Hispanic male who immigrated to United States from Mexico City with his two children—10-year-old Maria and 6-year-old Carlos—after his first wife died. One year after his move, he married Sofia, a 29-year-old single mother of 8-year-old Camila. Sofia was born and raised in the United States after her parents emigrated from Monterrey, Mexico. Sofia is divorced from her daughter's father, who is Caucasian, and they share custody of their daughter. Juan, Sofia, and their three children now live in a large city in the Southwestern United States. Both Juan and Sofia hold jobs in the service industry to make ends meet, but are struggling financially, particularly because of childcare costs. Unfortunately, they do not live near any extended family (aside from Sofia's ex-husband). Sofia has a two-year community college degree, while Juan finished high school in Mexico.

Although the two have placed priority on strengthening their marriage and connecting their families, there has been increased tension in the marriage due to cultural differences. Juan is a strict Catholic and has raised both of his children in that faith, while Sofia, although raised Catholic, rarely attends services. Additionally, Juan and his two children's first language is Spanish, and they want to speak Spanish in the home. Sofia's parents never formerly taught her Spanish because they believed she needed to know English to succeed in the United States. Although she can understand Spanish, she has never taught it to her daughter. Sofia also does not get along with her in-laws, as she feels judged for not only divorcing her first husband, but also for her daughter being "half White." Even so, Juan and Sofia have been trying to figure out the best way to raise their three children biculturally, and with respect to both Hispanic and American culture.

Juan and Sofia's family situation demonstrates the challenges of blending a family that is experiencing different levels of enculturation versus acculturation, especially in the face of financial stress.

Analyzing the scenario:

- In what ways does the interaction between Sofia and Juan illustrate the unique elements of familism, gender roles, and religion in Hispanic stepfamilies?
- How do differences in Juan and Sofia's journey into their stepfamily shape their current experience?
- What strengths could a practitioner draw upon when working with this family to help them transition to a successful stepfamily?

Aging, Familism, Gender Roles, LGBTQ+ Stepfamilies, and Religion

Aging

There are many considerations that involve aging and stepfamilies. For example, some stepfamilies are formed in later life when an older parent with adult children remarries or re-partners. Other stepfamilies, formed when the children were young, grow older or "age in place." Additionally, having children and adolescent stepchildren differs significantly from having adult stepchildren in the amount of contact, responsibility, and type of relationship that a new stepparent will have. Specifically, it is important to understand the role of aging in Hispanic culture and then the role of aging within Hispanic stepfamilies.

The median age among Hispanic individuals living in the United States has increased from age 25 in 2000 to age 28 five years later (Pew Research Center, 2015). Migration into the United States, which tends to involve younger ages, has slowed, increasing the average age of Hispanics. Additionally, the Hispanic population in the United States is living longer than previous generations. These statistics also demonstrate a particularly young demographic for Hispanic individuals in comparison with other minorities in America. As life expectancy has increased, there are more years for individuals to be married or remarried throughout their lifetime. When older parents remarry, they are sometimes termed "late-life recouplers," and this phenomenon will become

Grandparents and extended family members have an important role to play in Hispanic stepfamily dynamics.

more common as life expectancy continues to increase (Paper-now, 2013). Aging parents are often physically cared for by their adult children and may receive substantial emotional and financial support, and within a stepfamily this can lead to unique complications.

There is a lack of research that focuses specifically on aging issues within Hispanic stepfamilies in the United States. Overall research on aging in stepfamilies, however, indicates that public welfare programs have been increasingly taking care of older adults, rather than children (Coleman & Ganong, 2000). This represents a societal shift in the United States and it can directly clash with the cultural idea of familism in Hispanic families. Also, Hispanic stepfamilies may experience confusion based on who should care for aging parents as they navigate new relationships. This intersection between cultural values and stepfamily dynamics is discussed in the next section.

Familism

One of the most broadly known and supported cultural values found within the literature is the idea of *familism*, defined as a collective orientation that makes family roles highly valued, supportive, and important so that individuals are more focused on the needs of the broader family unit than their own personal desires (Campos, Perez, & Guardino, 2016; Landale & Oropesa, 2007; Santiago-Rivera et al., 2002; Rumbaut & Portes, 2001). Familism contributes to a strong sense of reciprocity, loyalty, and solidarity within extended families. This cultural value may be the key to the higher percentages by race of Hispanic children who live in two biological-parent households, as divorce, separation, and remarriage is discouraged in this highly collective environment. For example, in the vignette presented earlier, Sofia faced social repercussions and disapproval from her in-laws about her decision to get divorced. Divorce reflects an individualistic orientation and personal desires, and therefore goes against the core of this collectivist familism that is so prevalent in Hispanic cultures.

Additionally, familism extends and expands family networks beyond the nuclear family to include others such as grandparents and aunts and uncles (Coltrane et al., 2008; Coltrane & Collins, 2001; Griswold del Castillo, 1984). Familism could cause complications for Hispanic stepfamilies in two ways: (a) the discontinuation of a marriage and subsequent remarriage or cohabitation may spawn strong negative emotions among extended family members who had formed strong bonds with the former couple. This could lead them to become frustrated with their biological family member and their new companion; and (b) newly married couples may feel obligated to be actively involved in extended family members' activities and family gatherings, causing emotional strain as the couple struggles to adjust to their new obligations.

Familism also affects the way in which family members address one another. Papernow (2013) noted that although stepfamily *relationships* appear to be similar in many ways across Hispanic and White families, how they speak about their stepfamilies differs. The term "stepfamily" is rarely, if ever, used in the Spanish language. Furthermore, terms such as "stepmother" or "stepfather" are rarely used within households. Some studies have found that Hispanic step-couples refer to both biological children and stepchildren as "our children" or "my son," etc. (Adler-Baeder & Schramm, 2006.) Research suggests the lack of acknowledgement surrounding stepparents and children demonstrates that these families want to appear as nuclear families, perhaps to maintain an appearance of stability and an intact family (Skogrand et al., 2009).

Gender Roles

As is the case for all racial, ethnic, and religious groups, gender roles are important to Hispanic culture. The terms *machismo* and *marianismo* are commonly used to describe the traditional polarized gender expectations of males and females, respectively (Pina-Watson, Lorenzo-Blanco, Dornhecker, Martinez, & Nagoshi, 2016). Machismo is understood to emphasize male hypermasculinity, risk taking, and courage, while marianismo is exemplified by pious, gentle, and submissive women (Castillo, Perez, Castillo, & Ghosheh, 2010). Recent research has demonstrated that adherence to these roles is correlated with high levels of negative emotions and cognitions in Hispanic culture. While following traditional gender roles has become less common due to globalization and increased employment and education opportunities for women in some parts of the world (Hirsch, 2003; Nehring, 2005), they continue to have a strong influence on individual behaviors and expectations within the Hispanic culture (Kulis, Marsiglia, Nuno-Gutiérrez, Lozano, & Medina-Mora, 2017; López, & Lobo Da Costa, 2008). Our vignette about the differing gender roles of Juan and Sofia demonstrates potential challenges. Juan, being raised and having lived in Mexico

City most of his life, may be more likely to have more traditional gender role expectations than Sofia, who was born and raised in the United States.

For Hispanic stepfamilies, navigating new gender role expectations may be a substantial challenge. While it is not uncommon for new couples to struggle as they figure out how to cohabitate, differing gender role expectations among Hispanic parents could have serious implications for the success of the family. For example, when women who held jobs and shared cooking, cleaning, and parenting duties with their spouse in a former marriage become part of a new stepfamily relationship, there might be differing expectations among partners. In a scenario where traditional *machismo* and *marianismo* views are valued by their new partner and his or her extended family, these colliding expectations could lead to role confusion and frustration. The reverse (men transitioning from a traditional gender relationship to a more liberal environment) may also produce negative emotions as they adjust to increased expectations that they perform "feminine" tasks. This is particularly salient for Hispanic stepfamilies where parent and child roles are typically carried out through traditional ways. Thus, navigating differences in gender role expectations adds a layer of complexity for a new stepfamily to manage. Due to this added complexity, Hispanic stepfamilies may need increased flexibility compared to other stepfamilies when it comes to fulfilling stereotypical gender roles. This flexibility may enhance the Hispanic stepfamily's strength as members learn to create their own unique identity outside of typical Hispanic gender roles.

Religion

Historically, religion has been an important aspect of Hispanic families, with the spiritual practices of certain groups (e.g., Mexican Americans) dating back more than 400 years in some parts of the Southwestern United States (Espinosa & García, 2008). A 2003 study found that 94% of Hispanics identified as being religious, the majority of whom were Catholic (Espenosa, Elizaondo, & Miranda, 2003). Because Catholicism is so prevalent among Hispanic families, many Catholic values have merged with the cultural values of Hispanic families (Santiago-Riveria et al., 2002). As such, the overlap between religion and culture is so great that religious ceremonies are often considered social events (Hovey, 1999). This blend of values extends to beliefs about major family decisions such as family size, marriage, and divorce (Falicov, 1998). This strong religious influence can have both benefits and challenges, particularly for youth who are raised with or adopt such values. In particular, strong cultural and religious values can help youth promote resilience, foster prosocial behaviors, nurture strong mental health, and improve academic performance (Armenta, Knight, Carlo, & Jacobson, 2011; Berkel et al., 2010; Coohey, 2001; Gonzales et al., 2008).

For Hispanic stepfamilies, the strong connection between religiosity and culture may also present challenges. For example, divorce can be a taboo subject because marriage is regarded as highly sanctified, such that breaking up a marriage may cause intense feelings of guilt and failure (Skogrand, Barrios-Bell, & Higginbotham, 2009). As with other social expectations in Hispanic cultures, such failure to comply with cultural norms could lead to an unfavorable perception by the community, and subsequent alienation (see Kandel & Massey, 2002). This was evidenced in the vignette, as Sofia felt judged by her in-laws for being divorced from her daughter's father. On the other hand, sharing the same religion and religious involvement may serve as fertile ground wherein new stepfamilies can find common interest and strength. For example, Hispanic families may find their priest a resource in navigating the challenges of stepfamily life. Family spirituality and faith—often seen as the responsibility of a Hispanic mother to foster and promote within the family (Rodriguez, 2002)—can also help stepfamilies overcome personal and family hardship (Campesino & Schwartz, 2006) and strengthen familial relationships (Wolfinger, Wilcox, & Hernández, 2010).

LGBTQ+ Hispanic Stepfamilies

An interesting intersection of religiosity, familism, and traditional gender roles in Hispanic culture is found in LGBTQ+ families and stepfamilies. Due to the strict gender roles and strong Catholic values, Hispanic individuals who identify as LGBTQ+ often have to navigate between two identities with very different norms and values (Gray, Mendelsohn, & Omoto, 2015). While research on this topic is limited, in one study LGBTQ+ Hispanic immigrants identified their strong family ties—based in *familism*—as a supportive and protective factor in the coming out process and navigating the challenges of being LGBTQ+ in the Hispanic community (Gray et al., 2015). Furthermore, in research with individuals of color, religiosity and spirituality has also been identified as a protective factor for LGBTQ+ individuals struggling with heterosexism and discrimination in American society (Murphy & Hardaway, 2017). Therefore, while there may be tension between the traditional Hispanic values and the LGBTQ+ community, the strong religious and family values may also be a protective factor for LGBTQ+ Hispanic individuals.

Both an LGBTQ+ family and a stepfamily are considered nontraditional, especially in Hispanic culture—thus, LGBTQ+ stepfamilies have to navigate this dual challenge. Within the context of stepfamilies there is limited research on individuals with LGBTQ+ identities, either with LGBTQ+ children or two LGBTQ+ parents. One case study focusing on two gay Hispanic fathers found they spoke more to the cultural challenges of raising a child together than raising a child in a LGBTQ+ stepfamily (Lev & Sennott, 2012). Although more research needs to be done on LGBTQ+ Hispanic stepfamilies, it is important for practitioners working with these stepfamilies to not only consider the LGBTQ+ identity but also the cultural orientation of the stepfamily.

Cultural Orientation

Knight and colleagues (2009) proposed two types of cultural adaption that both affect the psychosocial development of immigrant families and define an individual's cultural orientation: acculturation and enculturation. *Acculturation* is the degree to which individuals adopt the values and behaviors of the majority or host culture, while *enculturation* is the adherence to the values and behaviors of the native culture (Knight, Jacobson, Gonzales, Roosa, & Saebz, 2009). These two socialization processes greatly influence the individual and familial identity of immigrants. For example, the different rates of cultural adaption by family members causes varying cultural expectations, which can result in tension and conflict among family members (Szapocsnik & Kurtines, 1980). Given that the Hispanic population is the fastest-growing minority group in the United States (Ramirez, 2004), the issue of cultural adaption presents a unique challenge for Hispanic families. Literature suggests that when remarriage is combined with immigration, the challenges of each major life event are exacerbated (Berger, 1997; Berger, 2000).

Berger (2000), in her analysis of Russian stepfamilies and their immigration experiences, suggested that both remarriage and immigration each presented families with various difficulties, such as past orientation (i.e., attitudes toward relocation) and choosing a focal subsystem (i.e., which family a member feels more connected to). When both life transitions are experienced together, stepfamilies thus experience what Berger terms a "double burden" of issues. Berger (2000) identifies three issues stepfamilies commonly face: past orientation, acceptance or rejection of differences, and focal sub-systems. Both *past orientation* (the degree to which the previous family system continues to affect the rules and expectations of the new family) and *acceptance or rejection of differences* (the degree to which stepfamilies see themselves as different than traditional families) have been compared to the acculturation process (Berger, 2000). Both life transitions require the family to shift and adapt from one culture to another, whether it be from one country to another or one family unit to another. When experienced together, stepfamilies are not only trying to navigate a new familial culture, but also a new societal culture, which aggravates the stressors associated with each life event. Although these findings were derived from Russian couples, the principle of a double burden is an important one to consider when forming a theoretical base from which to examine Hispanic stepfamilies' cultural orientation. With this is mind, the following section explores the influence of acculturation, enculturation, and bicultural identity on Hispanic families in the United States.

Acculturation

Acculturation is a process of learning and adapting nonnative cultural norms and behaviors that take place at an individual and family level. As it is a process that happens for both the individual and the family, children and parents can have different levels of acculturation. Berry (1997), using findings from a variety of studies, created a conceptual framework for acculturation defining four distinct levels: marginalization, separation/segregation, assimilation, and integration (see Figure 4.4). Berry approached the issue of acculturation by asking two questions with yes or no answers: (a) Is it of value for one to maintain native cultural identity? and (b) Is it of value for one to adapt to the majority culture? He suggested that if there is little interest in keeping one's native cultural identity, and also little interest

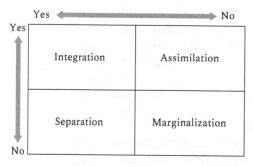

FIGURE 4.4   Horizontal: "Is it considered to be of value to maintain one's identity and characteristics?" Vertical: "Is it considered to be of value to maintain relationships with the larger society?" (Berry, 1997, pg. 10.)

in adapting to the host culture (no answers to each question), then marginalization happens.

On the opposite side, if there is a desire to adapt to norms of the host culture, while still maintaining aspects of one's native culture (yes answers to each question), then integration happens. If one maintains his or her native culture without adapting to any of the host culture (yes/no answers), then segregation occurs, whereas, if one adapts fully to the host culture without maintaining any of one's native culture (no/yes answers), then assimilation occurs. Some research suggests that integration has the most positive outcomes (Perez, Dawson, & Suarez-Orozco, 2011), but requires both the nonnative population and the host society to reach a type of mutual acceptance. The minority culture must take on aspects of the majority culture, and the majority culture must also make steps to integrate minority cultural norms to make institutions accessible to immigrants (Berry, 1997).

Acculturative stress is any stress associated with the acculturation process due to losses felt from leaving a native culture, more colloquially known as "culture shock" (Caplan, 2007), and can occur as individuals transition between different levels of acculturation (Miranda, Bilot, Peluso, Berman, & Van Meek, 2006). Acculturative stress has been associated with many negative psychosocial outcomes for Hispanic immigrants, including adolescent substance use, anxiety and depression, and physical effects such as obesity (Caplan, 2007). Putting acculturative stress into a family context, increased family stress will most likely occur when family members are at dissimilar stages of acculturation. For example, older generations of immigrants (parents and grandparents) are more likely to remain in the segregation stage while children and adolescents tend to reach assimilation and acculturate at much faster rates than their peers (Telzer, Yuen, Gonzales, & Fuligni, 2016). This creates interfamilial tension because as children adapt cultural norms of the host culture, they transgress traditional family rules, roles, and expectations, which increases the likelihood for decreased family cohesion (Miranda, Estrada, & Firpo-Jimenez, 2000). These stressors, however, can be offset by positive coping skills and family dynamics, which decrease acculturative stress (Miranda et al., 2006). For example, Papernow (2013) suggests that if a stepparent is of a third-plus generation, the stepparent may be able to soften the acculturative conflict between acculturated children and their biological first- or second-generation parent.

Furthermore, family dysfunction is associated with higher acculturative stress and more negative outcomes (Arbona et al.,

2014). In his systematic review, Amato (2010) found that family dysfunction is many times increased with remarriage, due to the effect multiple transitions have on child development. Studies in the review found the number of family transitions in childhood was associated with problem behaviors, drug use, academic achievement, and even dysfunctional relationships in adulthood. Consequently, concerning Hispanic immigrant families in particular, research suggests stepfamilies tend to have weaker family bonds, which may lead to the inability to utilize the family unit as a protective factor for family stresses (Chassin et al., 2016). Due to the unique challenges remarriage presents, stepfamilies may be at an increased risk for acculturative stress because of the historically high rates of immigration and associated assimilation difficulties.

Our current sociopolitical climate may be particularly problematic for Hispanic stepfamilies, regardless of immigration status. Widespread discussion about the legality of the Deferred Action for Childhood Arrivals, or DACA (an American immigration policy that makes children who were brought to the United States illegally eligible to receive higher education and a work permit [see Lee, 2006]); increased raids by Immigration and Customs Enforcement (ICE) in cities with large Hispanic populations; and constant references by President Donald Trump about "building a wall" and Mexican immigrants "flooding our borders" have put unwanted attention on all Hispanic families in the United States, and added another layer of stress on the aforementioned double burden of Hispanic families. Nevertheless, relative to other federal regulations and policies regarding stepfamilies, the United States immigration system has a liberal definition of "immediate relatives" for the purpose of family unification. Although federal law for the most part does not legally recognize stepparent-stepchild relationships, stepchildren and stepparents are considered immediate relatives as long was the parents are married and the marriage took place before the stepchild's 18th birthday and therefore can be brought to the country (Menjivar, Leisy, & Schmalzbauer, 2016; Whitlock, 2016). As discussed later, however, the laws are complicated and many restrictions apply.

Enculturation

Enculturation is defined as the process by which a family passes down its native culture. The degree to which an individual remains enculturated or conversely becomes acculturated can be understood using the socialization model, first described by

Knight, Bernal, Carza, and Cota (1993). The socialization model states that an individual's cultural orientation and/or ethnic identity (i.e., on the continuum of enculturated to acculturated) is shaped by the family background and structure, which influences relationship formation with familial and nonfamilial agents. As family structure is the key part of an individual's ethnic identity, it is worth considering the influence a stepfamily has on the enculturation of a family, and vice versa.

Studies have found that high enculturation is correlated with better individual outcomes for Hispanic immigrants (Roosa et al., 2009). This is perhaps related to the themes of *familism*—trust of, loyalty to, and orientation to the family—and *respeto*, which promotes positive familial relationships and maintains harmony, as they both increase family cohesion and values in traditional Hispanic families (Miranda et al., 2000). Although high enculturation inherently creates some stress related to balancing one set of cultural norms inside the home and another without (Roosa et al., 2009), enculturation may enhance Hispanic family cohesion. Hispanic immigrant families that have acculturated to American culture see a decrease in both *familism* and *respeto*, which has been found to increase problem behaviors of individual family members and increases family conflict (Gil et al., 2000).

Because *familism* and *respeto* emphasize family cohesion, harmony, and the importance of the family unit, enculturated Hispanic stepfamilies may experience less transitional stress with remarriage than do American stepfamilies. On the other hand, most stepfamilies today are formed through divorce or a nonmarital birth followed by marriage or cohabitation (as opposed to the death of a spouse), which goes against *familism* (Coltrane, Gutierrez, & Parke, 2008). The situation may be further complicated if one of the spouses or partners has a different cultural background, which makes enculturation to the Hispanic culture less likely and acculturation to American culture more likely (consider Juan and Sofia's relationship in the vignette). Furthermore, there is less stigma against stepfamilies in American culture versus Hispanic culture. For example, White Americans remarry and re-partner at much higher rates than do Hispanic Americans

Religiosity and spirituality is often intertwined with cultural norms and everyday life in Hispanic families.

(McNamee & Raley, 2011). Therefore, it may be more apropos for a Hispanic stepfamily to acculturate to reduce stress associated with negative attitudes from the community. Thus, traditional assumptions about the benefits of acculturation versus enculturation among Hispanic families in the United States may not apply to stepfamilies or may unfold differently. Additional research specifically addressing the enculturation to acculturation spectrum in relation to Hispanic stepfamilies is needed.

Bicultural Identity

There has been a recent shift toward using a bidimensional acculturation model, which assumes the dual process of enculturation and acculturation in understanding the experiences of Hispanic immigrants in the United States (Perez et al., 2011). On the continuum between enculturation and acculturation, this *bicultural identity* refers to dual involvement in both the mainstream and native cultures, without sacrificing the benefits of either (Berry, 1997). Some research suggests that bicultural identity has positive outcomes for Hispanic adolescents, including lower depression and school dropout rates, and higher levels of self-esteem (Dennis, Fonseca, Guiterrez, Shen, & Salazar, 2016).

The effect of bicultural identity on children's well-being may be mediated by other factors. Biculturalism may increase family cohesion and lower acculturative stress, thus leading to more positive outcomes (Perez, 2011). Indeed, an individual's ability to obtain biculturalism is dependent upon the support of the family to reinforce bicultural lessons and behaviors (Dennis et al., 2016). For example, Dennis and her colleagues explored the bicultural experiences of what they termed the 2.5 generation—when there is one American-born parent and one parent from another country. They found that individuals in the 2.5 generation have higher rates of biculturism than traditional second- or third-generation Hispanics because of their unique family structure. Supporting this finding, in their analysis of the March Current Population Survey, Litcher, Carmalt, and Qian (2011) found that "third-plus" generation Hispanics in the United States had lower rates of intermarriage (i.e., marrying someone who also identifies as Hispanic), which would increase biculturism.

Although few studies look specifically at biculturism in Hispanic stepfamilies, the hypothesis can be made that the stepfamily's unique family structure may influence their biculturism. Each stepfamily is inherently bicultural (regardless of parent birthplace), as the two families that come together bring with them two distinct family cultures—and perhaps two distinct cultural orientations that could be passed down to create a bicultural identity of their children. Hispanic stepfamilies may be more likely to have a mix of parents with different generational statuses due to remarriage after immigration, increasing the chance for bicultural identity formation. Therefore, it could be argued the unique structure of a stepfamily, as it promotes biculturism, may be a protective factor for the acculturative stressors.

In sum, differing cultural orientations (i.e., acculturated, enculturated, or bicultural) appear to influence family dynamics. Available research suggests that enculturation and bicultural involvement are correlated with positive family outcomes, whereas acculturation and its associated stressors may lead to negative family outcomes. For Hispanic stepfamilies, these general trends may hold true; however, there are unique challenges stepfamilies face that may leave them more at risk for acculturative stress and less equipped to cope. It is perhaps less likely that a Hispanic stepfamily would remain enculturated due to the heavy stigmatization of divorce and out-of-wedlock childbearing in traditional Hispanic culture. Therefore, Hispanic stepfamilies may be more likely to acculturate, and experience the stressors associated with acculturation while still developing a stepfamily unit. On the other hand, a stepfamily structure lends itself more to biculturism than a traditional family structure, which may increase biculturism and its positive outcomes. Clearly, more research is needed to understand the effect of different cultural orientations on family processes in Hispanic stepfamilies.

Socioeconomic Inequality and Hispanic Stepfamilies

In addition to the influence of culture, the role of socioeconomic status has been a focus of Hispanic family research (Umana-Taylor & Updegraff, 2013). While this text focuses heavily on culture, the following section reviews the effect socioeconomic status has on Hispanic stepfamilies. Hispanic families in the United States have historically been disadvantaged socioeconomically. Currently, 22% of the Hispanic population in the United States lives in poverty (Flores, Lopez, & Radford, 2017), including 26% of Hispanic children, which is more than twice the amount of White children (Annie E. Casey Foundation, 2017). Living in poverty has dire effects on life outcomes for adults and children, including lower levels of education, higher incarceration rates, and negative mental and physical health outcomes.

Tellingly, 61% of Hispanics living in the United States only have a high school diploma or less (Flores et al., 2017). Poverty statistics suggest, however, that the more generations Hispanics are removed from initial immigration, the higher their level of education and the less likely they will be living in poverty (Fry & Passel, 2009). For example, 43% of first-generation Hispanic parents have less than a high school diploma, compared with 40% of second-generation parents, and only 16% of third-or-more-generation parents; similarly, 34% of first-generation Hispanic families live in poverty, compared with 26% of second-generation families and 24% of third-plus-generation families.

Unfortunately, many studies that compare the family outcomes of different racial and ethnic groups do not account for persistent social and economic disadvantages faced by non-White groups that are associated with lower levels of well-being, attributing their worse outcomes to their own culture and choices (Umana-Taylor & Updegraff, 2013). Alternatively, the family stress model suggests that if a family faces economic hardship there will be a higher likelihood of poor family functioning, which decreases positive parenting, family relationships, and child outcomes (Neppl, Senia, & Donnellan, 2015). As poverty levels decrease over the generations, one might expect that Hispanic families of third-plus generations may have better family outcomes than first-generation immigrant families. Indeed, one study did find that higher acculturated (i.e., third-plus generation) Hispanic families had higher socioeconomic status, which was linked to better outcomes for children (Garu, Azmitia, & Quattlebaum, 2009). Among first-generation Hispanic immigrant families, however, those with more access to resources were found to have better outcomes than their peers with less access to resources (Umana-Taylor & Updegraff, 2013), highlighting the potential moderating influence of socioeconomic status on the relationships among migration, culture, generational status, and family and individual outcomes.

Marriage, including remarriage, is associated with higher incomes. Single parents are more likely to live in poverty than those in two-parent households (Lin & Harris, 2009). For Hispanic Americans, the average per capita income is $24,000 (Flores et al., 2017), which is barely above the poverty line for a family of three, and below the poverty line for a family of four; however, the average income among households with two or more working adults for Hispanic Americans is $44,000, which is above the poverty line. Thus, from an economic standpoint, there are clear incentives for Hispanic individuals to form partnerships, such as marriage or remarriage. Stepparents bring in additional resources to the household, including extra income.

U.S. families of all races and ethnicities are increasingly cohabiting and having children outside of marriage (Gibson-Davis, 2016). Cohabitation is high among Hispanic stepfamilies, with one study suggesting that more than 50% of Hispanic American stepfathers were not married to the mother (Coltrane et al., 2008). In some Hispanic subcultures, this may be due to the similarity of informal unions to marriage. For example, a study of Puerto Rican women showed that informal relationships, such as cohabitation, were just as meaningful and valued as legal marriage (Landale & Fennelly, 1995). Cohabitation may reduce the chances of minority children living in poverty, at least temporarily; however, research shows that cohabiting couples do not share resources as married families do, and thus a cohabiting partner's additional financial resources do not improve a family's economic status at the same rate (Brown, 2004). Therefore, cohabitors have lower incomes than do married couples, and cohabiting partners do not receive the economic benefits of marriage, including tax incentives and long-term, stable financial planning, and the accumulation of shared financial assets that lead to sustained wealth (Gibson-Davis et al., 2018). For example, one study found that its sample of first-time *fragile families* (cohabiting couples with children) had $9,645 less in financial assets than their married peers, and serial cohabitors (who have cohabited in more than one relationship) had $8,763 less than their married peers (Britt-Lutter, Dorius, & Lawson, 2018).

Another risk factor stepfamilies face for lower socioeconomic status is that one or both parents may also have financial obligations to another family system. Research suggests that stepparents may not invest as much into stepchildren, because they prioritize their resources for their biological children with previous partners (Ganong & Coleman, 2017). For example, in one sample of Hispanic stepfathers in the United States (married or cohabiting), nearly two-thirds were paying child support to children in other households—thus significantly reducing the potential benefits of that stepparent's extra income (Coltrane et al., 2008). This may even introduce new economic stressors, such as inability to pay bills due to lack of funds. Illustrating this financial effect, in the same sample of Hispanic stepfathers, the authors found that in 60% of all stepfamilies both the mother and stepfather were working to meet the financial needs of the family, and nearly 16% of all stepfamilies were living with other family members (i.e., uncles, grandparents, cousins, etc.) due to financial necessity. As Coltrane, Gutierrez, and Parke (2008) put it, "One of the most distinctive historical features of Mexican American family life is reliance on extended networks of kinfolk for emotional and material support" (p. 100).

The financial challenges facing stepfamilies are severe even when race and ethnicity are removed from the equation. The economic deprivation hypothesis states that children of divorce, regardless of race and ethnicity, are disadvantaged compared with their peers in traditional two-parent households (Mackey, 2005). Supporting this hypothesis are findings by the National Bureau of Economic Research that suggest the family income of children whose parents divorce falls by 40% to 45% (2018). While recognizing that additional research comparing financial differences between step and biological parent households is needed, Manning and Brown (2006) suggest that cohabiting stepparent families could be financially worse off because they may not share in the cohabiting partner's economic resources.

Therefore, it is important when considering the challenges Hispanic stepfamilies face to take into account the unique challenges related to culture (e.g., *acculturative stress*) separately from challenges related to low education and income. Think of the family presented in the case study. The fact that Maria and Juan cannot find childcare is related to their low education and income, while the tension stemming from whether to raise their children in the Catholic Church has more to do with culture and degree of acculturation. Thus, for a simplified example, it would be inappropriate to relate the fact they cannot find childcare to different cultural orientations, as they represent different challenges the stepfamily is facing resulting from two causes.

Implications and Recommendations

Recommendations for Future Research

As a deeper understanding of Hispanic stepfamilies is reached, it is imperative that researchers continue to explore the complexity of stepfamilies and recognize the limitations of research. Various limitations are worth noting before recommendations are provided. As with other minority groups in the United States, there are considerable cultural differences among the subgroups within the Hispanic population. The term "Hispanic" contains a broad array of groups including Mexicans, Guatemalans, Cubans, and

Dominicans, just to name a few of the most populous subgroups (U.S. Census Bureau, 2010). While the information we have presented will be useful when considering differences between Hispanics and other ethnic groups, practitioners should be careful not to make general assumptions or decisions affecting Hispanic clients based exclusively on the information presented herein. Another limitation worth noting is the dearth of research specific to Hispanic stepfamilies. This lack of research has required us to make assumptions about Hispanic stepfamilies in the United States based on knowledge we have about unique characteristics, traits, patterns, and nuances within their culture.

Despite these limitations, the information provided is critical for advancing stepfamily research agendas aimed at better understanding individual and family dynamics among the fastest-growing minority group in the United States. To further our understanding of the topics presented in this chapter, researchers should consider the following questions: (a) How might Hispanic stepfamilies best navigate the community perceptions of their family structure as it relates to cultural gender roles, familism, and religiosity? (b) Does increased religiosity/spirituality protect Hispanic stepfamilies from some of the challenges associated with the creation and maintenance of a stepfamily? (c) How does high religiosity/spirituality among extended family members influence their treatment and perception of those in stepfamilies? (d) Does acculturation, enculturation, and bicultural identity affect Hispanic stepfamilies differently than other migrant families? (e) How powerful is socioeconomic status as a predictor of quality of life among Hispanic stepfamilies, and does increasing income counteract the negative effect of other cultural, environmental, biological, social, and natural challenges they face? Answering these and other questions will help inform practitioners and policy makers with information needed for providing resources and services to these often overlooked families.

Recommendations for Practice

From a direct practice vantage point, social workers, counselors, mental health providers, and other professionals serving Hispanic stepfamilies should listen carefully for indications that unique cultural influences may or may not be sources of strength or difficulty. For example, expectations from community members regarding adherence to culturally prevalent views of familism and gender roles may help explain interpersonal behaviors and decisions within the stepfamily. Given the broad interpretation of "family" within

Hispanic culture, practitioners should be careful not to underestimate the influence of expectations from extended, nonbiological family members. Furthermore, when working with stepfamilies that mirror traditional Hispanic gender roles (i.e., *machismo* and *marianismo*), helping professionals should be mindful of their own cultural values so that personal or mainstream U.S. ideals do not unintentionally influence their recommendations.

Religiosity and spirituality, while not always overtly evident, may be sources of strength and resilience on which to build or, alternatively, sources of guilt and shame. The influence of strong religious values instilled in Hispanic youth has been found to have positive benefits, while feelings of guilt and shame may be strong among those who do not appear to be following religious cultural norms. Practitioners should carefully consider inquiring about the importance and effects of religiosity within Hispanic stepfamilies to determine its influence within the family, and whether it could be tapped to benefit the family.

Finally, the immigration situations of stepfamily members—particularly when there are differing immigration statuses—may be a source of stress and difficulty. For those who are undocumented, the fear of being separated from their children, obtaining sustainable employment, and trying to procure basic services such as education or healthcare may be significant causes of strain that exacerbate typical stepfamily stresses. Helping professionals should be informed about the legal rights of migrants, and be prepared to refer them to local human rights advocates and competent legal services as applicable. Regardless of immigration status, significant acculturation differences between parents and children may be present among first-, second-, and third-generation immigrants. Counselors should be careful not to assume that stepfamily challenges are inherently due to family structure when acculturation differences, immigration status, socioeconomic, and other factors may be more directly associated with their struggles.

Relevant Laws and Policies

The speed of growth amid the U.S. Hispanic population necessitates recognition and action on the part of lawmakers at all levels of government, particularly in such areas as the Southwest where Hispanics form the population majority in many cities and towns. Thoughtfully addressing the needs of this large and growing population can benefit all Americans. Looking beyond the divisive rhetoric focused on migration, employment, and education issues that affect (directly or indirectly) all U.S. Hispanics, it cannot be denied the Hispanic population is a large and integral part of who we now are as a nation.

Within this already marginalized minority group, we can see that Hispanic stepfamilies are particularly vulnerable because of cultural norms around divorce and the overlooking of stepfamilies as a legitimate family structure. Local, statewide, and national policies—or the lack thereof—can exacerbate these challenges. For example, recent actions by the executive and judiciary branches of our national government regarding the separation and subsequent reunification of migrant families coming to the United States make no overt considerations for parents and children in nontraditional family structures (Flores v. Sessions, 2018; Jordan & Fernandez, 2018). Considering immigration, one issue that may affect immigrant Hispanic stepfamilies is laws surrounding the I-130 form, the Petition for Alien Relative (United States Citizenship and Immigration Services, 2017). This form is used when a legal citizen in the United States needs to legally prove a relationship with an individual who wants to immigrate into the United States. This process, however, becomes more complicated for stepfamilies. As noted previously, according to U.S. law, a stepparent-stepparent child relationship is created if a natural parent and stepparent are married before the child turns 18. If the stepparent is a natural citizen, the stepparent can petition for citizenship for the stepchild (U.S. Citizenship and Immigration Services, n.d.). The step-relationship is terminated with a divorce, but remains if either of the parents are deceased. It is important to note that if a stepchild gains citizenship with petition by the stepparent, the child can then petition for either of the natural parents, regardless of their marriage status. Although this offers a good avenue to citizenship for members of stepfamilies, it is contingent on marriage, which would not include the high percentage of Hispanic stepfamilies with cohabiting parents. Furthermore, if a parent is deported, legal guardianship over the stepchildren becomes complicated, especially if the stepchild or stepchildren have not been legally adopted by the stepparent. One way some immigrant families have been addressing this issue is by using standby guardian laws to appoint temporary guardianship to a friend or family member in case of deportation of the natural parent (Wiltz, 2018). But standby guardianship was initially put into place in the case of the death of a natural parent (Child Welfare Information Gateway, 2018), therefore there is limited legal precedent for using the law in deportation cases, and currently only New York and Maryland have passed specific deportation standby guardianship laws (Wiltz, 2018). Without explicit instructions on how to act, law enforcement officers, social workers, and local judges may be forced to make case-by-case decisions that are influenced by personal opinions, leading to inconsistent treatment across stepfamilies.

Just as ignoring stepfamilies in the creation of policies can lead to confusion, uncertainty, and subsequent anxiety, a purposeful approach by policy makers to consider the unique situations of stepfamilies would be an acknowledgement of their existence, importance, and value to our communities. Such recognition would benefit all stepfamilies, and would be of particular importance to Hispanic stepfamilies who struggle for recognition within their unique ethnic culture. This type of change does not happen by chance, and must be part of a collaborative and purposeful effort from community leaders and sympathizing nonprofit organizations. Of particular importance will be the voices of Hispanic step-couples and stepchildren who can utilize their experiences to inform positive change.

Questions for Discussion

1. Consider how the recent immigration, cultural orientation, acculturative stress, socioeconomic status, religious and cultural differences, and lack of an extended family support system may be affecting the family in the vignette. What are some potential strengths and limitations of the family as they try to navigate their new situation as a stepfamily?

2. Why are familism and other cultural values important to consider with respect to family dynamics and processes in Hispanic stepfamilies? How are these cultural values different from or similar to other cultures?

3. Consider Berger's (2000) double burden on immigrant stepfamilies. How are the stressors of immigration similar to the stressors of remarriage and stepfamily formation? How are they different?

4. What are some reasons it is important to consider the issues of culture and race/ethnicity separately from the issues of socioeconomic status for Hispanic stepfamilies?

Additional Resources

Alfaro, E. C., Umaña-Taylor, A. J., & Bámaca, M. Y. (2006). The influence of academic support on Latino adolescents' academic motivation. *Family Relations, 55,* 279-291.

Harwood, R., Leyendecker, B., Carlson, V., Asencio, M., & Miller, A. (2002). Parenting among Latino families in the US. In M. H. Bornstein (Ed.) *Handbook of parenting* (pp. 21-46). Mahwah, NJ: Lawrence Erlbaum.

Jensen, T. M., & Shafer, K. (2013). Stepfamily functioning and closeness: Children's views on second marriages and stepfather relationships. *Social Work, 58,* 127-136.

McLoyd, V. C. (1998). Changing demographics in the American population: Implications for research on minority children and adolescents. In V. C. McLoyd & L. Steinberg (Eds.) *Studying minority adolescents: Conceptual, methodological, and theoretical issues* (pp. 3-28). Mahwah, NJ.: Lawrence Erlbaum.

Olmedo, E. L. (1979). Acculturation: A psychometric perspective. *American Psychologist, 34,* 1061-1070.

Umaña-Taylor, A. J., & Bámaca, M. Y. (2004). Conducting focus groups with Latino populations: Lessons from the field. *Family Relations, 53,* 261-272.

Umaña-Taylor, A. J., & Updegraff, K. A. (2013). Latino families in the United States. In G. W. Peterson & K. R. Bush (Eds.) *Handbook of marriage and the family* (pp. 723-747). New York, NY: Springer U.S.

References

Alfaro, E. C., Umaña-Taylor, A. J., & Bámaca, M. Y. (2006). The influence of academic support on Latino adolescents' academic motivation. *Family Relations, 55,* 279-291.

Amato, P. (2010). Research on divorce: Continuing trends and new developments. *Journal of Marriage and Family, 72,* 650-666.

Armernta, B. E., Knight, G. P., Carlo, G., & Jacobson, R. P. (2011). The relation between ethnic group attachment and prosocial tendencies: The mediating role of cultural values. *European Journal of Social Psychology, 41,* 107-155.

Arbona, C., Olvera, N., Rodriguez, N., Hagan, J., Linares, A., & Wiesner, M. (2012). Acculturative stress among documented and undocumented Latino immigrants in the United States. *Hispanic Journal of Behavioral Sciences, 32,* 362-384.

American Psychological Association. (2015). *Demographics of the US psychology workforce: Findings from the American Community Survey.* Washington, DC: American Psychological Association. Author.

Annie E. Casey Foundation. (2017). *Children in poverty by race and ethnicity.* Retrieved February 10, 2019, from https://datacenter.kidscount.org/data/Tables/44-children-in-poverty-by-race-and-ethnicity

Berger, R. (1997). Immigrant stepfamilies. *Contemporary Family Therapy, 19,* 361–370.

Berger, R. (2000). When remarriage and immigration coincide. *Journal of Ethical and Cultural Diversity in Social Work, 9,* 75–96.

Berkel, C., Murry, V. M., Hurt, T. R., Chen, Y.-F., Brody, G. H., Simons, R. L. (2009). It takes a village: Protecting rural African American youth in the context of racism. *Journal of Youth and Adolescence, 38,* 175–188.

Berry, J. W. (1997). Immigration, acculturation, and adaption. *Applied Psychology: An International Review, 46,* 5–68.

Britt-Lutter, S., Dorius, C., & Lawson, D. (2018). The financial implications of cohabitation among young adults. *Journal of Financial Planning, 31.*

Brown, S. L. (2004). Family structure and child well-being: The significance of parental cohabitation. *Journal of Marriage and Family, 66,* 351–367.

Campesino, M., & Schwartz, G. E. (2006). Spirituality among Latinas/os: Implications of culture in conceptualization and measurement. *Advances in Nursing Science, 29,* 69–81.

Caplan, S. (2007). Latinos, acculturation, and acculturative stress: A dimensional concept analysis. *Policy, Politics, & Nursing Practice, 8,* 93–106.

Castillo, L. G., Perez, F. V., Castillo, R., & Ghosheh, M.R. (2010). Construction and initial validation of the Marianismo Beliefs Scale. *Counselling Psychology Quarterly, 23,* 163–175.

Cauce, A. M., & Domenech-Rodriguez, M. (2002). Latino families: Myths and realities. In J. Contreras, A Neal-Barnett, & K. Kerns (Eds.) *Latino children and families in the United States: Current research and future directions* (pp. 3–26). Westport, CT: Praeger.

Chassin, L., Haller, M., Lee, M. R., Handley, E., Bountress, K., & Beltran, I. (2016). Familial factors influencing offspring substance use and dependence. In K. J. Sher (Ed.) *The Oxford handbook of substance use and substance use disorders* (pp. 449–482). New York, NY: Oxford University Press.

Child Welfare Information Gateway. (2018). *Standby guardianship.* Web. January 15, 2019.

Coleman, M., Ganong, L., & Rothrauff, T. (2006). Racial and ethnic similarities and differences in beliefs about intergenerational assistance to older adults after divorce and remarriage. *Family Relations, 55,* 576–587.

Coltrane, S., Gutierrez, E., & Parke, R. D. (2008). Stepfathers in cultural context: Mexican American families in the United States. In J. Pryor (Ed.) *The international handbook of stepfamilies: Policy and practice in legal, research, and clinical environments.* (pp. 100–121). Hoboken, NJ: John Wiley & Sons.

Coltrane, S., & Collins, R. (2001). *Sociology of marriage & the family: Gender, love, and property.* New York, NY: Wadsworth/ Thomson Learning.

Coohey, C. (2001). The relationship between familism and child maltreatment in Latino and Anglo families. *Child Maltreatment, 6,* 130–142.

Dennis, J. M., Fonseca, A. L., Guiterrez, G., Shen, J., & Salazar, S. (2016). Bicultural competence and the Latino 2.5 generation. *Hispanic Journal of Behavioral Sciences, 38*(3), 341–359.

Elliott, D. B., & Simmons, T. (2011). *Marital events of Americans: 2009.* American Community Survey Reports, ACS-13, U.S. Census Bureau, Washington, DC, 2011. Retrieved February 10, 2019, from https://www2.census.gov/library/publications/2011/acs/acs-13

Espinosa, G., Elizondo, V. and Miranda, J. 2003. *Hispanic churches in American public life: Summary of findings.* Notre Dame, IN: Institute for Latino Studies, University of Notre Dame.

Espinosa, G., & García, M. T. (2008). *Mexican American religions: Spirituality, activism, & culture.* Durham, NC: Duke University Press.

Falicov, C. J. 1998. *Latino families in therapy: A guide to multicultural practice,* New York, NY: Guilford Press.

Flores, A., Lopez, G., & Radford, J. (2017). *Facts on Latinos, 2015.* Retrieved February 10, 2019, from Pew Research Center website: http://www.pewhispanic.org/2017/09/18/facts-on-u-s-latinos-current-data/

Flores v. Session, Case No. CV 85-4544-DMG (AGRx) (DC 2018). Retrieved February 10, 2019, from https://www.politico.com/f/?id=00000164-8176-d66b-a166-8bf6cdaa0000

Fry, R., & Passel, J. S. (2009). *Latino children: A majority are U.S.-born offspring of immigrants.* Retrieved February 4, 2019, from http://www.pewhispanic.org/files/reports

Ganong, L. H., & Coleman, M. (2017). *Stepfamily relationships.* Boston, MA: Springer.

Gibson-Davis, C. M. (2016). Single and cohabitating parents and poverty. In D. Brady & L. M. Burton (Eds.) *The Oxford handbook of social science of poverty* (pp. 417–437). Oxford, UK: Oxford University Press.

Gil, A. G., Wagner, E. F., & Vega, W. A. (2000). Acculturation, familism, and alcohol use among Latino adolescent males: Longitudinal relations. *Community Psychology, 28,* 443–458.

Gonzales, N. A., Germán, M., Kim, S. Y., George, P., Fabrett, F. C., Millsap, R., & Dumka, L. E. (2008). Mexican American adolescents' cultural orientation, externalizing behavior and academic engagement: The role of traditional cultural values. *American Journal of Community Psychology, 41,* 151–164.

Grau, J. M., Azmitia, M., & Quattlebaum, J. (2009). Latino families: Parenting, relational, and developmental processes. In F. A. Villarruel, G. Carlo, J. M. Grau, M. Azmitia, N. J. Cabrera, & T. J.

Chahin (Eds.) *Handbook of U.S. Latino psychology* (pp. 153–170). Thousand Oaks, CA: Sage.

Gray, N. N., Mendelsohn, D. M., Omoto, A. M. (2015). Community connectedness, challenges, and resilience among gay Latino immigrants. *American Journal of Community Psychology, 55,* 202–214.

Griswold del Castillo, R. (1984). *La familia.* Notre Dame, IN: University of Notre Dame Press.

Harwood, R., Leyendecker, B., Carlson, V., Asencio, M., & Miller, A. (2002). Parenting among Latino families in the US. In M. H. Bornstein (Ed.) *Handbook of parenting* (pp. 21–46). Mahwah, NJ: Lawrence Erlbaum.

Hirsch, J. S. (2003). *A courtship after marriage: Sexuality and love in Mexican transnational families.* Berkeley and Los Angeles: University of California Press.

Hovey, J. D. (1999). Religion and suicidal ideation in a sample of Latin American immigrants. *Psychological Report, 85,* 171–177.

Jensen, T. M., & Shafer, K. (2013). Stepfamily functioning and closeness: Children's views on second marriages and stepfather relationships. *Social Work, 58,* 127–136.

Jordan, M., & Fernandez, M. (2018, July 9). Judge rejects detentions of migrant families, dealing Trump another setback. *The New York Times.* Retrieved February 4, 2019, from https://www.nytimes.com/2018/07/09/us/migrants-family-separation-reunification.html

King, V., Thorsen, M. L., & Amato, P. R. (2014). Factors associated with positive relationships between stepfathers and adolescent stepchildren. *Social Science Research, 47,* 16–29.

Knight, G. P., Bernal, M. E., Garza, C. A., Cota, M. K., & Ocampo, K. A. (1993). Family socialization and the ethnic identity of Mexican-American children. *Journal of Cross-Cultural Psychology, 24,* 99–114.

Knight, G. P., Jacobson, R. P., Gonzales, N. A., Roosa, M. W., and Saenz, D. S. (2009). An evaluation of the psychological research on acculturation and enculturation processes among recently immigrating populations. In R. L. Dalla, J. DeFrain, J. Johnson, & D. Abbot (Eds.) *Strengths and challenges of new immigrant families: Implications for research, policy, education, and service* (pp. 9–31). Lanham, MD: Lexington.

Knight, G. P., Roosa, M. W., & Umaña-Taylor, A. J. (2009). *Studying ethnic minority and economically disadvantaged populations: Methodological challenges and best practices.* American Psychological Association.

Kulis, S. S., Marsiglia, F. F., Nuno-Gutiérrez, B. L., Lozano, M. D., & Medina-Mora, M. E., (2017). Traditional gender roles and substance-use behaviors, attitudes, exposure, and resistance among early adolescents in large cities of Mexico. *Journal of Substance Use.* doi:10.1080/14659891.2017.1405088

Landale, N. S., & Fennelly, K. (1992). Informal unions among mainland Puerto Ricans: Cohabitation or an alternative to legal marriage? *Journal of Marriage and the Family, 54*, 269–280.

Landale, N. S., & Oropesa, R. S. (2007). Hispanic families: Stability and change. *Annual Review of Sociology, 33*, 381–405.

Lee, Y. (2006). To dream or not to dream: A cost-benefit analysis of the development, relief, and education for alien minors (DREAM) act. *Cornell JL & Pub. Pol'y, 16*, 231.

Lev, A. I., & Sennott, S. L. (2012). Clinical work with LGBTQ parents and prospective parents. In A. E. Goldberg & K. R. Allen (Eds.) *LGBT-parent families: Innovations in research and implications for practice* (pp. 241–260). New York, NY: Springer.

Lewis, J. M., & Kreider, R. M. (2015). *Remarriage in the United States: American Community Survey reports.* United States Census (Report No. ACS0-30). Retrieved February 4, 2019, from https://www.census.gov/content/dam/Census/library/publications/2015/acs/acs-30.pdf

Lichter, D. T., Carmalt, J. H., & Qian, Z. (2011). Immigration and intermarriage among Hispanics: Crossing racial and generational boundaries. *Sociological Forum, 26*, 241–264.

Lin, A. C., & Harris, D. R. (2009). *The colors of poverty: Why racial & ethnic disparities persist.* National Policy Center (Report #16). Retrieved February 4, 2019, from http://www.npc.umich.edu/publications/policy_briefs/brief16

López. K. S. G., & Lobo Da Costa, J. M. (2008). Conducta antisocial y consume de alcohol en adolescenteds escolares. *Revista Latino-Americana De Enfermagem, 16*, 299–305.

Mackey, R. (2005). The impact of family structure and family change on child outcomes: A personal reading of research literature. *Social Policy Journal of New Zealand, 24*, 111–133.

Malia, S. (2005). Balancing family members' interests regarding stepparent rights and obligations: A social policy challenge. *Family Relations, 54*, 298–319.

Manning, W. D., & Brown, S. (2006). Children's economic well-being in married and cohabiting parent families. *Journal of Marriage and Family, 68*, 345–362.

McLoyd, V. C. (1998). Changing demographics in the American population: Implications for research on minority children and adolescents. In V. C. McLoyd & L. Steinberg (Eds.) *Studying minority adolescents: Conceptual, methodological, and theoretical issues* (pp. 3–28). Mahwah, NJ.: Lawrence Erlbaum.

McNamee, C. B., & Raley, K. R. (2011). A note on race, ethnicity and nativity differentials in remarriage in the United States. *Demographic Research, 24*, 293–312.

Menjívar, C., Abrego, L. J., & Schmalzbauer, L. C. (2016). *Immigrant families.* UK: Polity Press.

Miranda, A. O., Bilot, J. M., Peluso, P. R., Bernman, K., & Van Meek, L. G. (2006). Latino families: The relevance of the connection among acculturation, family dynamics, and health for family counseling research and practice. *The Family Journal: Counseling and Therapy for Couples and Families, 14,* 268–273.

Miranda, A. O., Estrada, D., & Firpo-Jimenez, M. (2000). Differences in family cohesion, adaptability, and environment among Latino families in dissimilar stages of acculturation. *The Family Journal: Counseling and Therapy for Couples and Families, 8,* 341–350.

Murphy, J., & Hardaway, R. (2017). LGBTQ adolescents of color: Consideration for working with youth and their families. *Journal of Gay & Lesbian Mental Health, 21,* 221–227.

National Bureau of Economic Research. (2018). *Income declines after divorce.* Retrieved February 4, 2019, from http://www.nber.org/digest/jul02/w8786.html

Nehring, D. (2005). Reflexiones sobre la construcción cultural de las relaciones de género en México. *Papeles de Población, 11,* 221–245.

Neppl, T. K., Senia, J. M., & Donnellan, M. B. (2015). The effects of economic hardship: Testing the family stress model over time. *Journal of Family Psychology, 30,* 12–21.

Olmedo, E. L. (1979). Acculturation: A psychometric perspective. *American Psychologist, 34,* 1061–1070.

Papernow, P. L. (2013). *Surviving and thriving in stepfamily relationships: What works and what doesn't?* New York, NY: Routledge.

Payne, K. K. (2018a). Change in the U.S. remarriage rate, 2008 & 2016. *Family Profiles,* FP-18-16. Bowling Green, OH: National Center for Family & Marriage Research. doi: 10.25035/ncfmr/fp-18-16

Payne, K. K. (2018b). First divorce rate in the U.S., 2016. *Family Profiles,* FP-18-15. Bowling Green, OH: National Center for Family & Marriage Research. https://doi.org/10.25035/ncfmr/fp-18-15

Perez, R. M., Dawson, B. A., & Suárez-Orozco, C. (2011). Understanding acculturation, depressive symptoms, and the protective role of family involvement among Latino(a) immigrant families. *Journal of Family Social Work, 14,* 429–445.

Pew Research Center tabulations of 2015 American Community Survey (1% IPUMS). *Statistical portrait of Hispanics in the United States,* 2015.

Piña-Watson, B., Lorenzo-Blanco, E. I., Dornhecker, M., Martinez, A. J., & Nagoshi, J. L. (2016). Moving away from a cultural deficit to a holistic perspective: Traditional gender role values, academic attitudes, and educational goals for Mexican descent adolescents. *Journal of Counseling Psychology, 63,* 307–318.

Ramirez, R. R. (2004). *We the people: Hispanics in the United States.* Washington, DC: U.S. Department of Commerce, Economic and Statistics Administration, U.S. Census Bureau.

Rodriguez, J. (2002). Latina activists: Toward an inclusive spirituality of being in the world. In M. Aquino, D. Machado, & J. Rodriguez.

(Eds.) *A reader in Latina feminist theology* (pp. 114–130). Austin, TX: University of Texas Press.

Roosa, M. W., Liu, F. F., Torres, M., Gonzales, N. A., Knight, G. P., & Saenz, D. (2009). Sampling and recruitment in studies of cultural influences on adjustment: A case study with Mexican Americans. *Journal of Family Psychology, 22,* 293–302.

Rumbaut, R. G., & Portes, A. (2001). *Ethnicities: Children of immigrants in America.* Berkeley, CA: University of California Press.

Santiago-Rivera, A. L., Arredondo, P., & Gallardo-Cooper, M. (2002). *Counseling Latinos and la familia: A practical guide.* Thousand Oaks, CA: Sage.

Skogrand, L., Barrios-Bell, A., & Higginbotham, B. (2009). Stepfamily education for Latino families: Implications for practice. *Journal of Couple & Relationship Therapy, 8,* 113–128.

Stykes, J. (2012). Nonresident father visitation. *Family Profiles,* FP-12-02. Bowling Green, OH: National Center for Family and Marriage Research. Retrieved February 4, 2019, from www.bgsu.edu/content/dam/BGSU/college-of-arts-and-sciences/NCFMR/documents/FP/FP-12-02.pdf

Szapcoznik, J., & Kurtines, W. M. (1989). Acculturation, biculturalism and adjustment among Cuban Americans. In A. M. Padilia (Ed.) *Acculturation: Theory, models, and some new findings* (pp. 139–159). Boulder, CO: Westview Press.

Telzer, E. H., Yuen, C., Gonzales, N., & Fuligni, A. J. (2016). Filling gaps in the acculturation gap-distress model: Heritage cultural maintenance and adjustment in Mexican-American families. *Journal of Youth and Adolescence, 45,* 1412–1425.

Umaña-Taylor, A. J., & Bámaca, M. Y. (2004). Conducting focus groups with Latino populations: Lessons from the field. *Family Relations, 53,* 261–272.

Umaña-Taylor, A. J., & Updegraff, K. A. (2013). Latino families in the United States. In G. W. Peterson and K. R. Bush (Eds.) *Handbook of marriage and the family* (pp. 723–747). New York, NY: Springer U.S.

United States Census Bureau. (2011). *Section I: Population.* Retrieved February 10, 2019, from https://www.census.gov/library/publications/2010/compendia/statab/130ed/population.html

United States Census Bureau. (2012–2016). *American Community Survey 5-Year PUMS file.* Retrieved February 10, 2019, from http://www.census.gov/programs-surveys/acs/data/pums.html

United States Census Bureau. (2018). *Hispanic Origin.* Retrieved February 10, 2019, from https://www.census.gov/topics/population/hispanic-origin.html

United States Citizenship and Immigration Services. (2017). *I-30, petition for alien relative.* Retrieved February 10, 2019, from https://www.uscis.gov/i-130

United States Citizenship and Immigration Services. (n.d.). *21.4 petition by citizenship or lawful permanent resident for child, son or daughter.*

Retrieved February 10, 2019, from https://www.uscis.gov/ilink/docView/AFM/HTML/AFM/0-0-0-1/0-0-0-3481/0-0-0-4805.html

Wiltz, T. (2018). If parents get deported, who gets their children? *PEW*. Retrieved from https://www.pewtrusts.org/en/research-and-analysis/blogs/stateline/2018/10/25/if-parents-get-deported-who-gets-their-children

Whitlock, J. Blended families and immigration. Retrieved February 4, 2019, from http://www.amigalawyers.com/posts/2016/10/10/blended-families-and-immigration-common-issues-for-foreign-born-step-parents-and-step-children

Wolfinger, N. H., Wilcox, W. B., & Hernández, E. I. (2010). Bendito amor ("blessed love"): Religion and relationships among married and unmarried Latinos in urban America. *The Journal of Latino-Latin American Studies, 3*, 171–188.

CHAPTER FIVE

American Indian Stepfamilies

Ryan Turner, MSW, Brigham Young University
Gordon Limb, PhD, Brigham Young University
Susan Stewart, PhD, Iowa State University

Introduction

There have been dramatic changes in the demography of American families in the last half century. Increased rates of divorce, remarriage, nonmarital childbearing, and cohabitation have forever altered family structure and dynamics. These changes have created new family forms, including stepfamilies, defined as married or cohabiting couple households containing children from previous relationships. About 42% of adults have at least one step-relative—30% have a step- or half-sibling, 18% have a living stepparent, and 13% have a stepchild (Pew Research Center, 2011). Moreover, approximately 40% of children in the United States will spend at least some of their youth living in a stepfamily household (Norris, Vines, & Hoeffel, 2012). Families of all racial and ethnic groups in the United States have undergone these changes, including American Indians.[1]

Although interest in scholarly work on American Indians and Alaska Natives has increased over the past few decades, research on structural diversity in American Indian families and its effect on family dynamics and well-being remains sparse (U.S. Census Bureau, 2012a; Knaster, Fretts, & Phillips, 2015; Strong, 2015; Narduzzi, 2015; Donnermeyer, Edwards, Chavez, & Beauvai, 2016). The traditional definition of a stepfamily, which assumes stepfamilies are formed through widowhood and remarriage alone, tends to leave out racial and ethnic minority stepfamilies because they are formed in ways other than widowhood and remarriage—such as through a first marriage following a nonmarital birth or through cohabitation before a marriage or after a divorce. The result is that racial and ethnic minorities, including American Indian stepfamilies, are vastly underrepresented in the literature on stepfamilies.

For example, based on data from the American Community Survey, 25,000 children in married or cohabiting American Indian/Alaska Native households were reported as stepchildren from 2009–2011. American Indians represent only a tiny percentage (1%) of all stepchildren in the United States (Kreider & Lofquist, 2014).[2] American Indians, however, have high rates of cohabition, and cohabiting partners are less likely than married partners to identify their spouse's children as "stepchildren." Therefore, the number of American Indian stepchildren is likely greatly underestimated. Given the number of American Indian children who are stepchildren is small relative to other groups, most programs, policies, and interventions are designed for White, married, middle-class stepfamilies, and do not currently meet the needs of American Indians (Stewart, 2007).

There are roughly five million American Indians living in the United States, representing 1.7% of the American population (Norris et al., 2012; U. S. Census Bureau, 2010b). There is a common misperception that the American Indian population is in decline. Despite lower fertility, the American Indian population is growing as a result of increasing life expectancy and more Hispanics claiming American Indian heritage (Nittle, 2017). Indeed, many are surprised to learn that the American Indian population grew nearly three times the rate of the total U.S. population between 2000 and 2010 (27% among American Indians versus 10% for the general population; Child Trends, 2015).

Also contrary to popular notions of American Indians, most do not live on reservation lands (Norris et al., 2012). In 2010, only 21% of American Indians lived on reservations, while 2% lived in Alaska Native village areas, and 78% lived off reservation lands (Norris et al., 2012). Furthermore, while American Indians share many characteristics, they are not a monolithic racial/ethnic group and "there is no pan-Indian way of doing things" (National Healthy Marriage Resource Center, 2016). There are currently 567 federally recognized tribes (40% of which are Alaska Native) with more than 200 native languages spoken among them, each with a distinct culture and traditions (Bureau of Indian Affairs, 2017), including language origins, migration patterns, diet, and warfare practices (Bureau of Indian Affairs, 2017; Sue & Sue, 2012).

In the following sections, we discuss distinctive features of American Indian families in terms of their history, culture, religion, and traditions, and how these features affect interpersonal relationships in stepfamilies and the well-being of stepfamily members. Next, we discuss what is currently known about family patterns among American Indians at the national level, based on data from the U.S. Census Bureau, National Center for Health Statistics, and other government surveys. We provide a deeper understanding of American Indian stepfamily relationship and well-being dynamics based on original data from the Stepfamily Experiences Project (STEP). This follows with a discussion of implications for policy and practice and our recommendations for future research.

American Indian History

There is no doubt that American Indian family patterns have been shaped by historical trauma and institutionalized disruptions of family units. White colonists drastically fragmented and essentially destroyed the American Indian diaspora, and today American Indians are arguably the most marginalized, poor, and vulnerable group in the United States. For example, prior to 17th-century American colonization, American Indians reared and educated their children in a communal fashion. Through mandated attendance at boarding schools during the mid-20th century, however, American Indian children were taught to reject their indigenous culture and replace it with a more "civilized" mainstream Christian culture.

Such indoctrination created mistrust and tension between many Native children and parents. Although tribal nations today have a unique relationship with the federal government that includes many elements of sovereignty, decades of routine family and cultural disruption have contributed to social problems among American Indians such as unemployment, child maltreatment, alcohol and drug use, and mental health problems. Being situated between traditional and mainstream culture, in particular religious and spiritual culture versus growing secularism in the United States, continues to shape how American Indian family members interact with one another and outsiders in both positive and negative ways (National Resource Center for Healthy Marriage and Families, 2015).

Religion and Spirituality

A unique aspect of American Indian culture that positively contributes to family relationships are spiritual principles such as harmony, bravery, humility, and interconnectedness (Robbins, Robbins, & Stennerson, 2013). For example, research shows that regularly attending worship services, reading from and living values taught in the Bible, receiving prayers or blessings, and seeking and incorporating counsel from elders and medicine men helps American Indian couples, particularly Navajo couples, understand and resolve challenges in marriage (Skogrand et al., 2008).

Although many American Indians today attend Christian churches and abide by principles common to Christianity in general, mental health practitioners and family counseling professionals should be aware that there are many American Indians who continue to participate in traditional American Indian ceremonies and abide by spiritual principles that are unique to American Indians. As is the case for Karissa and Walt in the following vignette, stepfamilies often contain nonpracticing family members who may not share their beliefs. Family members' participation in traditional American Indian spiritual ceremonies without the support of a nonpracticing stepparent, spouse, or other stepfamily member may introduce stress and disrupt family integrity because of religious-based conflict and disagreements. In addition to spiritual practices, other cultural considerations unique to American Indians that influence family relationships are discussed later.

Karissa Nashoba is a 24-year-old Choctaw from Oklahoma with an 8-year-old son and 5-year-old daughter. She did well in high school, but dropped out during her junior year to marry Sal, the children's Caucasian father. Karissa, Sal, and their two children lived with her aunt and grandmother on the reservation off and on for three years. During this time, Karissa worked full time and finished her GED. Her general preference was to live with the relatives who provided childcare and emotional support for her during the problem periods of her marriage. Upon her divorce from Sal, Karissa decided to enter the local tribal college so that she could provide financially for her children. Karissa discussed these plans with her aunt and grandmother, and with a Native American social services counselor who had worked with the family in the past.

While taking classes at the tribal college, Karissa met and married Walt, a divorced Choctaw father who had custody of his three-year-old son. Bringing together this unique stepfamily made it clear to Karissa that she would need to rely on her family supports to make this relationship work. When moving in with Walt, Karissa was emphatic that they rent an apartment where they would be more independent from her aunt and grandmother yet close to the support network she had relied on since she was born. By moving into an apartment next door to her aunt and grandmother, Karissa was able to satisfy her need for independent financial security from her family relatives, and at the same time maintain continued contact with her family nearby.

A few months after her marriage to Walt, however, Karissa faced some expected resistance from her children toward her new husband. Her children refused to connect or play with Walt or follow his instructions on home discipline. They often visited next door to complain to their aunt and grandmother about Walt's difficult rules. Fortunately, the aunt and grandmother would often respond by listening to the children and telling them it was perfectly acceptable for them to trust Walt because he was familiar with their family's tribal values, history, and culture. Thanks to the support of extended family members, the children learned to accept and then later embrace their stepfather's presence in their lives.

Analyzing the scenario:

1.   How does Karissa's story demonstrate the unique features of American Indian stepfamilies, such as harmony, humility, and interconnectedness?

2.   If you were a counselor working with American Indian stepfamilies like Karissa and Sal's, what strengths could you draw upon to help them? What potential challenges do they face?

American Indian Culture

Many American Indians have traditionally had a strong sense of collectivism and community (Padilla, Ward, & Limb, 2013).[3] American Indian values include mutual respect and responsibility to care for the children, elderly, the disabled, and vulnerable members of the community. There is also a strong sense of care and responsibility for extended family members—grandparents, nieces, nephews, aunts, uncles, cousins, etc. As illustrated in the vignette, rather than Karissa and Walt moving away from their extended family after they married, they chose to live within very close geographical proximity, interact regularly, and participate together in family and tribal rituals. At the same time, Karissa and Walt wanted to support themselves economically.

While the majority culture tends to conceive of relationships in linear terms, American Indians often think of relationships in circular terms, especially concerning the need to maintain balance and harmony among body, mind, and spirit (Hodge, Limb, & Cross, 2009). For example, among Northwestern tribes in the United States, salmon is not only the primary source of protein in their diet, but also a primary way for family members to commemorate spiritual rituals. During fish-run seasons, individuals sacrifice significant amounts of personal time collaboratively fishing to meet physical and spiritual needs by uniting their family and tribal community (National Resource Center for Healthy Marriage and Families, 2015). Furthermore, rather than adhering to a linear concept of time, spending time with family members or elders from the community is almost always prioritized over adhering to strict time schedules. The prioritization of time spent with family or community members over strict time schedules is often interpreted as a sign of laziness by non-American Indians as opposed to a sign of deep, conscientious respect for tribal members. Indeed, there are many differences between American Indians and the dominant culture that are often misunderstood. We next discuss more of these differences in an attempt to distinguish long-held stereotypes from cultural practices of this population.

LGBTQ+ Considerations

Social rejection is a common challenge facing children, adolescents, and adults with nonconforming sexual or gender identities, such as those who identify as gay, lesbian, non-binary, sexually fluid, transgender, or some other identity (LGBTQ+). Parents, extended families, friends, teachers, and others are often confused and unsupportive, at least initially, when a loved one "comes out" or when their gender or sexual identity is somehow discovered. Unfortunately, American Indians have not been exempt from such challenges in recent history (Papernow, 2013). For example, more than half (54%) of American Indian LGBTQ+ youth have reported physical violence at school (NCAI Policy Research Center, 2015). On the other hand, variations in gender and sexual identity among Native people are often treated with respect and acceptance among tribal elders, community leaders, and family members, allowing for a greater feeling of safety in transparency (Red Horse, 1997; Wilson, 1996). For example, the Navajo have a four-gender system: male, female, male with a female essence, and female with a male essence (Nibley, 2011).

Therefore, instead of remaining "closeted" at school or in their community, children, adolescents, and adults who identify as something other than "cisgender" (defined as "male" or "female" and heterosexual) may be more comfortable disclosing their identity while also expecting to receive more social and emotional support than individuals of other racial and ethnic groups. A "two-spirit" person, for example, is a Native person who identifies with both masculine and feminine traits and a non-heterosexual orientation. While the concept was coined in the early 1990s, it has existed for centuries and played a central and respected role among Native people (Walters et al., 2006).

Despite the U.S. Supreme Court's decision in 2015 to legalize gay marriage, same-sex parental rights have continued to be dependent upon the nonuniform, patchwork collection of state laws. While some states legally recognize the presumption of parentage, others require co-parent or second-parent adoptions (McKinley, 2019), and yet others have no legal specifications, making decisions regarding adoption or parental rights the responsibility of the courts on a case-by-case basis (A Family for Every Child, 2018). While most tribal laws do not directly address the issue of LGBTQ+ adoption, there are some exceptions, including legislation of the Confederated Tribe of Siletz Indians, which permits domestic partners or married spouses who maintain a home together to petition for adoption or second-parent adoption. Similar legal specificity is found among the Tulalip Tribes' Paternity and Child Support Code, the Northern Arapaho Family Support Ordinance, and various other tribal codes (Native American Program of Legal Aid Services of Oregon et al., 2013). As is the case with all racial and ethnic groups, American Indian stepfamilies formed through cohabitation are described as fragile families due to their legal and social vulnerabilities, which contribute to greater union instability relative to marriage.

Stigma and Stereotypes

Stigmatization refers to a phenomenon in which people who share norms of ability, appearance, or membership in a particular social group are labeled as deviant (Henslin, 2010). Stereotypes are widely held, oversimplified, and often exist in the form of negative images in the mind of a dominant group which denies access to opportunities or rewards to another group. Stepfamilies and American Indians are two groups that both have a long history of stigmatization and stereotypes. Despite their prevalence, stepfamilies are still often considered dysfunctional and typified by tumultuous relationships, weak parent-child attachment, and poor child outcomes, even though data show that any differences are small and the result of factors outside of stepfamily dynamics themselves, such as poverty (Muraru & Turliuc, 2012; Phillips et al., 2013; Stewart, 2007).

American Indians are stigmatized on the basis of many factors, including low socioeconomic status, being from a non-English-speaking home (Jacobs, 2013; DeVoe, Darling-Churchill, & Snyder, 2008), alcoholism and drug abuse, poor mental health (Grandbois, 2005; Kleinman, 1996; Thompson, Walker, & Silk-Walker, 1993), low educational attainment, out-of-wedlock childbearing, and high rates of single motherhood (Christensen & Manson, 2001). Unfortunately, rather than considering the role of structural barriers that limit American Indians' choices, many people attribute these problems to American Indians' personal failings.

Low socioeconomic status is a persistent feature of life among American Indians. The percentage of American Indians living in poverty is similar to other disadvantaged racial and ethnic groups at 26%, compared with 11% for Whites, 28% for Blacks, 25% for Hispanics, and 13% for Asians. American Indians also have above average high school dropout rates, with 11% of American Indians ages 16 to 24 dropping out of high school, compared with 5% of Whites, 9% of Blacks, 13% of Hispanics, and 3% of Asians. Consequently, American Indians also have low levels of educational attainment and high levels of unemployment. The percentage of American Indians over age 25 with a bachelor's

Portrayals of American Indian culture are fraught with stereotypes and are far from the lived experiences of American Indian families.

degree or higher in 2014 was only 15%, compared with 33% for Whites, 19% for Blacks, 14% for Hispanics, and 51% for Asians. Four in 10 American Indian young adults (44%) aged 18 to 24 are neither working nor enrolled in school, compared with 17% of Whites, 24% of Blacks, 21% of Hispanics, and 18% of Asians of the same age (U.S. Bureau of the Census, 2013a; 2012b).

Another issue associated with American Indian stigmatization is the relatively high rate of alcohol consumption. The prevalence of heavy drinking has historically been highest among American Indians compared with Whites and Hispanics. American Indians also rank highest for binge drinking at 30%, compared with 26% for Whites, 26% for Hispanics, and 21% for Blacks (Chartier & Caetano, 2010; Robbins et al., 2013). Drinking during pregnancy among American Indian women has given rise to high levels of fetal alcohol syndrome, with recent prevalence rates at 8.5 per 1,000 births compared with 2.2 per 1,000 births for the general U.S. population (May, McCloskey, & Gossage, 2002). American Indians' alcoholism death rates are five times higher than the national average (Indian Health Service, 2011).

While these numbers often reinforce the sigma of American Indians and alcohol use, it is important to understand a historical context for this. The results of historical trauma and American Indian–White treaties and regulations (including reservations, boarding schools, child-removal policies, etc.) made it very challenging for many American Indian families. Thus, alcohol abuse became one of the most severe health challenges facing many American Indian families, resulting in an increase in deaths by alcohol-related injuries, alcohol-related automobile accidents, and alcohol-related suicides (American Indian Development Associates [AIDA], 2000). Over the past 50 years, research has made significant progress in understanding the prevalence and correlates of alcohol use among American Indians in an effort to develop successful intervention strategies. Any discussion of alcohol use among this population, however, must include negative socioeconomic effects and the presence of historical trauma (see Brave Heart & DeBruyn, 1998; Manson & Altschul, 2004).

American Indians also experience high rates of physical violence in the home. Domestic violence most often occurs between partners and spouses, which negatively influences family relationships and erodes children's sense of safety and self-efficacy (Robbins et al., 2013). Child abuse and neglect rates are higher among American Indians (one in every 30 children) than the national average (one in every 58 children), with neglect appearing to be more common than abuse; however, because state reporting requirements do not typically extend to persons living on tribal lands, numbers regarding American Indian abuse and neglect may be inaccurate or underrepresented (Fox, 2003).

American Indians are also at high risk for mental health problems. For example, although varying widely by tribe, the suicide rate among American Indians/Alaska Natives is 30% higher than that of the general population and has been steadily increasing in recent years. According to the 2013 Youth Risk Behavior Survey, lifetime rates of having attempted suicide reported by adolescents ranged from 22% among girls to 12% among boys, and suicide is the second-leading cause of death among youth aged 10 to 24 (Suicide Prevention Resource Center [SPRC], 2013). Moreover, historical trauma, alienation from the dominant culture, discrimination, and violence have had serious adverse effects on Indians' connection to their reservation community, family and friends, and broader society, leading to high rates of mental health problems and suicide (Sarche & Spicer, 2008; SPRC, 2013).

American Indians also face stigma for their parenting practices. While White parents tend to impose consequences (e.g., grounding) upon their children for the breaking of rules, American Indian parents allow children to learn from their behavior through the flow of natural consequences in relation to their social network. Indeed, American Indian child-rearing practices are seen as a shared responsibility across multiple parental figures, including aunts, uncles, grandparents, or even adult friends. While the majority culture might consider Natives' parenting style to be indulgent or neglectful, American Indian parents view such practices as empowering and optimal for their children's healthy development (Glover, 2001). A further explanation on American Indian parenting styles is contained in the "Biological Parent-Child Relationships" section later in the chapter. Given this, American Indians' open and inclusive family dynamics can make stepfamily formation seem natural and feel normal, rather than deviant or pathological, especially from the child's perspective (Lewis, 1970). Such a process of normalization would most likely ease at least part of the burden of stigma that American Indians would otherwise experience by transitioning into a stepfamily (Adler-Baeder, Robertson, & Schramm, 2010).

In sum, stepfamily life among American Indians is particularly challenging because of the double burden of stigma they bear: as members of a stepfamily and as a result of their American Indian heritage. Moreover, family life for American Indians plays out in the context of historical trauma and persecution, such as forced relocations, removal of children from the home to boarding schools, and prohibition of practicing one's native language and religious traditions passed down through multiple generations (Brave Heart & DeBruyn, 1998).

Although American Indians would benefit from interventions, stigmatized groups are often too ashamed to seek help and support, which may help explain American Indians' low level of help-seeking for financial, mental health, and other federal, state, and local services, which in turn undermines stepfamily well-being (Spear et al., 2013). Although American Indians on average have higher rates of social, emotional, and financial difficulties than other racial and ethnic groups, superficial understanding of Natives' history and challenges encourages a "blaming the victim" mentality among the dominant culture, rather than encouraging a strengths-based perspective of the resources already inherent in American Indian stepfamilies to deal with challenges common to stepfamily formation.

Family Formation, Dissolution, and Reorganization

Knowledge of American Indian family patterns, specifically with respect to marriage, nonmarital childbearing, cohabitation, divorce, residential arrangements, and remarriage of American Indians is vital to understanding American Indian stepfamily life. Finding family data on American Indians, however, can be a challenge. Because their numbers are small, data are often presented in a vague form (i.e., lumped in with other similarly small racial/ethnic groups), are omitted from analysis of family patterns by racial and ethnic group, or are simply left out of data sets of other racial and ethnic groups (i.e., Whites, Hispanics, Asians), making comparisons of standard measures of family structure and well-being across groups often impossible. Nevertheless, we have pieced together data on the unique structure of American Indian stepfamilies based on what data is available.

Marriage

Compared with Whites and Asians, American Indians have low marriage rates. From 2008 to 2012, 60% of American Indians had ever been married, compared with 53% of Blacks, 60% of Hispanics, 73% of Whites, and 70% of Asians. A number of factors influence marriage rates among American Indians, including low levels of education and income (Raley, Sweeney, & Wondra, 2015), high rates of substance use, historical trauma that has eroded traditional marriage practices, and institutionalized disruptions of family units (Brave Heart & DeBruyn, 1998).

When they do marry, American Indians are quite likely to choose a spouse of a different race. More than half (56%) of American Indians today marry a partner of a difference race (the most common being White, followed by African American), which introduces challenges associated with cultural differences into the stepfamily (National Healthy Marriage Resource Center, 2016). As with Karissa and Walt, many Indian families navigate these challenges by spouses (and extended family members) acquiring a knowledge of both tribal and modern ways. Values of sharing, cooperation, noninterference, present-focused time-orientation, spirituality, and nonverbal communication skills have been noted to be of special importance for strengthening marriage and family among American Indian mixed-race marriages (Sue & Sue, 2013).

Fertility and Childbearing Outside of Marriage

American Indians currently have the lowest fertility rates in the United States, with the average American Indian family having 1.3 children, compared with 1.8 for Whites, 1.9 for Blacks, 2.2 for Hispanics, and 1.7 for Asians. American Indians also have high rates of nonmarital births, second only to African Americans. In 2014, 71% of African American births, 66% of American Indian

American Indian stepfamilies are often multiracial.

births, 53% of Hispanic births, 29% of White births, and 17% of Asian births occurred outside marriage (Child Trends, 2015). Indeed, the number of births to unmarried women of all ages in the United States has been significantly higher among American Indians compared with Whites throughout history, perhaps because of informal marital ceremony practices (U.S. Census Bureau, 2012a). Because of the high number of births occurring outside of marriage among American Indians, combined with high rates of cohabitation, American Indians have a high likelihood of forming stepfamilies in nontraditional ways, such as through first marriages and cohabitation, a pattern also seen among Hispanics and Blacks (Lonczak et al., 2007; Stewart, 2007).

As with other nonwhite groups (except Asians), teen childbearing is high among American Indians. The American Indian teen birthrate is 31 births per 1,000 women—higher than the rate for Whites (17 per 1,000) and Asians (nine per 1,000), but lower than the rate for Hispanics (42 per 1,000) and Blacks (39 per 1,000). Similar to other groups with high levels of teen births, the driving factors are low levels of education, poverty, and low access to community health resources (Ispa, Thornburg, & Fine, 2006). Despite these adverse contextual factors, the difficulty of raising a child outside of marriage among American Indian mothers, especially for teenage mothers, may be "softened" through extended family support networks, as was the case for Karissa before her marriage (Krogstad, 2014). For example, one study showed that among Navajo teenage mothers aged 15 to 19, it was common to receive childcare, financial assistance, and emotional support from extended families and their communities (Dalla & Gamble, 1998; Eitle et al., 2013).

Cohabitation

Cohabitation of unmarried partners is common among American Indians. As is the case for African Americans, this pattern is very likely related to American Indians' history of informal marriages and/or marriages not sanctioned by prevailing laws. According to data from the American Community Survey, American Indians have the highest rate of unmarried cohabitation of any racial or ethnic group in the United States (Elliott & Lewis 2010; Lesthaeghe, Lopez-Colas, & Neidert, 2016; U.S. Census Bureau, 2010a,b). One-third (33%) of American Indian/Alaska Native women are in a cohabiting union, compared with 23% of Whites, 31% of Blacks, 20% of Mexicans, and 17% of Chinese (Lesthaeghe et al., 2016).

Divorce

Divorce rates among American Indians are among the highest of all racial and ethnic groups in the United States. Data from 2008–2012 in the American Community Survey indicates that among American Indian-married women aged 25 to 29, 52 out of every 1,000 had divorced, compared with 39 for Whites, 44 for Blacks, 27 for Hispanics, and 13 for Asians. Common factors predicting divorce include low education levels, low socioeconomic status, unemployment, a history of union instability, and interracial marriage, all of which are factors disproportionately present among American Indians compared with the general population (Fu & Wolfinger, 2011; Kuroki, 2017; Pryor, 2013).

Biological Parent-Child Relationships

Parenting across households is a common practice among many American Indian families. For example, grandparents often temporarily care for grandchildren during episodes of parental substance abuse in order to provide adequate care for them (Holmes, 2013). Fifty-two percent of American Indian children live in households headed by a single parent, compared with 35% of the general population (Kids Count Data Center, 2018). As is the case for all children, American Indian youth who are not raised by both biological parents are at higher risk for multiple problem behaviors, including gang involvement, suicide, crime, and substance use (Lonczak et al., 2007). Even after controlling for age, gender, and family financial problems, substance abuse is higher among American Indian youth raised by a single parent. The harm this may cause, however, may be attenuated by a strong extended family support system that American Indians tend to have, including the expectation that fathers remain strongly involved in their children's lives following divorce and union disruption (Padilla et al., 2013).

Research indicates that authoritative parenting, a parenting style in which expectations for children are high along with a similarly high level of nurturing and involvement, is often preferred for positive child development (Larzelere, Morris, Harrist, & Cavell, 2013). This "give and take" type of parenting is generally associated with better academic outcomes for children in both two-biological-parent families and stepfamilies. Yet, parenting style may operate differently for families of different races. For example, children raised in African American and Asian American stepfamilies have higher academic performance when raised within an authoritarian parenting style, a "top-down" type of parenting in which children have less say over decisions (Steinberg, Dornbusch, & Brown, 1992). For American Indians, Ayers (n.d.) has found that parenting relies heavily on extended family, that teaching and child-rearing practices utilize observation, nonverbal communication, patience, and role-playing modeling and storytelling, and that children are viewed as autonomous and competent in making their own decisions, with parents often permitting their children to develop in their own time and with minimal rules. She notes that traditionally this style has been very successful in the nurturing and raising of American Indian children.

Thus, while there are often similarities in many parenting styles between American Indians and other groups, distinct differences are also prevalent and incorporated within Native culture. Regarding American Indian stepfamilies, there is little corresponding research; however, American Indian parents in all family formations often delegate child discipline to extended members to preserve the parent-child bond and simultaneously strengthen extended family involvement (LaFramboise & Low, 1998).

Most stepfamily households consist of a biological mother and stepfather, but an important part of stepfamily dynamics is the biological father. In general, the quality of the biological father-child relationship is mediated by the father's relationship with the mother. A poor relationship between the parents often translates into poor relationship quality between the nonresidential biological father and the child (Townsend, 2002). Again, while a father's absence often leads to a poor quality father-child relationship, the socioemotional risks that children face in such cases can be offset by the added support that American Indian children receive from an extended family system (Padilla, Ward, & Limb, 2013).

Stepparents and Stepchildren

Existing research indicates that stepfamily functioning is enhanced when the biological parent takes the lead in child-rearing, with the stepparent adopting the role of an "intimate outsider," intimate enough to serve as a confidant and outside enough to provide advice, support, and mentoring in areas too threatening to share with the biological parent (Papernow, 2015). Indeed, the majority of research indicates that the stepparent-child relationship is more stable when the stepparent takes a less active role than the biological parent in child discipline during the first few years after the stepfamily formation (Bray & Hetherington, 1993; Browning & Artelt, 2012). This may not be the case, however, for American Indian stepfamilies as children are generally already acclimated to the ubiquitous presence and active parenting role of extended family in their lives. In other words, if fictive kin (non-blood-related friends or family members) are living in the family prior to stepfamily formation, it is possible that the integration of a stepparent into the family will be perceived by children as less of an abrupt transition into stepfamily living. Even when stepchildren are open to integrating a stepparent into the family, non-Indian stepparents (or Indian stepparents of other tribes) may find it difficult to do so themselves, particularly when there are major lifestyle differences such as extensive grandparent child-raising, rituals and ceremonies, and hunter-gatherer activities.

Later Life Changes

Adult children often provide for their aging parents' and stepparents' financial needs. Overall, Americans' attitudes about economic and social support between older and younger generations is that stepfamily members, compared with family members who are biologically related, are less obligated to one another and that any such exchanges are optional (Ganong & Coleman, 1999). Furthermore, for more than one-third of adult children living at home (Vespa, 2017), stepparents are more likely to voice concerns that children's dependence on the family is being enabled by their "overly soft" biological parent. American Indians, however, typically expect and value continued parent-child interdependence throughout the lifespan.

As stepfamilies progress toward end-of-life stages, wills and estate inheritances can be an overlooked source of conflict among previously friendly relationships (Papernow, 2013). For example, according to the American Indian Probate Reform Act of 2004, without a written will, two-thirds of a person's estate is transferred to the children (the Act refers only to "children" and does not make it clear whether stepchildren are considered children) and one-third to the surviving spouse (i.e., cohabiting partners are excluded). With a will, a person can transfer his or her estate to anyone, including stepchildren and non-Indian individuals, as long as such persons are specified in the will (McCulley, 2005). Although American Indians often share cultural values that prioritize family unity, when it comes to estates and inheritances, especially regarding stepchildren and nonbiologically related kin who are not considered children or family by default law, it is important for them to be aware of their legal options and plan accordingly to avoid unnecessary emotional or legal conflict among surviving family members.

Step-Grandparents and Step-Grandchildren

Commonly referred to as "elders" in American Indian families, grandparents play a much more active role in grandchildren's lives than do grandparents in most other U.S. families. Fifty-four percent of American Indian grandparents report living with and having childcare responsibility for their grandchildren, compared with 40% of Whites, 48% of Blacks, 15% of Asians, and 31% of Hispanics (U.S. Census Bureau, 2013b). For many American Indian families and stepfamilies, grandparents are one of the principal ways in which traditional tribal ceremonies are modeled to grandchildren and the way that tribal values and principles are transmitted from one generation to the next.

American Indian grandparents actively participate in childcare roles, including the discipline and teaching of their grandchildren (Henslin, 2010). Accordingly, both the parents and stepparents of American Indian stepfamilies who live in a home with a grandparent may face conflicts with the grandparent concerning child discipline styles, family financial decisions, home responsibilities, and parental roles in general. On the other hand, the presence of a grandparent may add to the stepfamily's financial and emotional support for child-rearing, resulting in an easier transition into stepfamily living.

Risk and Resiliency in American Indian Stepfamilies

Like all stepfamilies, American Indian stepfamilies are at increased risk of negative outcomes. Research based on nationally representative data reveals that, on average, American Indian marriages are of lower quality than White marriages (Gray, Shafer, Limb, & Busby, 2013).

Grandparents tend to play a key role in the rearing of grandchildren among American Indians.

Furthermore, heavy involvement of extended family members can negatively affect routine stepfamily dynamics and functioning (Pasley & Lee, 2010). For example, in one study of American Indian families conflict arose between grandparents and parents living in the same home concerning child discipline styles, family financial decisions, home responsibilities, and parental roles in general (Robbins, Scherman, Holeman, & Wilson, 2005).

Although American Indians are statistically at greater risk than other races for union disruption, they are also in a historically more resilient position than the general population to maintain familial stability following divorce. After more than 500 years of historical and institutional trauma, including recurrent familial and cultural destruction, American Indians have maintained cultural and family ties through the support of extended kin networks (Limb, Shafer, & Sandoval, 2014). Such a communal sense of identity has been shown to maintain unity within populations that have faced historical opposition, discrimination, and cultural genocide (LaFromboise, Hoyt, Oliver, & Whitbeck, 2006). In addition to a sense of communal identity, all indigenous languages have a word that means resilience, such as the Lakota word *wacan tognaka* (meaning strong will) or the Ho-Chunk word *wa nah igh mash jah* (meaning strong mind) (Goodluck & Willeto, 2009). Because American Indians value an inclusive group orientation over an individual orientation, "cultural resilience" (as opposed to "statistical risk") may be a more accurate way of understanding American Indian people's resilience and healing following opposition—including socioemotional opposition that accompanies stepfamily formation (Goodluck & Willeto, 2009).

According to interviews with American Indians conducted by Goodluck and Willeto (2009), the source of American Indians' resiliency can be categorized into seven themes: ethos and values, religion and spirituality, language, extended family, responses from culture, sense of humor, and moving forward to the seventh generation. Many American Indians report that being raised to show unconditional respect to all people, engaging in religious ceremonies, and staying connected to ancestors and extended family through traditional stories and language are crucial aspects that help them survive and thrive in the face of opposition. Other reports confirm these same themes and practices to be protective factors against trauma and opposition for American Indians (Alexie, 2005; Werner & Smith, 1992).

Furthermore, given that American Indians place heavy emphasis on balancing spiritual and physical needs (Red Horse, 1997), it is possible that marital or family breakup would be viewed by

American Indians as one's destiny as contrasted with a deficit or personal failure. There is the belief that everything and everyone was created with a specific purpose to fulfill, which may suggest the belief that no one has the authority to interfere or impose on others the path that they should follow, including a couples' marital dissolution, perhaps making stepfamily formation less stigmatizing for American Indians from their own perspective (Garrett & Garrett, 1994). In sum, resiliency is an important part of American Indian heritage and lifestyle, and just as it has helped many remain strong in the face of historical trauma, it will very likely continue to support American Indian individuals, families, and communities to remain strong in the face of familial separation and stepfamily formation (Robbins et al., 2013).

STEP Findings on American Indian Stepfamilies

The Stepfamily Experiences Project (STEP) is a cross-sectional, retrospective quota sample of 1,593 emerging adults (aged 18 to 30) who reported having lived in a stepfamily before the age of 18 (STEP, 2017). The goal of the survey is to look back on children's experiences with living in a stepfamily to understand what makes stepfamilies successful, to reduce risks in stepfamilies, and to strengthen stepfamily relationships. Stepfamily membership was defined broadly to include participants who lived with a biological parent and his or her partner (same sex or opposite sex), whether married or cohabiting. The STEP also includes detailed information on biological, half- and step-siblings, residential mobility, and relationships with and between resident biological parents, nonresident biological parents, resident stepparents, and nonresident stepparents. Participants also provided assessments of their adaptation to stepfamily life, their social and emotional well-being (e.g., depression, attachment, substance use), and their current attitudes about relationships and family life. A unique feature of this data set, and important for this study, is that the STEP data, although not nationally representative, includes an oversample of 342 American Indians. The following tables summarize stepfamily relationship and well-being differences between American Indians and other racial and ethnic groups, noting statistical significance when present.

Table 5.1 reveals that American Indian young adults who have lived in stepfamilies reported poorer relationship quality among stepfamily members than respondents of other racial groups. Only 34% of American Indian young adult stepchildren agreed that they shared a "positive, close, and warm" relationship with their residential stepmother compared with 53% of Whites, 66% of Blacks, 49% of Hispanics, and 56% of Asians. Results were less dramatic for relationships with resident stepfathers, at 41% for American Indians, 52% for Whites, 54% for Blacks, 48% for Hispanics, and 66% for Asians. American Indians also had significantly less close relationships with their resident and nonresident parents and stepsiblings. See Table 5.1 for a full description of adult stepchildren's description of the quality of their relationships between and among family members.

Similarly, many aspects of American Indian young adult stepchildren and their stepfamily's well-being was lower in quality compared with other racial and ethnic groups (Table 5.2). For example, only 35% of American Indian young adult stepchildren reported that everyone in the household "adjusted well" to the new stepfamily arrangement compared with 52% of Whites, 55% of Blacks, 54% of Hispanics, and 53% of Asians. They were also less likely to agree that their nonresident biological parent was able to adapt well to the new arrangement. American Indians were significantly more likely to report that their relationship with their stepparent was distant or a continuous struggle, at 53%, compared with 36% of Whites, 36% of Blacks, 35% of Hispanics, and 23% of Asians. American Indian and Hispanic stepchildren were more likely than Whites, Blacks, and Asians to report that they were sad, lonely, or depressed, at 12%, 14%, 8%, 8%, and 4%, respectively. Counter to stereotypes of heavy alcohol consumption, there was no statistically significant difference between American Indian young adult stepchildren and other races, and engaging in risky sexual and drug-related behaviors was found to be slightly lower among American Indians compared with Black and Hispanic respondents. The full array of well-being variables can be found in Table 5.2.

In summary, the STEP data reveals important information regarding stepfamily relationships, dynamics, and well-being of American Indian young adults who grew up in stepfamilies. Overall, the data illustrate that American Indians who grew up in a stepfamily reported more difficulties in relationships and lower individual and family well-being compared with respondents of other racial and ethnic groups. These differences are not insignificant in their magnitude. As will be discussed later in this chapter, it is important to take into account that external factors such as low education levels, low socioeconomic status, and high unemployment rates are disproportionately present among American Indians. As a result, these may be negatively influencing

TABLE 5.1   Selected Stepfamily Relationship Characteristics by Race and Ethnicity

VARIABLE (AGREE OR STRONGLY AGREE THAT ...)	AMERICAN INDIAN[1]	WHITE (NON-HISPANIC)	BLACK	HISPANIC	ASIAN	STATISTICAL SIGNIFICANCE[2]
... biological parent was happy in his or her romantic relationship.	53%	63%	57%	63%	70%	AI<W,H,A
... stepparent was happy in his or her romantic relationship.	61%	69%	64%	68%	72%	AI<W
... they would like their own romantic relationship to be like the relationship between their parent and stepparent.	25%	35%	32%	31%	47%	AI<W,A
... they shared a warm, close, and positive relationship with their residential biological parent.	57%	70%	63%	63%	72%	AI<W
... their residential biological parent was not as interested in their well-being after the stepfamily formed.	32%	26%	27%	26%	13%	AI<W,A
... they shared a positive, close, and warm relationship with their nonresidential biological parent.	34%	47%	49%	37%	40%	AI<W,B
... they shared a positive, close, and warm relationship with their residential stepfather.	41%	52%	54%	48%	66%	AI<W,B,A

continued

TABLE 5.1 *(continued)*

VARIABLE (AGREE OR STRONGLY AGREE THAT …)	AMERICAN INDIAN[1]	WHITE (NON-HISPANIC)	BLACK	HISPANIC	ASIAN	STATISTICAL SIGNIFICANCE[2]
… they shared a positive, close, and warm relationship with their residential stepmother.	34%	53%	66%	49%	56%	AI<W,B
… their relationship with their biological siblings worsened as a result of their stepfamily forming.	23%	19%	20%	17%	20%	————
… they were able to form close and warm relationships with their step-siblings.	42%	51%	62%	52%	72%	AI<W,B,A
… they were able to communicate effectively and openly with step-siblings.	43%	53%	62%	53%	67%	AI<W,B,A
Median age	29	25	23	23	23	————
Number of respondents	342	875	146	136	47	————

1 American Indian includes "alone" or "combined with another race."

2 Significant differences between groups at p < .05.

TABLE 5.2 Selected Stepfamily Wellbeing Characteristics by Race and Ethnicity

VARIABLE (AGREE OR STRONGLY AGREE THAT …)	AMERICAN INDIAN[1]	WHITE (NON-HIS-PANIC)	BLACK	HISPANIC	ASIAN	STATISTICAL SIGNIFICANCE[2]
… everyone in the household adjusted well to the new stepfamily arrangement.	35%	52%	55%	54%	53%	AI<W,B,H,A
… the residential biological parent's emotions were the same after the stepfamily formed, compared with before.	34%	46%	52%	35%	56%	AI<W,B,A
Reported that relationship with residential stepparent was distant or a continuous struggle (as opposed to in continuous positive regard, deterioration and recovery, or gradual improvement).	53%	36%	36%	35%	23%	AI<W,B,H,A
… nonresidential biological parent was able to adapt well to the new stepfamily arrangement.	32%	45%	50%	38%	50%	AI<W,B,A
Reported most or all of the time feeling sad, lonely, or depressed as an adult in the last week.	12%	8%	8%	14%	4%	AI<W
As an adult reported 3–5 times or more a week drinking more than four drinks within two hours.	4%	4%	3%	5%	0%	——

continued

TABLE 5.2 *(continued)*

VARIABLE (AGREE OR STRONGLY AGREE THAT ...)	AMERICAN INDIAN[1]	WHITE (NON-HISPANIC)	BLACK	HISPANIC	ASIAN	STATISTICAL SIGNIFICANCE[2]
As an adult reported 3–5 times or more a week using marijuana.	12%	1%	17%	13%	1%	AI<W,A
As an adult reported 3–5 times or more a week using other illegal drugs (e.g., cocaine, heroin, crystal meth, mushrooms, etc.).	2%	1%	3%	1%	0%	——
As an adult reported 3–5 times or more a week riding in a car driven by someone who had been drinking.	1%	1%	3%	2%	0%	AI<B
As an adult reported 3–5 times or more a week hooking-up sexually with someone he or she just met.	2%	1%	3%	1%	0%	——
Median age	29	25	23	23	23	——
Number of respondents	342	873	145	134	47	——

1 American Indian includes "alone" or "combined with another race."
2 Significant differences between groups at p < .05.

relationship quality and other well-being indicators in nuanced ways that our analysis does not capture.

Implications for Laws, Policies, and Practice

Laws and policies that affect American Indian children are of utmost importance when considering the well-being of tribal nations because American Indians follow a combination of federal, state, and tribal laws, depending on the locality and tribe. Therefore, this section focuses on the laws and policies already in place that benefit American Indian children and their families and those that are less beneficial or currently do harm. Then, we make recommendations regarding how existing and new policies and laws would be helpful to American Indian children and families in the future.

Recommendations for Laws and Policies

A complicating factor for promoting American Indian stepfamilies' well-being is that they are governed by laws created within their own legal jurisdiction that can be distinct from the laws that govern the people of the United States. For example, the Indian Removal Act of 1830 designated specific plots of land as reservations where American Indians would dwell and govern themselves outside of the purview of federal laws, and the Marshall Court cases led to greater sovereignty for American Indians. These laws allowed tribes to levy taxes on their own tribal members, hold court cases, and even create their own laws to govern the members of their tribes. Furthermore, the American Religious Freedom Act of 1978 protects American Indians' right to practice their own religious ceremonies, and a 1994 addendum to this act legalized the consumption of peyote among tribal members for religious purposes, which previously was illegal.

Regarding child custody, the Indian Child Welfare Act (ICWA) of 1978 prioritized the placement of American Indian children with tribal family members or individuals. Prior to this law, it was not uncommon for Indian children to be removed from Indian homes (even if from an intact family) and placed in a non-Indian home. With the passage of ICWA, American Indian children are now considered a "ward of the tribe" and under its jurisdiction if desired. This legislation has contributed to the growth of adopted families, stepfamilies, and other nontraditional families, though the numbers are unclear. The most common form of adoption is that of a stepchild by a stepparent, and ICWA may have increased the number of American Indian stepfamilies since it was enacted into law 40 years ago.

Despite helping maintain cultural and social integrity among American Indian individuals and families, the ICWA policy has created unintended consequences in recent years. Because more than half (56%) of American Indians today marry a partner of a different race, the process of a non-Indian stepparent adopting an Indian child can be significantly challenged, if not made impossible altogether (National Healthy Marriage Resource Center, 2016). This is the case even if the non-Indian stepparent is married to the child's biological Indian mother. In the United States, stepparents do not currently enjoy physical or legal custody rights of their stepchildren, even when legally married to their stepchildren's biological parent. More than anything, current laws and public policies may require that stepparents have financial obligations, but they are almost never afforded step-parental rights (Engel, 2003). These barriers to involvement of stepparents in their children's lives are even greater for American Indians.

Among Alaska Natives, villages are often separated by great distances, making child visitation more difficult because of time and costs associated with such visitations. Furthermore, when Alaska Native parents are unable to care for their children, many are forced to place children in non-Indian foster care homes because of the limited number of licensed Native foster care families. The Administration of Children and Families (within the Department of Health and Human Services) has the ability to leverage funding that assists the state of Alaska's Office of Children's Services to meet its goal, which is making more available appropriate tribal-specific foster care home recruitment and licensing. Progress, however, has been slow (Attorney General's Advisory Committee, 2014).

The Native Culture, Language, and Access Act of 2011 enables tribes to organize and direct their own education system. This will most likely positively affect stepfamilies because it will allow tribal governments, which know their communities and culture better than any non-Indian entity or institution, to reform educational policies that will meet their tribal members' needs. For example, schools could introduce policies to facilitate American Indian stepparents' involvement and decision-making ability with respect to the education of their stepchildren that are not more broadly allowable in the United States. Furthermore, tribes are allotted a portion of federal TANF (Temporary Assistance to

Needy Families) funding each year, which they are able to distribute to tribal members as flexibly as they see fit. This may allow American Indian stepfamilies access to programs that will strengthen their family ties (National Congress of American Indians [NCAI], 2018).

Recommendations for Practitioners

American Indians have marital and family counseling needs and preferences that can be unique in comparison with those of other racial and ethnic groups (Cross, 1998). For example, use of a relaxed, client-centered listening style and capitalizing on the power of nonverbal forms of communication will more likely lead to more successful and satisfying outcomes for American Indian clients (Sue & Sue, 2013). This is not to say that American Indian stepfamilies do not share similarities with other groups. For example, in one study both White and Navajo couples reported keeping their marriage strong by regularly taking inventory of their financial security and communicating clearly to resolve mistakes and misunderstandings with their spouse (Skogrand et al., 2008).

In either case, approaching clients "where they are" and then utilizing culturally appropriate evidence-based treatment strategies are effective ways to show respect for this important—but often overlooked—population. Social workers, marriage and family therapists, caseworkers, and others working with American Indian individuals or families would do well by helping their clients work toward balance and harmony in their stepfamily. A number of a spiritual assessment tools have been developed that help clinicians utilize spiritual strengths when working with American Indian clients, including spiritual genograms, spiritual life maps, spiritual eco-maps, and spiritual eco-grams (Hodge & Limb, 2010). Such tools are especially useful when working with children.

Another important intervention approach with American Indian clients is to recognize the unique strengths that American Indian stepfamilies carry within themselves and then help clients capitalize on these. For example, nontraditional family systems are traditionally viewed by American Indians as not pathological but acceptable and normative. Counselors and other helping professionals should be careful not to problematize and make assumptions about stepfamily relationships. For example, single motherhood is more acceptable because of the involvement of a large network that surrounds the mother and her children. In sessions, counselors could discuss issues not just of concern to immediate stepfamily members but also to grandparents, aunts, uncles, and other members of the community such as tribal elders. There are other norms unique to American Indians that require consideration. For example, gender and sexual fluidity are acceptable in many tribes (Red Horse, 1997). Practitioners should not hesitate to be accepting of nontraditional behaviors and social structures and build an atmosphere of celebration and acceptance of nontraditional family structures.

Conclusion

American Indian stepfamilies share many characteristics of non-Native stepfamilies but also have unique strengths, including collectivism and community. On the other hand, American Indian stepfamilies face many challenges, including unemployment and poor mental health. More American Indian children are raised in single-parent homes compared with the general population, divorce rates are among the highest of all racial and ethnic groups, and unmarried cohabitation rates are higher than any other racial group. Child abuse and neglect rates are high, and alcohol and drug abuse along with mental health problems are prevalent among the American Indian population.

Our analysis of the STEP data revealed that American Indians have lower quality relationships and well-being than the other racial and ethnic groups examined (except for a few outcomes in which the data are similar to Hispanics and/or African Americans). For example, American Indian adult stepchildren perceived their relationships with their stepparents to be of lower quality than did White stepchildren. It is important to remember that many factors associated with stepfamily relationship difficulties—low education levels, low socioeconomic status, unemployment, history of union instability, and interracial marriage—are experiences that are disproportionately present among American Indians compared with the general population. Controlling for the influence of these factors on stepfamily relationships and well-being is an important direction for future research to clarify what strengths and treatment approaches should be emphasized among this population. For example, developing policies to address American Indians' large high school dropout rates would help reduce unemployment. Investing in programs to address drug and alcohol abuse would reduce child abuse and neglect. Improving the lives of American Indians would no doubt work toward improving stepfamily relationships and well-being.

Our review of existing studies of American Indian history, culture, and traditions combined with our own findings provide important baseline data for the development of policies, practices, and resources for American Indian stepfamilies. Although Native people would most likely benefit from culturally responsive interventions, stigmatized groups are often too ashamed to seek help and support, which may help explain American Indians' low level of help-seeking for financial, mental health, and other federal, state, and local services, which in turn undermines stepfamily well-being (Spear et al., 2013). One strategy would be to work closely with tribal leaders and elders, providing resources and guidance to encourage families to reach out.

We hope that this chapter communicates how crucial it is for practitioners, policy makers, and the general public to appreciate the resilience of this population in the face of historical trauma and opposition, and to encourage the use of the strengths already inherent in American Indian family systems to deal with the challenges common to stepfamily life.

Questions for Discussion

1. What are some strengths of American Indian stepfamilies? What challenges do they face?
2. In addition to those discussed in the chapter, what are some policies and practices you believe would help American Indian stepfamilies?
3. How are stepfamilies among American Indians similar to and different from other racial and ethnic groups? How do extended family systems affect relationships between American Indian family members?

Additional Resources

Davis, B., Dionne, R., & Fortin, M. (2014). Parenting in two cultural worlds in the presence of one dominant worldview: The American Indian experience. In *Parenting across cultures* (pp. 367–377). Netherlands: Springer.

National Healthy Marriage Resource Center. http://www.healthy-marriageinfo.org/research-and-policy/marriage-facts/culture/native-americans/index.aspx

Stepfamily Experience Project (STEP). https://step.byu.edu/Pages/home.aspx

Notes

1   What to call Indigenous peoples of the United States has long been a subject of controversy. Recent interviews with members of this group, however, reveal a wide range of preferences, with most preferring to identify with their specific tribe (Blackhorse, 2017). For ease of comparison with the other racial, ethnic, and religious groups covered in this book, we chose "American Indian," which is the official federal government term used in treaties and official dealings with American Indian peoples or First Nations in the United States. This being the case, we will use the term *American Indian*, and occasionally *Native* or *Native American* (also common in the literature), to refer to this group of people throughout this chapter.

2   Because the American Community Survey only assessed the relationship between the child and the primary householder (and not additional adults in the household), such estimates underestimate the prevalence of stepparent-stepchild relationships.

3   We recognize that American Indians are not the only minority group with collectivist family patterns. It is well known that African Americans, Hispanics, and Asians display higher levels of involvement with extended family members than do Whites and have a stronger sense of obligation to them (Kim & McKenry, 1998). Similar to American Indians, these groups have a history of legal, economic, and social oppression. In addition to American Indians, we also draw on studies of other racial and ethnic groups in our discussion of the implications of collectivist culture on American Indian stepfamilies.

References

A family for every child. (2018). *Diversity.* Retrieved from https://www.afamilyforeverychild.org/diversity/

Adler-Baeder, F., Robertson, A., & Schramm, D. G. (2010). A conceptual framework for marriage education programs for stepfamily couples with considerations for socio-economic context. *Marriage and Family Review, 46,* 300–322.

Alexie, S. (2005). *The Lone Ranger and Tonto fistfight in heaven.* New York, NY: Grove Press.

American Indian Development Associates. (2000). *Promising practices and strategies to reduce alcohol and substance abuse among American Indians and Alaska Natives.* Retrieved from http://www.aidainc.net/Publications/Alcohol%20promise.pdf

Attorney General's Advisory Committee. (2014). *Ending violence so children can thrive.* Retrieved from https://www.justice.gov/sites/default/files/defendingchildhood/pages/attachments/2014/11/18/finalaianreport.pdf

Ayers, S. (n.d.). *Measures of positive parenting for American Indian and Alaska Native adolescents in urban contexts.* Retrieved from https://www.researchconnections.org/files/childcare/pdf/ai-an/Ayers_P2WParenting Measures.pdf

Blackhorse, A. (2017). *Native American? American Indian? Nope.* Retrieved from https://newsmaven.io/indiancountrytoday/archive/blackhorse-native-american-american-indian-nope-hNAQB_MRSk-07Cw1hAF8Xw/

Bray, J. H., & Hetherington, E. M. (1993). Families in transition: Introduction and overview. *Journal of Family Psychology, 7,* 3-8.

Brave Heart, M. Y. H., & DeBruyn, L. M. (1998). The American Indian holocaust: Healing historical unresolved grief. *American Indian and Alaska Native Mental Health Research, 8,* 60-82.

Browning, S., & Artelt, E. (2012). *Stepfamily therapy: A 10-step clinical approach.* Washington, DC: American Psychological Association.

Bureau of Indian Affairs. (2017). Indian entities recognized and eligible to receive services from the United States Bureau of Indian Affairs. *Federal Register, 33.* Retrieved from https://www.gpo.gov/fdsys/pkg/FR-2017-01-17/pdf/2017-00912.pdf

Chartier, K., & Caetano, R. (2010). Ethnicity and health disparities in alcohol research. *Alcohol Research Health, 33,* 152-160.

Child Trends. (2015). *Racial and ethnic composition of the child population.* Retrieved February 7, 2019, from https://www.childtrends.org/wp-content/uploads/2016/07/60_Racial-Composition.pdf

Christensen, M., & Manson, S. (2001). Adult attachment as a framework for understanding mental health and American Indian families: A study of three family cases. *The American Behavioral Scientist, 44,* 1447-1465.

Cross, T. L. (1998). Understanding family resiliency from a relational world view. In H. McCubbin, E. Thompson, A. Thompson, & J. Fromer (Eds.) *Resiliency in American Indian and immigrant families.* (143-157). Thousand Oaks, CA: Sage.

Dalla, R. L., & Gamble, W. C. (1998). Social networks and systems of support among American Indian Navajo adolescent mothers. In H. McCubbin, E. Thompson, A. Thompson, & J. Fromer (Eds.) *Resiliency in American Indian and immigrant families* (183-198). Thousand Oaks, CA: Sage.

Davis, B., Dionne, R., & Fortin, M. (2014). Parenting in two cultural worlds in the presence of one dominant worldview: The American Indian experience. In *Parenting across cultures* (pp. 367-377). Netherlands: Springer.

DeVoe, J. F., Darling-Churchill, K. E., & Snyder, T. D. (2008). Status and trends in the education of American Indians and Alaska Natives: 2008. *U.S. Department of Education,* September 2008. Retrieved from http://files.eric.ed.gov/fulltext/ED502797.pdf

Donnermeyer, J. F., Edwards, R. W., Chavez, E. L., & Beauvais, F. (2016). Involvement of American Indian youth in gangs. *Free Inquiry in Creative Sociology, 28*, 73–80.

Elliott, D. B., & Lewis, J. M. (2010). *Embracing the institution of marriage: The characteristics of remarried Americans.* PAA Annual Meeting, Dallas, TX.

Engel, M. (2003). *United States law degrades stepfamilies.* Retrieved February 7, 2019, from http://www.stepfamilies.info/key-advocacy-issues.php

Ganong, L., & Coleman, M. (2004). *Stepfamily relationships: Development, dynamics, and interventions.* New York, NY: Kluwer/Plenum.

Ganong, L., Coleman, M., & Jamison, T. B. (2011). Patterns of stepchild-stepparent relationship development. *Journal of Marriage and Family, 73*, 396–413.

Garrett, J. T., & Garrett, M. W. (1994). The path of good medicine: Understanding and counseling American Indians. *Journal of Multicultural Counseling and Development, 22*, 134–144.

Glover, G. (2001). Parenting in American Indian families. In N. B. Webb (Ed.) *Culturally diverse parent-child and family relationships: A guide for social workers and other practitioners* (205–231). New York, NY: Columbia University Press.

Goodluck, C. W., & Willeto, A. A. (2009). *Seeing the protective rainbow: How families survive and thrive in the American Indian and Alaska Native community.* Seattle: WA: Annie E. Casey Foundation.

Grandbois, D. (2005). Stigma of mental illness among American Indian and Alaska Native nation: Historical and contemporary perspectives. *Issues in Mental Health Nursing, 26*, 1001–1024.

Gray, A. C., Shafer, K., Limb, G., & Busby, D. M. (2013). Unique influences on American Indian relationship quality: An American-Indian and Caucasian comparison. *Journal of Comparative Family Studies, 44*, 589–608.

Henslin, J. M. (2010). *Sociology: A down-to-earth approach.* Boston, MA: Pearson.

Hodge, D. R., & Limb, G. E. (2010). An American Indian perspective on spiritual assessment: The strengths and limitations of a complementary set of assessment tools. *Health & Social Work, 35*, 121–131.

Hodge, D. R., Limb, G. E., & Cross, T. L. (2009). Moving from colonization toward balance and harmony: An American Indian perspective on wellness. *Journal of Social Work, 54*, 211–219.

Holmes, W. M. (2013). Substance abuse and mental health issues within American Indian grandparenting families. *Journal of Ethnicity in Substance Abuse, 12*, 210–227.

Indian Health Service. (2004). *Trends in Indian health—2000-2001.* Rockville, MD: Indian Health Service.

Ispa, J. M., Thornburg, K. R., & Fine, M. A. (2006). *Keepin' On: The everyday struggles of young families in poverty.* Baltimore, MD: Brookes.

Jacobs, M. D. (2013). Remembering the "forgotten child": The American Indian child welfare crisis of the 1960s and 1970s. *The American Indian Quarterly, 37*, 136–159.

Kids Count Data Center. (2018). *Children in single-parent families by race in the United States.* Retrieved from https://datacenter.kidscount. org/data/tables/107-children-in-single-parent-families-by#detailed/1/any/false/870,573,869,36,868,867,133,38,35,18/10,11,9,12,1,185,13/432,431

Kim, H. K., & McKenry, P. C. (1998). Social networks and support: A comparison of African Americans, Asian Americans, Caucasians, and Hispanics. *Journal of Comparative Family Studies, 29*, 313–34.

Knaster, E. S., Fretts, A. M., & Phillips, L. E. (2015). The association of depression with diabetes management among urban American Indians/Alaska Natives in the United States. *Ethnicity & disease, 25*, 83–89.

Kreider, R. M., & Lofquist, D. A. (2014). *Adopted children and stepchildren: 2010. Population characteristics.* Washington DC: U.S. Census Bureau.

Kleinman, A. (1996). How is culture important for DSM-IV? In J. E. Mezzich, A. Kleinman, H. Fabrega, & D. L. Parron (Eds.) *Culture & psychiatric diagnosis: A DSM-IV perspective* (pp. 17–18). Washington, DC: American Psychiatric Press.

Krogstad, J. M. (2014, June 13). One-in-four American Indians and Alaska Natives are living in poverty. *Pew Research Center.* Retrieved from http://www.pewresearch.org/fact-tank/2014/06/13/1-in-4-native-americans-and-alaska-natives-are-living-in-poverty/

LaFramboise, T. D., & Low, K. G. (1998). American Indian children and adolescents. In Gibbs, Huang, & Associates (Eds.) *Children of color: Psychological interventions with culturally diverse youth* (pp. 112–142). San Francisco, CA: Jossey-Bass.

LaFromboise, T. D., Hoyt, D. R., Oliver, L., & Whitbeck, L. B. (2006). Family, community, and school influences on resilience among American Indian adolescents in the upper Midwest. *Journal of Community Psychology, 34*, 193–209.

Larzelere, R. E., Morris, A., Harrist, A. W., & Cavell, T. A. (2013). *Authoritative parenting: Synthesizing nurturance and discipline for optimal child development.* Washington, DC: American Psychological Association.

Lesthaeghe, R., Lopez-Colas, J., & Neidert, L. (2016). The social geography of unmarried cohabitation in the USA, 2007-2011. In A. Esteve & R. Lesthaeghe (Eds.) *Cohabitation and marriage in the Americas* (pp. 101–132). New York, NY: Springer.

Lewis, C. (1970). *Indian families of the Northwest coast: The impact of change.* Chicago, IL: University of Chicago Press.

Limb, G. E., Shafer, K., & Sandoval, K. (2014). The impact of kin support on urban American Indian families. *Child & Family Social Work, 19*, 432–442.

Lonczak, H. S., Fernandez, A., Austin, L., Marlatt, G. A., & Donovan, D. M. (2007). Family structure and substance use among American Indian youth: A preliminary study. *Families, Systems, & Health, 25*, 10–22.

Manson, S., & Altschul, D. (2004). *Meeting the mental health needs of American Indians and Alaska Natives.* Retrieved from http://www.azdhs.gov/bhs/pdf/culturalComp/ccna.pdf

May, P. A., McCloskey, J., & Gossage, J. P. (2002). Fetal alcohol syndrome among American Indians: Epidemiology, issues, and research. In P. D. Mail, S. Heurtin-Roberts, S. E. Martin, & J. Howard (Eds.) *Alcohol use among American Indians: Multiple perspectives on a complex problem* (pp. 321–369). Bethesda, MD: National Institute on Alcohol Abuse and Alcoholism.

McCulley, K. L. (2005). The American Indian Probate Reform Act of 2004: The death of fractionation or individual Native American property interests and tribal customs? *American Indian Law Review, 30*, 401–422.

McKinley, I. (2019). *LGBT parental rights and adoption.* Retrieved from https://www.mckinleyirvin.com/resources/same-sex-marriage-parenting-divorce-in-washingto/lgbt-parental-rights-adoption/

Muraru, A. A., & Turliuc, M. N. (2012). Family-of-origin, romantic attachment, and marital adjustment: A path analysis model. *Social and Behavioral Sciences, 33*, 90–94.

Narduzzi, J. L. (2015). *Mental health among elderly Native Americans (Psychology Revivals).* New York, NY: Routledge.

National Healthy Marriage Resource Center. (2016). *Research and policy, marriage facts, culture, Native Americans.* Retrieved from http://www.healthymarriageinfo.org/research-and-policy/marriage-facts/culture/native-americans/index.aspx

National Resource Center for Healthy Marriage and Families. (2015). *Working with American Indian and Alaska Native individuals, couples, and families.* Retrieved from https://www.healthymarriageandfamilies.org/sites/default/files/Resource%20Files/Working%20with%20American%20Indian%20and%20Alaska%20Native.pdf?_ga=2.202809298.253644693.1549314992-371194401.1549314992

Native American Program of Legal Aid Services of Oregon, Indigenous Ways of Knowing Program at Lewis & Clark Graduate School of Counseling and Education, Western States Center, the Pride Foundation, and Basic Rights of Oregon. (2013). *Tribal equity toolkit 2.0: Tribal resolutions and codes to support two spirit and LGBT justice in Indian country.* Retrieved from https://graduate.lclark.edu/live/files/15810-tribal-equity-toolkit-20

National Congress of American Indians. (2018). *Child welfare and TANF.* Retrieved from http://www.ncai.org/policy-issues/education-health-human-services/child-welfare-and-tanf

National Congress of American Indians, Policy Research Center. (2015). *A spotlight on two spirit (Native LGBT) communities.* Retrieved from http://www.ncai.org/policy-research-center/research-data/prc-publications/A_Spotlight_on_Native_LGBT.pdf

Nibley, L. (2011). *Two spirits.* PBS television.

Nittle, N. K. (2017). *Interesting facts and information about the Native American population.* Retrieved from https://www.thoughtco.com/interesting-facts-about-native-americans-2834518

Norton, I. M. (1996). Research in American Indian and Alaska Native communities: Navigating the cultural universe of values and process. *Journal of Consulting Psychology, 64,* 856–860.

Norris T., Vines P., & Hoeffel, E. M. (2012). *The American Indian and Alaska Native population: 2010.* United States Census Bureau. Retrieved from http://www.census.gov/prod/cen2010/briefs/c2010br-10.pdf

Padilla, J., Ward, P., & Limb, G. E. (2013). Urban American Indians: A comparison of father involvement predictors across race. *Social Work Research, 37,* 207–217.

Papernow, P. L. (2015). *Becoming a stepfamily: Patterns of development in remarried families.* New York, NY: Routledge.

Papernow, P. L. (2013). *Surviving and thriving in stepfamily relationships.* New York, NY: Routledge.

Pasley, K., & Lee, M. (2010). Stress and coping within the context of stepfamily life. In S. Price & C. Price (Eds.) *Families and change* (4th ed., pp. 235–262). Thousand Oaks, CA: Sage.

Pew Research Center. (2011). *A portrait of stepfamilies.* Retrieved from http://www.pewsocialtrends.org/2011/01/13/a-portrait-of-stepfamilies/

Phillips, T., Wilmoth, J., Wall. S., Peterson, D., Buckley, R., & Phillips, L. (2013). Recollected prenatal care and fear of intimacy in emerging adults. *The Family Journal: Counseling and Therapy for Couples and Families, 21,* 335–341.

Raley, R. K., & Bumpass, L. (2003). The topography of the divorce plateau: Levels and trends in union stability since 1980. *Demographic Research, 3,* Article 8. Retrieved from http://www.demographic-research.org/Volumes/Vol8/8/8-8-.pdf

Red Horse, J. G. (1997). Traditional American Indian family systems. *Families, Systems, & Health, 15,* 243–250.

Robbins, R., Scherman, A., Holeman, H., & Wilson, J. (2005). Roles of American Indian grandparents in times of cultural crisis. *Journal of Cultural Diversity, 1,* 46–56.

Robbins, R., Robbins, S., & Stennerson, B. (2013). American Indian family resilience. In D. S. Becvar (Ed.) *Handbook of family resilience* (197–213). New York, NY: Springer.

Sarche, M., & Spicer P. (2008). Poverty and health disparities for American Indian and Alaska Native children: Current knowledge and future prospects. *Annals of the New York Academy of Sciences, 1136,* 126–136.

Skogrand, L., Mueller, M. L., Arrington, R., LeBlanch, H., Spotted Elk, D., Dayzie, I., Rosenband, R. (2008). Strong Navajo marriages. *American Indian and Alaska native Mental Health Research, 15,* 25–41.

Spear, S., Crevecoeur-MacPhail, D., Denering, L., Dickerson, D., & Brecht, M. (2013). Determinants of successful treatment outcomes among a sample of urban American Indians/Alaska Natives: The role of social environments. *The Journal of Behavioral Health Services and Research, 40,* 330–341.

Steinberg, L., Dornbusch, S. M., & Brown, B. B. (1992). Ethnic differences in adolescent achievement: An ecological perspective. *American Psychologist, 47,* 723–729.

Stepfamily Experience Project. (2017). Retrieved from https://step.byu.edu/Pages/home.aspx

Stewart, S. (2007). *Brave new stepfamilies: Diverse paths toward stepfamily living.* Thousand Oaks, CA: Sage.

Strong, P. T. (2015). *American Indians and the American imaginary: Cultural representation across the centuries.* New York, NY: Routledge.

Suicide Prevention Resource Center. (2013). *CDC releases 2013 youth risk behavior surveillance system data.* Retrieved from https://youth.gov/feature-article/cdc-releases-2013-youth-risk-behavior-surveillance-system-data

Sue, D. E., & Sue, D. (2003). *Counseling the culturally diverse: Theory and practice.* New York, NY: John Wiley & Sons.

Sweeney, M. M. (2007). Stepfather families and the emotional well-being of adolescents. *Journal of Health and Social Behavior, 48,* 33–49.

Thompson, J. W., Walker, R. D., & Silk-Walker, P. (1993). Psychiatric care of American Indians and Alaska Natives. In A. C. Gaw (Ed.) *Culture, ethnicity and mental illness* (pp. 189–243). Washington, DC: American Psychiatric Press.

Townsend, N. (2002). *The package deal: Marriage, work, and fatherhood in men's lives.* Philadelphia, PA: Temple University Press.

U. S. Bureau of the Census. (2013a). *Poverty rates for selected detailed race and Hispanic groups by state and place: 2007–2011.* Retrieved from https://www.census.gov/prod/2013pubs/acsbr11-17.pdf

U. S. Bureau of the Census. (2013b). *America's families and living arrangements: 2012.* Retrieved from https://www.census.gov/prod/2013pubs/p20-570.pdf

U. S. Bureau of the Census. (2012a). *Births, deaths, marriages, and divorce.* Retrieved from http://www.census.gov/compendia/statab/2012/tables/12s0086.pdf

U. S. Bureau of the Census. (2012b). *American Indian and Alaska Native Heritage month.* Retrieved from https://www.census.gov/newsroom/releases/archives/facts_for_features_special_editions/cb12-ff22.html

U. S. Bureau of the Census (2010a). *Adopted children and stepchildren: 2010*. Retrieved from http://www.census.gov/prod/2014pubs/p20-572.pdf

U. S. Bureau of the Census (2010b). *Households and families*. Retrieved from https://www.census.gov/prod/cen2010/briefs/c2010br-14.pdf

Vespa, J. (2017). *The changing economics and demographics of young adulthood: 1975-2016*. Washington, DC: US Department of Commerce, United States Census Bureau, 14.

Walters, K. L., Evans-Campbell, T., Simoni, J. M., Ronquillo, T., & Bhuyan, R. (2006). My spirit in my heart: Identity experiences and challenges among American Indian two-spirit women. *Journal of Lesbian Studies, 10*, 125-149.

Werner, E., & Smith, R. (1992). *Overcoming the odds: High risk children from birth to adulthood*. Ithaca, NY: Cornell University Press.

Willeto, A. A. A. (2002). *Native American kids 2002: Indian children's wellbeing data book for 13 states*. Seattle, WA: Casey Family Programs.

Wilson, A. (1996). How we find ourselves: Identity development and two spirit people. *Harvard Educational Review, 66*, 303-318.

CHAPTER SIX

East Asian Stepfamilies

Shinji Nozawa, MA, Meiji Gakuin University

Introduction

According to the 2009–2011 American Community Survey, there are slightly more than 35,000 Asian stepchildren under age 18 living in the United States, which consists of only 1.8% of all the stepchildren of this age (Kreider & Lofquist, 2010). Although there has been a great development in stepfamily research in the United States since the 1970s, stepfamilies of relatively small ethnic groups such as Asians in North America still remain understudied (Ganong & Coleman, 2018). Therefore, little is known about the distinctiveness of stepfamily dynamics among Asian Americans or the similarities and differences compared with stepfamilies of other racial and ethnic groups. Thus, this chapter will turn its main attention to findings from emerging stepfamily studies in East Asian societies. Family norms and dynamics among Asian stepfamilies in the United States, which are under different social, cultural, and political environments, should not be regarded as identical to those of stepfamilies in East Asian countries. Yet, the information provided in this chapter should be helpful in designing future research on stepfamilies within the U.S. Asian population.

Until around the turn of the century, stepfamilies in Asia remained a socially invisible and academically unexplored subject (Nozawa, 2008b). The divorce rate has risen during the past few decades among many societies in East Asia (Jones, 2015), resulting in a corresponding growth in the number of stepfamilies (Nozawa,

2015a). As a result, an increasing number of Asian family researchers and clinicians are studying stepfamily dynamics in Asian culture along with their unique aspects. Although the literature is still quite small, there is a growing body of research on Asian stepfamilies (Nozawa, 2015).

In an effort to add to the growing research in this area, the goals of this chapter are to present an overview of stepfamilies in Asian societies and to discuss both similar and distinct features in comparison with their Western counterparts. The chapter draws upon stepfamily research findings from selected East Asian societies, mainly from Japan, Hong Kong, South Korea, and Singapore.[1] There are at least two reasons to focus primarily on stepfamilies in these limited parts of Asia. First, Asia makes up a large percentage of the globe and contains a wide variety of nations and regions. Although there are similarities across many Asian cultures, societies in East Asia have distinct historical and cultural backgrounds and are at different stages of social and economic development. They also operate under very diverse political and judicial systems and religious backgrounds. Therefore, it is a large endeavor simply to identify traditional family patterns in some parts of Asia, let alone emerging family forms.

The second reason, as noted, is the relative scarcity of research on Asian stepfamilies. Stepfamily research in Asia is still in its infancy (Nozawa, 2015a) in comparison with that in the United States, which has nearly 50 years of scholarship in this field (Ganong & Coleman, 2018). In many Asian societies, stepfamilies remain socially hidden and their stories are largely untold. This is due to continued strong social stigma against nonmarital births, divorce, and remarriage. For example, there was no Japanese equivalent to the English word "stepfamily" until a new Japanese word—*suteppufamiri*—was adopted from English in 2001. This term was introduced when the Stepfamily Association of Japan (SAJ), the first nonprofit organization supporting stepfamilies in Japan, was founded, emulating the Stepfamily Association of America (Nozawa, 2008b). Although the imported new word now appears in some Japanese dictionaries, it is used among only a small part of the Japanese speaking population. Chinese and Korean languages are similarly lacking a common word to indicate a stepfamily in everyday conversations. Instead, stepfamily members try to "pass" as a nuclear family or describe their family situation only when necessary. As a result, there continues to be relatively little research on stepfamilies in Asia, in contrast with the wealth of stepfamily research in the United States (Ganong & Coleman, 2017). Similar to stepfamilies in the United States 40 years ago, Asian stepfamilies today remain "an incomplete institution" (Cherlin, 1978), as will be discussed later in more detail. Despite these difficulties, it is meaningful to review what is known about East Asian stepfamilies as a group, for whom many similarities in social and cultural backgrounds exist. Further, this chapter includes what is known about Asian stepfamilies in the United States. In the next section, I will briefly overview the marriage and family patterns of Asian societies, which will give readers important ideas in understanding stepfamilies in Asia. It should be noted, however, that premodern traditional marriage practices were quite diverse across Asian societies and that these family patterns in Asia are rapidly changing.

Marriage and Family Patterns in Asian Societies

Many societies in Asia, including China, Taiwan, Korea, and Japan, share the tradition of Confucianism and its family values. Originating in ancient China, Confucian family values emphasize the ethics or behavioral norms in familial and other human relations such as patriarchy and filial piety, which means that a child should respect the parents, especially the father (Ishii-Kuntz, 2015). It should be noted, however, that the degree of influence of Confucian ideas on families and their living arrangements are diverse among these countries. For example, premodern marriage in China was rigidly patriarchal, whereas in Thailand it was much more flexible. In both Japan and Korea there was an interplay of rigidly patriarchal and more flexible marriages since the late 18th century (Ochiai, 2015) with the advent of modernization. In Tokugawa (premodern) Japan, religion had no function in legitimizing a marriage, unlike most Christian countries where the church generally promoted marriage and prohibited (or at least strongly discouraged) divorce. Here, Confucian ideology was influential only among a small portion of the ruling-class population in Tokugawa Japan. Studies of marriage, divorce, and remarriage in 18th- to late-19th-century Japanese villages revealed that divorce and remarriage occurred more frequently and were much less stigmatized than in 20th-century Japan (Ochiai, 2015; Kurosu, 2007; Iwai, 2000; Takagi 1992).

In the process of modernization, promoted by the Japanese government after the Meiji Restoration in 1867, the practices and ideals of less flexible marriage and family relations based on Confucian and patriarchal values were institutionalized with the introduction of the Civil Code and the family register system, with more authority and power of the family being placed upon fathers/husbands. As a result, the divorce rate declined significantly during the late 19th and the early 20th centuries and remained quite low until the 1960s. Here, much more negative attitudes toward divorce and remarriage were spread across the population, mainly through the rigid educational institutions of modernizing Japan (Muta, 1996). The idea of less freedom in mate selection or mate changing, authoritarian fathers' control of marriage, and increased emphasis on chastity (particularly for women) became the norm. In sum, as marriage and childbirth have been institutionalized as more formal and inflexible life events, *de facto* marriage (cohabitation), divorce, remarriage, and nonmarital childbirth rapidly declined from the late 19th century until about the mid-20th century in Japan (Ochiai, 2015; National Institute of Population and Social Security, 2017).

In this context, an excellent ethnography by Ella Wiswell, an American anthropologist, is worth mentioning. She documented that women in an older generation in a Japanese farming village in the 1930s had flexible and rather positive views of divorce and remarriage and behaved accordingly, and were not affected by the new conservative family ideology at that time (Smith & Wiswell, 1982). Thus, it should be emphasized that diversity and complexity did exist in patterns in marriage, divorce, and remarriage among East Asian societies throughout history.

Despite the differences in political systems and ethnic diversity, there are many similarities across Asian societies stemming from recent social and demographic changes that affect family life. Japan, South Korea, Hong Kong, Taiwan, and Singapore have experienced rapid economic growth in recent decades. Japan's economic growth began earlier, after World War II, followed by economic growth in South Korea, Hong Kong, Taiwan, and Singapore that began in the 1970s and is continuing. During this transition, particularly among the growing middle-class, college-educated population in urban areas, the nuclear family model emerged, one based on a romantic love between spouses instead of an arranged marriage with heavy involvement of couples' parents and other relatives. This model is the new standard for younger generations (for more discussion on the Japanese case, see Ochiai, 1997).

Japan, South Korea, Hong Kong, Taiwan, and Singapore show strikingly similar demographic changes in family life. Over the past 40 years, all have seen a shift toward later marriages with fewer men and women opting to marry (Quah, 2015). All have experienced rapid declining trends in fertility, with the average couple across all five having less than two children (1.1 to 1.4 in 2013; Cheung, 2015). Divorce rates in these societies rose during the 1990s, followed by the same trend in China in the early 2000s, though they have declined slightly or leveled off later, as shown in Figure 6.1 (Jones, 2015). In the meantime, it should be noted that the prevalence of cohabitation is much lower in East Asian societies than in the United States and European countries, though there are some studies reporting upward trends on cohabitation in Japan, Taiwan, and South Korea (Kobayashi & Kampen, 2015; Raymo et al., 2015). Nonmarital childbearing in East Asia is also very low compared with Western countries (Raymo et al., 2015). Only 2.3% of babies in Japan and 1.9% in South Korea are born to unmarried mothers, in contrast with 40.2% in the United States (OECD, 2014). Thus, these Asian societies share similarities in that the institution of marriage, in which the bearing and rearing of children is still confined, continues to be socially valued, with lowered marriage and fertility rates and a lower divorce rate.

Corresponding with the rise in divorces and remarriages, the number of stepfamily households in these Asian societies appears to be increasing (Nozawa, 2008b). A recent search found that there were no official statistics on counting or estimating the exact number of stepfamilies in Asia. Thus, the growth in step-families is based on anecdotal observations and conversations with family researchers and other professional colleagues in Asia. For example, there are rising social interests and concerns about stepfamilies among family social workers and family therapists in these societies. Asian family professionals are in need of understanding stepfamily dynamics as they are gradually becoming aware of the limitations in following the nuclear family model in marital relationships and parenting.

In the following sections I present two competing and conflicting theoretical stepfamily models shared by many family researchers and professionals, and among many stepfamily members. The first and older of these two models, in particular,

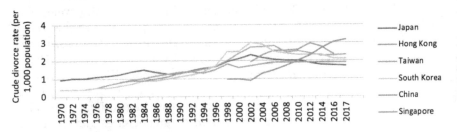

FIGURE 6.1   Crude Divorce Rate, East Asia and Singapore, 1970–2017

has been incorporated into many social and legal institutions in Japan. Meanwhile, the second and newer one is being alternatively adopted into the recent reforms of family laws and related policies in Japan and elsewhere. Thus, findings from stepfamily research in Japan and some of the Asian societies cited previously will be reviewed in light of the two stepfamily models.

Theoretical Perspectives: Old and New Stepfamily Models

Cherlin (1978) sees stepfamilies, formed through the remarriage or cohabitation of couples in which one or both partners have children from previous relationships, as "an incomplete institution." This theoretical perspective is particularly useful in observing stepfamilies in Asia. He attributes the relative instability of couple relationships in stepfamilies to the lack of social norms guiding stepfamily relationships, and to the lack of institutional supports for the specific needs of stepfamily members. According to Cherlin's hypothesis, difficulties that stepfamily members face in their daily lives are largely ignored due to the lack of guidance and social support in intra-family and interfamily interactions, along with the lack of proper names and labels for that particular family form and the people in them. Medical and educational professionals, including doctors and schoolteachers, and family therapists and social workers also lack knowledge relevant to stepfamilies. The vast majority of what is known about stepfamilies comes from studies conducted in North America, Europe, Australia, and New Zealand (Ganong & Coleman, 2017). Therefore, there are far more resources, including self-help books and educational programs, available in the United States and other Western countries (see Coleman & Nickleberry, 2009). In contrast, there are few resources available in Asian societies, though family professionals and researchers in Asia are increasingly interested in learning about and researching stepfamilies.

Although Cherlin's "incomplete institution" was developed in response to the dramatic increase in stepfamilies in the United States beginning 50 years ago it remains an important theory for understanding stepfamilies. Even in the United States, where there are large numbers of stepfamilies, they remain misunderstood, stigmatized, and undefined (Ganong & Coleman, 1997, 2017). Similarly, incomplete institutionalization is a problem among stepfamilies in Asian societies and limits our understanding of the realities of stepfamily life and whether—and how—these families will become integrated into Asian societies.

In this context, it is not surprising that stepfamilies in Asia tend to model themselves after an already institutionalized family form—the "nuclear family" consisting of a married couple and their shared biological (or adopted) children. For example, studies of stepfamilies in Japan reveal that they strongly encourage and assume that stepparents are the "new parents" of their stepchildren, and that their nonresidential biological parents should be *replaced by* their stepparents. Stepparents in Japan are more likely to behave as if they were the only father or mother of their stepchildren (Kikuchi, 2005; Nozawa, 2008b).

These stepfamilies more or less unconsciously adopt what I have labeled as the *scrap and build household model* in their process of stepfamily formation (Nozawa, 2011; Nozawa, 2015a). This stepfamily model assumes that separation of the parents means a breakdown of their original nuclear family with the children being forced to belong to only one of the two parents' households and kinship networks, and to cut ties to one parent's side. If and when a custodial parent re-partners, a new nuclear family household is built with the new spouse/partner replacing the former partner's parental position, essentially becoming a "new father/mother" with respect to the stepchildren (Kikuchi, 2005; Nozawa, 2008b). A similar process takes place should the noncustodial parent remarry or re-partner with someone who has his or her own children.

A new type of Japanese father ferrying his three children with a utility bicycle on the streets of Tokyo.

Stepfamilies are not only institutionally incomplete but also "institutionally guided" by laws and policies arising from norms supportive of traditional family life. In Japan, post-divorce joint custody (as either legal or physical joint custody) by both parents of a child is not legally allowed. Therefore, neither co-parenting nor frequent regular visitations of nonresidential parents after parental separation are common practices. The vast majority of divorce cases in Japan (87%, according to Japan's Vital Statistics 2016) are based on mutual agreement of the couple to divorce (so-called *kyogi rikon* in Japanese). As long as a married couple agree on the divorce and on who takes custody—in most cases, both legal and physical custody—of the children and submits a signed and sealed "Divorce Application Form" to the responsible local government office, the divorce becomes valid almost immediately without going through any judicial process at a family court or elsewhere. Thus, most Japanese divorce cases are more private and free of official or public interventions in contrast with divorce in the United States where courts play bigger parts.

As a result of both Japanese culture and laws (and probably those of many other Asian societies) that do not recognize the uniqueness of stepfamilies, ties between noncustodial parents and their children are very often lost. The National Survey of One Parent Households with a nationally representative sample of single parents' households conducted in 2016 (Japan, Ministry of Health, Labour and Welfare, 2017) demonstrates this tendency. Only 43% of the divorced single mothers reported having made either written or unwritten arrangements regarding child support payments by noncustodial fathers, and only 24% of them reported that their former partners (noncustodial fathers) paid child support. The same survey revealed that only 24% of the divorced single mothers made an agreement with respect to visitation arrangements, and that 65% of the children in these households had lost contact with their noncustodial parents. Although research is lacking, it is very likely that even more nonresident parent-child relationships discontinue after a custodial parent's remarriage because of cultural norms that encourage the stepparent to take on the biological parent's role, and also because adoption of a stepchild by his or her stepparent is easy and does not require the consent of the noncustodial parent (Hayano, 2006). The present legal and social systems in Japan, therefore, lead many stepfamilies to form themselves in accordance with the *scrap and build model*.

Nevertheless, a newer model of stepfamilies has been emerging in Japan (and possibly in the rest of Asia), just as it has in the

Western world. I have called this the *expanded and interconnected network model* of stepfamilies (Nozawa, 2011; Nozawa, 2015a). In contrast with stepfamilies following the *scrap and build model*, stepfamilies within this new model attempt to keep parents and kin members on both sides connected and in touch with children after parental separation and re-partnering. According to Australian family law researcher Patrick Parkinson (2011), this new model is based on the principle of being in "the best interest of children" and recognizing "the indissolubility of parenthood." He argues that over the past 40 years, the "indissolubility of parenthood" has replaced the "indissolubility of marriage" as the new social norm in Western, Christian societies. Joint custody and shared parenting by separated parents in post-divorced (and remarried) families have become a new standard in the West. Accompanying these norms have been changes in social institutions, family laws, and public services allowing for visitation and co-parenting arrangements. These changes have occurred in most Western nations and have produced an increasing number of post-divorce/separation stepfamilies in the form of an expanded network of kin and quasi-kin members across two or more households. They are interconnected through links to one or more focal children rather than stepfamilies composed of only one household (Allan et al., 2011).

Even in Japan and the rest of Asia where family norms based on the *scrap and build model* remain strong, new values and attitudes toward stepfamilies and other new family forms have begun to permeate. Fathers' attachments toward their children have been getting stronger in Asia as they have in the Western world (Ishii-Kuntz, 2015; Shwalb et al., 2010). In Japan, a nationally representative survey in 2006 found that significantly more people (72%) supported the notion that children need to be in contact with both parents even after their divorce, in comparison with 41% supporting the same idea from a comparable national survey conducted in 1986 (Kikuchi, 2008). The number of newly accepted applications for family conciliation at Japanese family courts over visitation issues

A Japanese motion picture, *After the Storm*, depicts the relationships among a school boy, his divorced non-resident father, (newly dating) resident mother, and a grandmother (father's mother).

of noncustodial parents and children has risen drastically since the late 1990s, up to approximately 12,000 cases in 2015, which is roughly six times more than the cases in 1998 (Harada, 2017). Therefore, it appears that norms about divorced families and stepfamilies in Japan and other Asian societies are in transition. There have been subsequent reforms in family laws concerning children in divorced families and stepfamilies, as will be discussed in detail later.

Many challenges faced by stepfamilies in Asia may be better understood by taking these competing and contesting implicit stepfamily models into consideration, along with the classic "incomplete institution" theory (Cherlin, 1978). In this regard, it should also be emphasized that Asian stepfamilies are neither culturally homogeneous nor historically immutable. Stepfamilies, just like other forms of families, are diverse across all societies in Asia. Stepfamilies have been and will be transformable in the course of history, being subject to political and social changes in each society not only in Asia but also in the rest of the world. This viewpoint is also useful in understanding the difference between stepfamilies in the East and the West (Nozawa, 2015a).

Stepfamily Dynamics in Asia: The Case of Japan

As noted earlier, stepparenting and stepparent-stepchild relationships have been a main focus of stepfamily research in the United States and other Western societies (Crosbie-Burnett, 1984; Pasley & Ihinger-Tallman, 1982; Felkeret al., 2002). Stepparenting is generally viewed as necessarily difficult and remains a stigmatized status even in Western countries where stepfamilies are common. It can be an ambiguous and challenging role with little guidance and few role models available (Ganong & Coleman, 1997; Stewart, 2007; Pryor 2014; Ganong & Coleman, 2017).

Stepmothers and Stepfathers

Stepmothering can be very stressful as motherhood is more demanding (with higher expectations for nurturing mothers) than it is for fathers. There is also greater stigma attached to stepmothers compared with stepfathers in Western societies (Levin, 1997; Nielsen, 1999; Coleman et al., 2008). Japanese stepmothers face similar difficulties. Initial stepfamily research in the early 2000s explored Japanese stepmothers' experiences, mainly because those researchers collaborated with SAJ, whose founding members were predominantly stepmothers (Kikuchi, 2005).

The first survey on stepfamilies in Japan was conducted between 2001 and 2003 using a convenience sample of 166 stepparents and biological parents recruited mainly through SAJ's seminars, publications, and its website (Nozawa, 2008a). Based on a subsample of 88 women (biological or stepmothers) who lived in a relatively new stepfamily household (less than 11 years old), it was found that residential stepmothers felt a significantly higher level of family role strain than biological mothers in stepfamilies (Nozawa, 2008a). Subsequent studies explored role identities of Japanese stepmothers and reasons why they tended to feel their situations were more difficult than those of biological mothers in stepfamilies. Kikuchi (2005) conducted interviews with five residential stepmothers and found that for three of the five, their initial role expectations were to both have a "honeymoon" marital relationship and also to become the new and only "mother" to their stepchildren. The three suffered from a gap between their expectations and the realities of their stepfamily life. As a result, their present role identities were in confusion, being unlike the initial expectations of "wife" and/or "mother." The other two stepmothers in the study were more cautious in taking on the "mother" role. They consciously avoided substituting themselves for their stepchildren's biological mothers, and accepted that the latter were the "real" mothers. The two stepmothers described their role identities to their stepchildren as being a "big sister" or a "caretaker" (for similar findings, see also Nozawa, 2008b). These studies in Japan suggest that the role identities of stepmothers were at least as difficult as in North America (Nielsen, 1999).

On the other hand, interviews with stepfathers in Japan found that they tended to feel more at ease than did stepmothers because the former were culturally allowed to be more flexible in parenting (Nozawa, 2008b). It should be noted that Kikuchi (2005) also found that stepmother identities are far from uniform within Japanese society, even though they might not be as diverse as in the West (Levin, 1997; Church, 1999; Coleman et al., 2008). It is particularly important for Japanese stepmothers to learn and share new ideas on how to behave in stepmothering through participation in the activities of supporting groups such as SAJ or through the Internet (Kikuchi, 2005; Nozawa, 2008a; Nozawa, 2008b).

Stepfamily dynamics in the West and in East Asia, however, do share common ground, such as the stigma attached to stepparents (Kikuchi, 2005; Lam-Chan, 1999). For example, Papernow (2013) argues that biological parents and their children tend to be "insiders" while stepparents tend to feel like "outsiders." It holds structurally true both in the East and the West. If a stepparent (an outsider) attempts to play an active role in disciplining a stepchild from the beginning based on the *scrap and build model*, such a role would very likely cause increased stress in the stepparent-stepchild and couple relationships on whichever side of the globe it occurred.

Stepparent-Stepchild Relationships

Studies on stepparent-stepchild relationship development from the young adult stepchildren's viewpoint also reveal similarities in stepfamily dynamics between Asia and the West. For example, there is considerable diversity in the quality of step-relationships in both regions. Emulating a study in New Zealand (Kinniburgh-White et al., 2010) and another in the United States (Ganong et al., 2011), Nozawa and Kikuchi (2014) conducted interviews with 19 young adult stepchildren aged 20–34 in Japan. They identified five patterns of stepchild-stepparent relationship development.

The first pattern, *continuously accepting as a parent with varying relationships*, described four of the participants. They tended to be young at the time of their parents' remarriage and accepted and regarded their stepparents as their "father" or "mother." Although one stepson had an easier time accepting the stepfather as his new father with no disciplining role in the household, the other three participants in this category described their stepparents as rather "strict" in disciplining them and with lower attachments to them. All of them, however, had continued to consider their stepparents as nothing but their parents.

In the second pattern, *accepting as a parent with deterioration in adolescence* (n = 2), participants regarded their stepfathers naturally as fathers, developing reasonably close relations with them in childhood similar to those cases in the first category. But they experienced some serious conflicts with their stepparents when they reached their teenage years, which drastically deteriorated their relationships with their stepparents. As is exemplified later in "Yoko's Story," the stepchildren in this category experienced sudden loss of trust and intimacy in their relations with stepfathers upon the collapse of (step)parent-child relationships. They saw the demise of their parent-child relationships not only with their stepfathers but also with biological mothers since their mothers supported only their spouses rather than daughters. Feeling strongly alienated, the stepchildren in this category stayed away from their original family and did not go on to college.

The third pattern found was *consistent avoidance* (n = 6). In these cases, there was little development in stepchild-stepparent relationships since the primary school days. There were few attempts from either side to interact personally, mainly because these stepparents were not interested in their stepchildren and also because the parents were not active in mediating stepparent-stepchild relationships. In the majority of the cases, parental remarriage occurred when the participants reached school age. In many of the cases, children refused to have conversations with stepfathers as they felt angry and alienated because of their custodial mothers' behaviors. Some mothers forced their children to treat stepfathers as a new authoritative father, while their children felt their feelings were disregarded and suffered from some internal or external behavior problems. In other cases, stepparent-child relationships did not develop at all, mainly because stepparents showed little interest in relations with stepchildren. One of the stepchildren in this category considered her stepfather as her "sponsor" for paying her money to go on to higher education.

The fourth pattern was *oppression/submission followed by breaking off ties* (n = 4). In these cases, the stepparent took on an authoritarian position as a new father/mother very early on, and became abusive physically, sexually, or psychologically toward the participants. The residential parents of the participants in this category behaved as if they approved of the conduct explicitly or implicitly, at least in the early days. If the residential parents realized the danger soon enough to protect their children, they felt more positive about their personality and life. On the other hand, if it was too late, the children tended to suffer from the deteriorated mother-child relationships and/or long-term mental health problems even after divorce/separation from their abusive partners.

The last pattern is *gradual development of non-parental role* (n = 4). Participants in this category began their step-relationships in their adolescence. While they did not regard their stepfathers as their "fathers," they said they felt more attached to their stepfathers than any participants in the other patterns. Residential mothers of this category's participants were cautious enough about their children's feelings toward their re-partnering. As a result, the participants developed mostly positive relationships with stepfathers and defined them as one of their most important family members. Residential mothers in this category were financially more independent and chose a more flexible and informal partnership pattern such as *de facto* marriage and/or commuting marriage.

YOKO'S STORY

This is the story told by a participant in the young adult stepchild interview study (Nozawa & Kikuchi, 2014). Yoko was in her mid-20s at the time of the interview and is categorized as one of the stepchildren in the second pattern discussed previously: "accepting as a parent with deterioration in adolescence." Her relationships with her stepfather changed drastically when she was a junior high school student.

In reflecting back upon her childhood, Yoko says she was very close to her stepfather, even closer than to her mother, when she was in primary and junior high school. He was a "kindhearted father" to her. But when she was 15 years old, having a school assignment to write her life history, she became curious about the biological father she lost contact with after her parents' divorce at the age of 5. She searched for her father's old photos in the house. Then her stepfather learned what she was up to. Explains Yoko: "He [stepfather] said something like, 'If you don't want be in this house any more, you can go anywhere.' ... He went on to say 'If you like your former father so much, you can move back to him.'" She continues, "There was some arguing between us, and I refused to talk with him for some years after that. Now I live apart from him and I have matured enough to talk a bit with him these days. Yet I cannot go back into the close relationship I had with him like in the early days after [my mother's] remarriage."

Yoko reflects that she was just curious about her long-lost biological father, intending nothing else. But her stepfather seems to have been hurt so much by her behavior that he reacted with offensive words, which in turn hurt her very much. Maybe Yoko's stepfather was living in his fictional ideal of an "ordinary/nuclear" family in which a child has only one father. This is a good example of stepfamily relationships built upon the *scrap and build model*, which made Yoko's biological father a taboo subject in the house. Yoko also says she had a feeling of resentment when her mother took the side of her husband without trying to understand her own daughter's feelings in the dispute. After the incident, she experienced some problems at school, including fighting with other students, and went out almost every night, returning home very late throughout her high school days and beyond. At that time, she was living in rebellion, attempting to irritate both her mother and her stepfather.

Yoko's story offers an excellent illustration on how painful it can be, particularly for children, if adult stepfamily members attempt to behave as if they were a nuclear family and give no room for children to maintain contact with, or at least to learn about, their noncustodial parent.

Analyzing the scenario:

- Explain how Yoko's story provides an example of two competing models of stepfamily life in East Asian societies: the *scrap and build model* and the *expanded and interconnected network model*.
- Describe some advantages and disadvantages of each model to Yoko's relationship with her biological father and her stepfather and suggest a new model that could improve each.

Although it should be noted there are limitations with this small number of interview cases, it is worth pointing to variations found in the quality of relationships. Overall, the stepchild-stepparent relationships in this last pattern were the most positively described ones, while the cases in the second and third patterns often brought negative effects on stepchildren's lives for extended periods, including lower levels of educational achievement and psychological well-being. This wide diversity in the quality of stepparent-stepchild relationships from stepchildren's perspectives across the five patterns suggest that too serious attempts by stepparents to be an instant "new father/mother" tend to cause difficulties in stepchildren's adaptation in stepfamily life.

As Ganong and Coleman (2017) argue, these five patterns of stepchild-stepparent relationships found in Japan (Nozawa, 2015a; Nozawa & Kikuchi, 2014) are strikingly similar to the patterns previously found in New Zealand (Kinniburgh-White et al., 2010) and in the United States (Ganong et al., 2011). The findings across sociocultural borders suggest that the easygoing and "affinity-seeking" type of role behavior by stepparents (Ganong et al., 1999) is more functional for stepchildren's adaptation. Disciplining by stepparents based upon a "new father/mother" role will very likely lead to more negative reactions. In other words, the findings suggest that stepparenting strictly confined within the *scrap and build model* tends to cause stepchildren's difficulties in adaptation, in both Asian and Western societies.

Nozawa (2015b) examined these same participants and discovered three patterns of residential stepparent-child relationships. The pattern named *positive regard for flexible supporting and mediating roles* (n = 8) signifies the most positive evaluation of the relationships from the children's view, while the pattern called *distrust and distance* (n = 5) is the most negative. The pattern in the middle in its quality evaluation is labeled as *disappointed and alienated by constant support for stepparent* (n = 6). The interview cases suggest that stepchildren's outcomes are related more to the quality of residential parent-child relationships than that of residential stepparent-stepchild relationships (argument of Nozawa,

2015b, summarized in English in Nozawa, 2017). Combined with the analysis on the stepchild-stepparent relationships above (Nozawa & Kikuchi, 2014), it is hypothetically argued that stepchildren's outcomes would be more positive if residential parents could play a careful and flexible gatekeeper role for their children, coping with whatever types of step-relationships they might have.

Conventional stepfamily research tends to focus more on children's relationships with their stepparents rather than biological parents (Crosbie-Burnett, 1984). More recent studies of stepfamilies in the United States, however, suggest the quality of the biological parent-child relationship is important to stepchildren's well-being (Jensen, Shafter, & Holmes, 2017). This appears to be the case in Asian stepfamilies as well. Children's behavioral problems such as those shown in "Yoko's Story" tend to appear if a residential biological parent does not remain central in supporting and protecting his or her children. If the biological parent lets the new partner (stepparent) behave as an instant "parent" in a disciplining team (as if they were a first-marriage nuclear family couple), their child is apt to feel deprived of intimacy and trust in relationships with his or her residential parent. This type of situation might cause children's feelings of alienation, isolation, and even betrayal, and trigger internal or external behavioral problems. These findings from the research in Japan (Nozawa, 2015b; Nozawa, 2017) are compatible with research on Western societies that emphasize the importance of biological parent-child relationships rather than stepparent-stepchild relationships (Cartwright, 2008).

Stepfamily Dynamics in Other Asian Societies

Stepfamily research in other Asian societies provides similar findings to those from Japan. Regarding the stepparents' view on stepparenting, Lam-Chan (1999) documented how stepmothers in Hong Kong go through difficulties in performing a stepmother role, particularly in childrearing, with little reward from their husband and/or stepchildren and in the face of strong and negative attitudes toward divorce and remarriage. These stepmothers tried hard to be a good "mother" to their stepchildren while struggling with role conflict and ambivalence about their situation. As for the children's view in Hong Kong, Lam (2006) reports there are negative attitudes toward stepfamilies even among primary and secondary school children. This was the case among both children in stepfamilies and children from traditional family households. A considerable percentage of stepchildren in Lam's study hid from their teachers and classmates the fact that they belong to a stepfamily. For example, two-thirds of stepchildren in senior primary schools had not disclosed their stepchild status to their teachers. In Hong Kong, as in Japan, adult and child members of stepfamilies live in the disguise of a first-marriage nuclear family at the risk of being without any social support, suggesting they feel forced to follow the *scrap and build model*.

In Seoul, South Korea, Lim (2006) conducted a survey about the emotional experiences of 43 adolescent children who lived in stepfamily households. More than half of these stepchildren hesitated to talk about the fact they belonged to a stepfamily, which implies there are negative social attitudes toward stepfamilies in that country. It should be noted, however, that there is quite a variety in the participants' reactions to their transitions into stepfamily life. For example, 40% of the participants answered that their stepparent (described as "new parent" in the original questions in Korean) is a "family member and parent" of theirs, while 30% said their stepparent is "a family member but not a parent." Another 14% described their stepparent as "neither a family member nor a parent," and the rest responded "I don't know" or gave no answer. About 40% of stepchildren reported being "satisfied" with their family life, another 40% reported being "a little dissatisfied," and 14% felt "more dissatisfied" (no stepchild reported being "satisfied very much").

The children in the study also described their feelings on many aspects of their stepfamily life in a series of open-ended questions. Some expressed negative feelings regarding changes in their residential parent's attitude, such as paying less attention to them while giving priority to new partners, being less understanding of them, or siding always with the stepparent and never with them. Others cited conflicts with stepparents when they tried to exert control over the stepchildren, difficulty in interacting with the stepparent, and an uncomfortable atmosphere in the house as negative experiences. But the children also listed positive feelings such as improvement in the household's financial situation, their parents being happier and less worried, and less pressure upon them to help with housework. The wide variety of stepchildren's emotional reactions found in Korea are compatible with studies conducted in Japan (Nozawa & Kikuchi, 2014; Nozawa, 2015a, 2015b, 2017), New Zealand (Kinniburgh-White et al., 2010), and the United States (Ganong et al., 2011).

Beyond the confines of Asian societies with the Confucian tradition, similar patterns are also found in the Malay (Muslim) community of Singapore. The multicultural nature of Singapore is reflected in its population composition of three main ethnic groups: Chinese, at 74%; Malays, 13%; and Indians, 9% (Singapore Department of Statistics, 2016). Based on interviews with 157 remarrying Malay couples and reinterviews with 40 of them three months after remarriage, Faroo (2012a) found the participants generally had positive views of remarriage. Many reported having some stepfamily friends and relatives, which suggests the prevalence of what Faroo calls "the culture of remarriage" in the Malay community, which may be related to the fact that Malay Muslim in Southeast Asia was one of the few "stable high-divorce (and probably high-remarriage) societies" until the mid-20th century (Cherlin, 2017). In Singapore, the divorce rate among the Malay Muslim population declined in the 1960s and 1970s with rising education (as in Japan in the late 19th and early 20th centuries), but it rose rather quickly in the 1990s as marriage became more one's own choice instead of a parental decision. Yet, the divorce rate has been always considerably higher among Malay Muslims than non-Muslim (mostly Chinese) populations in Singapore (Jones, 2015).

Most interesting is Faroo's finding that custodial parents tended to stick to the notion of stepfamilies as "normal/nuclear families," with attempts to treat stepparents as "real parents" of their children. They are also very likely to believe that "adjustment comes quickly," which suggests that the *scrap and build model* is also dominant in the Singaporean Muslim community. This might reflect the new ideal of family formation, along with marriage based on personal choice in a nuclear family household prevailing in many East Asian societies, including Japan, and in Western countries.

In another study, Faroo (2012b) interviewed 26 stepchildren aged between 10 and15 years in the Muslim section of Singapore. She classified their views of stepparents into three types: the "brother," the "parent-friend," and the "parent," with the first two representative more of friendliness and the last one more of "authority" or being "respectful but distant, lacking warmth." In fact, two participant stepchildren refused to develop any relationships with their stepfathers. These two cases virtually correspond to the patterns of "avoidance" (Nozawa & Kikuchi, 2014) and "distance" (Kinniburgh-White et al., 2010). Taken together, these four patterns of stepparent-stepchild relationships are also very similar to the patterns found in the studies in Japan, New Zealand, and the United States.

In sum, role expectations for stepparents and biological parents based on the *scrap and build model* will very likely cause children of stepfamilies difficulty in their adjustment in family transition processes. This tendency has been observed in the United States and other Western societies and also in Japan and other Asian societies. Although norms are loosening and the acceptability of stepfamilies is growing, incomplete institutionalization of stepfamilies can be seen in both Eastern and Western societies where the nuclear family model dominates (Cherlin, 1978).

Asian Stepfamilies in Comparison With the West

What differences in stepfamily dynamics between Asia and the West can be found? One difference is potentially greater involvement of extended kin members in stepfamily dynamics in Asia in comparison with the West. Interviews with members of stepfamilies in Japan and other Asian societies revealed a wider range of kin members, such as the grandparents of stepchildren. For instance, the qualitative studies of stepmothering cited previously (Nozawa, 2008b; Kikuchi, 2005; Lam-Chan, 1999) indicate that stepmothers experience stress from having to compete and cope with stepchildren's grandparents who intervene directly and/or indirectly in stepparenting. One example from the study included a new Japanese stepmother who complained about her situation in which her husband's mother regarded her as a "new mother" and expected her to discipline her stepdaughter, but the stepdaughter always respected the authority of her grandmother who had been mothering for some time before. In East Asian countries, there is the family tradition of parents and children living with grandparents and other extended family members. This is related to Confucianism, which emphasizes intergenerational ties rather than couple relationships. Western tradition emphasizes independent nuclear family units with couple relationships at the center.

In another example, one-fourth of 35- to 39-year-old divorced women in Japan co-reside with their parents compared with only 2% of divorced women in the United States (Raymo et al., 2004). According to more recent data from the 2016 National Survey of One Parent Households in Japan, 29% of divorced custodial mothers with children and 48% of divorced custodial single fathers lived with their parents (Japan Ministry of Health, Labour and Welfare, 2017). This seems to have a positive effect. A recent study also suggests that Japanese single mothers' co-residing with their parents improves their self-rated health (Raymo & Zhou, 2012).

These findings suggest that single parents' co-residing with their parents is normative behavior in Japan, while it is not in the United States. Thus, stepfamily dynamics in Japan also tend to involve more extended kin members in and around a household than in America.

Grandparents' involvement in grandchild care in Taiwan, South Korea, Singapore, and China may be even greater than in Japan (Xu & Chi, 2015). In those Asian societies where active grandparenting is more prevalent, grandparents of stepchildren are more likely to be incorporated into stepfamily dynamics than in Japan. The studies in the Malay community of Singapore cited are also relevant here. Based on the interviews with remarried Muslim couples, Faroo (2012a) suggests that the involvement of extended kin in stepfamily life is so prevalent in the Malay community that professional intervention efforts need to factor it into their treatment plans. In the study of stepchildren in the Malay community, Faroo (2012b) reports that some stepchildren lived with their grandmother or aunt instead of their parents and stepparents. In these types of situations, parenting by extended kin members such as grandparents rather than parents seems more acceptable in many Asian societies. It can be concluded that a wider range of kin members are involved in childcare in general and in stepfamily dynamics in Asia than in the United States and other Western countries.

With greater intergenerational interdependence, family boundaries in Asia tend to be different from those of their North American White, middle-class counterparts (Pasley, 1987; Stewart, 2005). It should be noted that joint custody and co-parenting are now more common in the United States and in many other Western societies than in Asia, and that stepfamily members' family boundaries are more likely to be ambiguous and sometimes in conflict among the members between two households of separated parents in the West. For example, children and their parents may have different perceptions as to who is in their family versus who is not. For example, in the United States, stepchildren's biological parents are significantly more likely to include their spouse or partner as a family member than are the child (Brown & Manning, 2009). While stresses in coping with the ambiguity in family boundary and role definition in many of the Western countries are *horizontal* in terms of co-parenting of parents and stepparents in the same generation (Cartwright & Gibson, 2013), difficulties in coping with the ambiguity are more concerned with generationally *vertical* members, such as stepparents and grandparents, in Asia (Nozawa, 2008b). This is a relatively unique aspect of Asian stepfamilies in comparison with their Western counterparts.

Changing Values, Laws, and Policies on Stepfamilies in East Asia

The *horizontal/vertical* dichotomy between the West and the East is transitional because of ongoing legal and other social institutional reforms. Coupled with changing family values, such as a new fatherhood culture and increased fathers' involvement (Ishii-Kuntz, 2015; Shwalb et al., 2010), family laws in East Asia have been revised in the direction of the *expanded network model* of stepfamilies.

In Japan, the revised Article 766 of the Civil Code came into force in 2012 to ensure that parents discuss and decide on child support payments and visitation of noncustodial parents based on the priority of the child's best interests at the time of divorce by mutual agreement. It should be noted, however, that this revised Civil Code Article has no means of legally enforcing its goal (Minamikata, 2014). Under the present system, there are no mechanisms for checking the outcome of the divorcing parents' discussions and decisions on the abovementioned issues, because most divorce cases in Japan are by mutual agreement without any family court procedure, as cited earlier.

But a comparison of the results from the 2016 National Survey of One Parent Households (Japan Ministry of Health, Labour and Welfare, 2017) and those in 2011 (Japan Ministry of Health, Labour and Welfare, 2012), the year before the reformed Civil Code Article 766 came into effect, demonstrates substantial changes in child support and visitation arrangements made by newly divorced single parents. Only 27% of single mothers who got divorced less than two years prior were receiving child support from noncustodial fathers, while the percentage rose to 40% in the 2016 survey (calculated using data in the Ministry of Health, Labour and Welfare 2012 and 2017 reports). According to the same survey, the percentage of the single mothers having their children visit their fathers in the same recently divorced group also increased, from 38% to 48%. This suggests that even gradual legal reforms could make differences in divorced (and possibly remarried) parents and their children's relationships.

South Korea also introduced more radical family law reforms in relation to children's rights and interests, hence moving much closer to Western social institutions. Korea once had an easy and quick judicial system of divorce by mutual agreement, similar to systems in Japan and Taiwan. The reform of the Korean Civil Code in 2007 made it compulsory to go through a series of interventions by a family court to achieve divorce by mutual agreement after three months (Chin et al., 2014). After filing for divorce, divorcing parents are required to attend sessions of guidance and post-divorce parenting education, and have to create an agreement document on custody and parenting after divorce (joint custody and/or co-parenting are available options) to be checked by a family court that can recommend parents attend counseling if necessary (Ninomiya, 2014).

The institutionalization of joint custody and co-parenting by divorced/separated parents is an emerging social and political issue in East Asia. The *scrap and build model,* which is now considered dominant in Japan and some other Asian countries, may be replaced by the *expanded network model* if the present social institutions regarding stepfamilies are reformed and reformulated. It should be kept in mind that cultural traditions are always being revised in the midst of ever-changing social, economic, and political milieus, both in the East and the West.

Recommendations for Practice

Based on the findings from the studies in Asia reviewed thus far, it is recommended that stepfamily practitioners and professionals, such as family social workers and family therapists, be mindful of any idealized or preconceived notions of family life they may have. This is difficult given the strong cultural and social pressures in Asian societies for stepfamilies to conform to the nuclear family model. In 2016, Asian women experienced the lowest first-divorce rate among Whites, Blacks, native-born Hispanics, and foreign-born Hispanics in the United States (Pyne, 2018). This implies that Asian families in the United States are under stronger pressure of the first-marriage family ideal in comparison with other American families, despite the recent rise in divorce rates in many East Asian societies cited previously. Many Asian people might unconsciously expect that stepparents should and could instantly perform a parental role (e.g., disciplining their stepchildren), and thus substitute for and replace their noncustodial parent. Yet, it is almost universal wisdom that this kind of expectation will become unrealistic and unreasonable for at least some members (children in particular) of a stepfamily (Pryor, 2014).

It is also advisable for family professionals working with Asian stepfamilies to focus more on a wider range of kin members being involved. It is more probable among Asian than other stepfamilies that not only biological parents of a stepchild but also grandparents and other kin members of a stepchild form a coalition of "insiders" when a stepparent feels isolated as an "outsider" (Papernow, 2013). This appears similar to findings from research done with American Indians (see Chapter 5). All the stakeholders in a stepfamily network should be included when there is talk about family rules, and the underlying stepfamily assumptions should be made flexible enough and workable.

Conclusion and Recommendations for Future Research

This chapter's conclusion remains somewhat tentative given that the studies reviewed are not only limited to a small number of societies in Asia but are also limited in scope and sample size. Nevertheless, the findings are rather consistent and can be summarized as follows: (a) stepfamilies in Asia remain an "incomplete institution" and are more often based on the *scrap and build household model,* which assumes the nuclear family ideal; (b) there is variation in stepparenting styles, stepparent-stepchild relationships, and residential parent-child relationships both in Japan and also some other East Asian societies; (c) stepfamily dynamics might have some universal ground in that parenting and stepparenting rigidly based on the *scrap and build household model* are more likely to bring difficulties and sometimes painfulness for both child and adult members in their adaptation to stepfamily life; (d) stepfamily dynamics in Asia tend to include more extended family members, such as grandparents of stepchildren, than in the United States and some other Western societies; and, (e) stepfamily dynamics are in transition and there exist ongoing revisions of family laws and family policies in societies in East Asia, just as in the rest of the world, that are hypothetically moving toward the *expanded network model.*

Suggested future stepfamily research in Asian countries should be multifold, since what has been explored so far is largely confined within limited issues such as stepparenting and stepparent-stepchild relationships. Parenting by residential and nonresidential parents in relation to stepparenting are important issues to be studied further. Grandparenting in stepfamilies is also important, particularly in the Asian social context. Research with a focus on joint custody and co-parenting in Asian stepfamilies would be a recommended new direction in connection with potential policy implications. There is also a need to collect basic information on the prevalence of stepfamilies in Asia and track trends in growth and acceptance. Information is also needed on the demographic characteristics of Asian stepfamilies, with respect to union formation (i.e., through marriage, nonmarital childbearing, and cohabitation) and rates of dissolution. Research into diverse Asian stepfamilies, including stepfamilies in later life and LGBTQ+ stepfamilies, is yet to come, and data on Asian stepfamilies in the United States are similarly lacking.

Most of the studies on Asian stepfamilies in the past are based upon qualitative data and descriptive rather than quantitative and relational data. Nationally representative data should be collected and analyzed to assess and evaluate the effect of different types of relationships along with different custody or visitation arrangements upon the well-being of children and adult members in these stepfamilies. Most anticipated in the near future are cross-cultural studies comparing stepfamily dynamics across countries in and beyond Asia.

Questions for Discussion

1. Which of the two stepfamily models (*scrap and build household model* and *expanded network model*) do you believe people in your own community tend to follow? Provide some examples supporting your observation.
2. Compare and contrast *horizontal* versus *vertical* boundary ambiguity found in West and East Asia, respectively. Do you agree with the author's assertion? Provide a brief explanation of your answer.
3. What kind of changes in family laws and policies are most likely to take place in the future in East Asian societies? How would stepfamily life be different as a consequence of such changes?

Additional Resources

Quah, S. (Ed.). (2015). *Handbook of families in Asia.* New York, NY: Routledge.

Faroo, F. (2012b) *"I'm getting married ... again!" Exploring children's understanding and experience of parental remarriage.* Singapore: PPIS (Singapore Muslim Women's Association).

Smith, R., & Wiswell, E. (1982). *The women of Suye Mura 1935-36.* University of Chicago Press.

Kore-eda, H. (2016). *After the storm (Umi Yori Mo Mada Fukaku).* Tokyo: Fuji Television/BANDAI/ AOI Pro/GAGA. (A Japanese family drama film written and directed by Hirokazu Kore-eda. The story is about a divorced noncustodial father visiting his son, who lives with his mother, now repartnering.) Available through FILM MOVEMENT's website at https://www.filmmovement.com/film-catalog/index.asp?MerchandiseID=526

Note

1 Singapore is usually considered one of the Southeast Asian countries rather than an East Asian ones. It is included in this chapter, however, because of the outstanding stepfamily research that has been done there and also because of its social and demographic similarities to the selected East Asian societies (Quah, 2015). Attempts were made to incorporate stepfamily studies from Taiwan and China, and a number of masters theses (in Chinese) on stepfamilies in Taiwan were found; however, they were not successfully incorporated in this chapter, mainly because of the limitation in the author's understanding of the literature. I thank Shuang Ning and Lichen Liu for their support in finding and translating stepfamily studies in Taiwan. My thanks also go to Kanako Nozawa for translating the Korean literature reviewed here.

References

Allan, G., Crow, G., and Hawker, S. (2011). *Stepfamilies.* Basingstoke, UK: Palgrave Macmillan.

Brown, S. L., & Manning, W. D. (2009). Family boundary ambiguity and the measurement of family structure: The significance of cohabitation. *Demography, 46,* 85-101.

Cartwright, C. (2008). Resident parent-child relationships in stepfamilies. In J. Pryor (Ed.) *The international handbook of stepfamilies: Policy and practice in legal, research, and clinical environments* (pp. 208-230). Hoboken, NJ: John Wiley & Sons.

Cartwright, C., & Gibson, K. (2013). The effects of co-parenting relationships with ex-spouses on couples in step-families. *Family Matters, 92,* 18-28.

Cherlin, A. (1978). Remarriage as an incomplete institution. *American Journal of Sociology, 84,* 634-650.

Cherlin, A. J. (2017). Introduction to the special collection on separation, divorce, repartnering, and remarriage around the world. *Demographic Research, 37,* 1275–1296.

Cheung, P. (2015). Fertility trends in Asia: Prospects and implications of very low fertility. In S. Quah (Ed.) *The Routledge handbook of families in Asia* (pp. 138–149). London, UK: Routledge.

Chin, M., Lee, J., Lee, S., Son, S., & Sung, M. (2014). Family policy in South Korea: Development, implementation, and evaluation. In R. Mihaela (Ed.) *Handbook of family policies across the globe* (pp. 305–318). New York, NY: Springer.

Church, E. (1999). Who are the people in your family? Stepmothers' diverse notions of kinship. *Journal of Divorce and Remarriage, 31,* 83–105.

Coleman, M., & Nickleberry, L. (2009). An evaluation of remarriage and stepfamily self-help literature. *Family Relations, 58,* 549–561.

Coleman, M., Troilo, J., & Jamison, T. (2008). The diversity of stepmothers: The influences of stigma, gender, and context on stepmother identities. In J. Pryor (Ed.) *International handbook of stepfamilies: Policy and practice in legal, research, and clinical environments* (pp. 369–393). Hoboken, NJ: Wiley & Sons.

Crosbie-Burnett, M. (1984). The centrality of the step relationship: A challenge to family theory and practice. *Family Relations, 33,* 459–463.

Faroo, F. (2012a). *Remarriage in the Malay community: An exploration of perceptions, expectations and adjustment to stepfamily living.* Singapore: PPIS (Singapore Muslim Women's Association).

Faroo, F. (2012b) *"I'm getting married ... again!" Exploring children's understanding and experience of parental remarriage.* Singapore: PPIS (Singapore Muslim Women's Association).

Felker, J. A., Fromme, D. K., Arnaut, G. L., & Stoll, B. M. (2002). A qualitative analysis of stepfamilies: The stepparent. *Journal of Divorce and Remarriage, 38,* 125–142.

Ganong, L. H., & Coleman, M. (1997). How society views stepfamilies. *Marriage and Family Review, 26,* 85–106.

Ganong, L. H., & Coleman, M. (2017). *Stepfamily relationships: Development, dynamics, and interventions* (2nd ed.). New York, NY: Springer.

Ganong, L. H., & Coleman, M. (2018). Studying stepfamilies: Four eras of family scholarship. *Family Process, 57*(1), 7–24.

Ganong, L. H., Coleman, M., Fine M., & Martin, P. (1999). Stepparents' affinity-seeking and affinity-maintaining strategies with stepchildren. *Journal of Family Issues, 20,* 299–327.

Ganong, L. H., Coleman, M., & Jamison, T. (2011). Patterns of stepchild-stepparent relationship development. *Journal of Marriage and Family, 73,* 396–413.

Harada, A. (2017). Family reorganization in the Japanese family conciliation system: Resolving divorce disputes involving minor children. *Japanese Journal of Family Sociology, 29,* 49–62 (in Japanese).

Hayano, T. (2006). Stepfamilies and the legal systems in Japan. In S. Nozawa, N. Ibaraki, T. Hayano, & Stepfamily Association of Japan (Eds.) *An introduction to stepfamilies* (pp. 39–53). Tokyo: Akashi Shoten (in Japanese).

Ishii-Kuntz, M. (2015). Fatherhood in Asian contexts. In S. Quah (Ed.) *The Routledge handbook of families in Asia* (pp. 161–358). London, UK: Routledge.

Iwai, N. (2000). Divorce in Japan: Historical changes and current issues. In R. R. Miller & S. L. Browning (Eds.) *With this ring: Divorce, intimacy, and cohabitation from a multicultural perspective* (pp. 53–77). Stamford, CT: JAI Press.

Japan Ministry of Health, Labour and Welfare (2012). *Report paper on the 2011 National Survey of One Parent Households.* Retrieved January 1, 2018, from Japan Ministry of Health, Labour and Welfare website (in Japanese): http://www.mhlw.go.jp/seisakunitsuite/bunya/kodomo/kodomo_kosodate/boshi-katei/boshi-setai_h23/

Japan Ministry of Health, Labour and Welfare (2017). *Report paper on the 2016 National Survey of One Parent Households.* Retrieved January 1, 2018, from Japan Ministry of Health, Labour and Welfare website (in Japanese): http://www.mhlw.go.jp/stf/seisakunitsuite/bunya/0000188147.html

Jensen, T. M., Shafer, K., & Holmes, E. K. (2017). Transitioning to stepfamily life: The influence of closeness with biological parents and stepparents on children's stress. *Child & Family Social Work, 22,* 275–286.

Jones, G. (2015). Divorce trends and patterns in Asia. In S. Quah (Ed.) *The Routledge handbook of families in Asia* (pp. 332–344), London, UK: Routledge.

Kreider, R. M., & Lofquist, D. A. (2010). Adopted children and stepchildren: 2010. *Adoption Quarterly, 13,* 268–291.

Kikuchi, M. (2005). Becoming a stepmother: The gap between expectations and realities. *Annals of Family Studies, 30,* 49–63 (in Japanese).

Kikuchi, M. (2008). Determinants of the value of visitation after divorce: From the data of JGSS-2006. In Institute of Regional Studies at Osaka University of Commerce & Institute of Social Sciences at University of Tokyo (Eds.) *JGSS Research Series No. 7: Japanese People's Attitudes and Behaviors* (pp. 93–105). Osaka, JP: Institute of Regional Studies at Osaka University of Commerce (in Japanese).

Kinniburgh-White, R., Cartwright, C., & Seymour, F. (2010). Young adults' narratives of relational development with stepfathers. *Journal of Social and Personal Relationships, 27,* 890–907.

Kobayashi, K. M., & Kampen, R. M. (2015). Cohabitation in Asia. In S. Quah (Ed.) *Handbook of families in Asia* (pp. 377–397). New York, NY: Routledge.

Kurosu, S. (2007). Remarriage in a stem family system in early modern Japan. *Continuity and Change, 22,* 429–458.

Lam, G. L. T. (2006). Difficulties of stepchildren from reconstituted families in a westernized society challenged by traditional Chinese culture. *International Social Work, 49,* 605-613.

Lam-Chan, G. L. T. (1999). *Parenting in stepfamilies: Social attitudes, parental perceptions and parenting behaviours in Hong Kong.* Aldershot, UK: Ashgate.

Levin, I. (1997). The stepparent role from a gender perspective. *Marriage and Family Review, 26,* 177-190.

Lim, C. (2006). The perception of stepfamily adolescents about their stepfamily relationship and the need for education program. *Korean Journal of Human Ecology, 15,* 743-760 (in Korean).

Minamikata, S. (2014). Dissolution of marriage in Japan. In J. Eekelaar, & R. George (Eds.) *Routledge handbook of family law and policy* (pp. 122-132). London, UK: Routledge.

Muta, K. (1996). *Families as strategies: The making of the modern Japanese nation state and women.* Tokyo, JP: Shin-yosha (in Japanese).

National Institute of Population and Social Security (Japan). (2017). *Population statistics of Japan 2017.* Retrieved from http://www.ipss. go.jp/p-info/e/psj2017/PSJ2017.asp

Nielsen, L. (1999). Stepmothers: Why so much stress? A review of the research. *Journal of Divorce & Remarriage, 30,* 115-148.

Ninomiya, S. (2014). Reforms in divorce by mutual agreement in Korea: Guidance, agreement document, counseling recommendation, and co-parenting booklet. In S. Ninomiya & S. Watanabe (Eds.) *Divorce dispute settlement by agreement and the importance of children's view* (pp. 266-278), Tokyo, JP: Nihon Kajo Shuppan (in Japanese).

Nozawa, S. (2008a). What does the internet bring about for families? Role strains and support networks among stepfamilies. In K. Miyata & S. Nozawa (Eds.) *Everyday life online: Any difference in social support exchange?* (pp. 79-116). Tokyo, JP: Bunkashobo Hakubunsha (in Japanese).

Nozawa, S. (2008b). The social context of emerging stepfamilies in Japan: Stress and support for parents and stepparents. In J. Pryor (Ed.) *The international handbook of stepfamilies: Policy and practice in legal, research, and clinical environments* (pp. 79-99). Hoboken, NJ: John Wiley & Sons.

Nozawa, S. (2011). Conflicts regarding stepfamilies and underlying two family models. *The Socio-Legal Studies on Family Issues, 27,* 89-94 (in Japanese).

Nozawa, S. (2015a). Remarriage and stepfamilies. In S. Quah (Ed.) *Handbook of families in Asia* (pp. 345-358). New York, NY: Routledge.

Nozawa, S. (2015b). Young adult children's views of the relationships with their residential parents in stepfamilies in Japan: A key factor of their adaptation to parental remarriage. *Seijo University Social Innovation Studies, 10,* 59-83 (in Japanese).

Nozawa, S. (2017). Japanese young adult stepchildren's views on their relationships with parents and stepparents: A new perspective of stepfamily dynamics and children's well-being. In C. Canali, J. Ma, & T. Vecchiato (Eds.) *New perspectives for outcome-based evaluation and research on family and children's services* (pp. 170–173). Padora, IT: Fondazione.

Nozawa, S., & Kikuchi, M. (2014). Japanese young adult stepchildren's views on stepchild-stepparent relationships: The variation in stepparents' role and stepchildren's adaptation. *Bulletin of Institute of Sociology and Social Work* (Meiji Gakuin University), *44*, 69–87 (in Japanese).

Ochiai, E. (1997). *The Japanese family system in transition: A sociological analysis of family change in postwar Japan.* Tokyo, JP: LCTB International Library Foundation.

Ochiai, E. (2015). Marriage practices and trends. In S. Quah (Ed.) *The Routledge handbook of families in Asia* (pp. 123–139). London, UK: Routledge.

OECD (2016). *OECD Family Database,* Paris: OECD. Accessed August 31, 2018, from http://www.oecd.org/els/family/database.htm

Papernow, P. L. (2013). *Surviving and thriving in stepfamily relationships: What works and what doesn't.* New York, NY: Routledge.

Parkinson, P. (2011). *Family law and the indissolubility of parenthood.* New York, NY: Cambridge University Press.

Pasley, K. (1987). Family boundary ambiguity: Perceptions of adult stepfamily members. In K. Pasley & M. Ihinger-Tallman (Eds.) *Remarriage and stepparenting: Current research and theory* (pp. 206–224). New York, NY: Guilford Press.

Pasley, K., & Ihinger-Tallman, M. (1982). Stress in remarried families. *Family Perspective, 16,* 181–190.

Payne, K. K. (2018). First divorce rate in the U.S., 2016. *Family Profiles,* FP-18-14. Bowling Green, OH: National Center for Family & Marriage Research. Accessed August 31, 2018, from https://doi.org/10.25035/ncfmr/fp-18-15

Pryor, J. (2014). *Stepfamilies: A global perspective on research, policy, and practice.* New York, NY: Routledge.

Quah, S. (2015). Families in Asia: A kaleidoscope of continuity and change. In S. Quah (Ed.) *The Routledge handbook of families in Asia* (pp. 3–22). London, UK: Routledge.

Raymo, J. M., & Zhou, Y. (2012). Living arrangements and the well-being of single mothers in Japan. *Population Research and Policy Review, 51,* 727–749.

Raymo, J. M., Iwasawa, M., & Bumpass, L. (2004). Marital dissolution in Japan: Recent trends and patterns. *Demographic Research, 11,* 395–419.

Raymo, J. M., Park, H., Xie, Y., & Yeung, W. J. (2015). Marriage and family in East Asia: Continuity and change. *Annual Review of Sociology, 41,* 471–492.

Shwalb, D. W., Nakazawa, J., Yamanoto, T., & Hyun, J. (2010). Fathering in Japan, China, and Korea: Changing contexts, images, and roles. In M. E. Lamb (Ed.) *The role of the father* (pp. 341–387). Hoboken, NJ: John Wiley & Sons.

Singapore Department of Statistics. (2016). *Population Trends 2016*. Retrieved January 1, 2018, from Department of Statistics, Ministry of Trade and Industry, Republic of Singapore website: http://www.singstat.gov.sg/docs/default-source/default-document-library/publications/publications_and_papers/population_and_popula-tion_structure/population2016.pdf

Smith, R., & Wiswell, E. (1982). *The women of Suye Mura 1935–36*. University of Chicago Press.

Stewart, S. D. (2005). Boundary ambiguity in stepfamilies. *Journal of Family Issues, 26*, 1002–1029.

Stewart, S. D. (2007). *Brave new stepfamilies: Diverse paths toward stepfamily living*. Thousand Oaks, CA: Sage.

Takagi, T. (1992). *Divorcing letters and sheltering temples: Reexamination of divorce in Edo Tokugawa era*. Tokyo, JP: Kodansha (in Japanese).

Xu, L., & Chi, I. (2015). Aging and grandparenting in Asia. In S. Quah (Ed.) *The Routledge handbook of families in Asia* (pp. 247–258). London, UK: Routledge.

CHAPTER SEVEN

Religious Diversity in Stepfamilies

Todd M. Jensen, PhD, MSW, Jordan Institute for Families and University of North Carolina at Chapel Hill

Rosa retained primary custody of her 16-year-old daughter, Selena, following her divorce from Selena's father. Rosa and Selena recently formed a resident stepfamily when Rosa's new partner, Jim, moved into the house. Rosa is a fairly devout Catholic, and Jim identifies as a conservative Protestant. Although she was religiously active during childhood, Selena no longer identifies as religious.

Selena and Jim get along fairly well, though there are occasional conflicts and misunderstandings. Tensions seem especially pronounced when Jim attempts to discuss his views on religion and the importance of attending religious meetings or services every week as a family. Rosa likes to attend Catholic Mass only on special occasions, and Selena does not ever attend religious meetings or services.

Another point of stepfamily conflict arose when, after several months of dating her boyfriend, Selena became pregnant. Both Rosa and Jim openly express their disappointment, as they believe God does not approve of Selena's life choices. In response, Selena feels judged and defensive. Selena eventually accuses Rosa and Jim of being hypocritical, given their choice to live together without getting married—something their religious communities generally frown upon. Rosa admits to feeling some guilt about her decision to live with Jim without being married, though having a partner is an important feature of her religious paradigm. Rosa also experiences some residual guilt from having divorced in the first place—she believes her divorce was an offense to God. These dynamics generate ongoing strain in the couple's relationship.

Over time, Rosa, Jim, and Selena began to navigate their disagreements skillfully, strengthen their relationships, and find common ground. Jim employs his religious values to bolster his commitment to being an empathetic, patient, and supportive stepfather and partner. Rosa and Jim joined together in adhering to various religious principles, including those centered on forgiveness and kindness. Rosa and Jim are also able to maintain connection through their joint practice of religious behaviors, such as prayer. They both possess religious beliefs that imbue family relationships with spiritual or transcendent properties, which continues to motivate them, and helps them exert greater effort and investment in the stepfamily.

Analyzing the scenario:

- In what ways can diversity of religious views strengthen a stepfamily? What challenges does it present?
- How can practitioners work with stepfamilies like Rosa and Jim with differing religious views from a strength perspective?
- What specific examples can you see of religious influence in the interactions between Rosa, Selena, and Jim?

Introduction

Family dynamics emerge within a rich intersection of culture, racial and ethnic identity, socioeconomic status, historical time and place, and, as shown in the opening vignette, religion. Although it can be challenging to disentangle the influence of one family context or characteristic from another (Cutrona, Russell, Burzette, Wesner, & Bryant, 2011), the ultimate goal of this chapter is to explore and explicate the potential role of religion in stepfamilies—a largely overlooked and understudied area (Marks, 2006). The opening vignette begins to illustrate how stepfamilies might interface with religion.

The landscape of family life in the United States has become increasingly complex and diverse over the last half century, and nearly one-third of youth are estimated to reside in a stepfamily household before reaching adulthood (Bumpass, Raley, & Sweet, 1995; Pew Research Center, 2011). A stepfamily is formed when one or both partners in a new committed relationship have a child or children from a previous relationship (Ganong & Coleman, 2017). Members of stepfamilies often grapple with unique demands, including conflict between youth and new stepparents, step-couple disagreements about parenting strategies, navigating co-parental relationships and child custody arrangements, disruptions in parent-child relationships, and ambiguity about family roles and boundaries (Jensen, 2017; Sweeney, 2010; Van Eeden-Moorefield & Pasley, 2013). These demands have implications for stepfamily functioning and individual well-being (King, 2006; Jensen & Harris, 2017a, 2017b; Jensen & Howard, 2015;

Jensen, Lippold, Mills-Koonce, & Fosco, 2018; Jensen & Shafer, 2013; Jensen, Shafer, & Holmes, 2017).

Given their increasing prominence and distinct experiences, stepfamilies receive notable attention among researchers and practitioners (Browning & Artelt, 2012; Ganong & Coleman, 2017; Papernow, 2013; Pryor, 2014; Stewart, 2007). Moving away from the historically predominant deficit-comparison approach, by which stepfamily outcomes are simply contrasted with those of biological nuclear families, researchers have begun to focus more on processes of resilience within stepfamilies (i.e., normative-adaptive approach; Coleman, Ganong, & Russell, 2013; Ganong & Coleman, 2017). Research has also begun to explore unique step-family dynamics within subgroups marked by specific racial and ethnic identities and cultures. Yet, the risk, protective, and pro-motive capacity of religion in the context of family transitions in general, and stepfamily life in particular, remains an area of scant empirical attention (Marks, 2006; Pryor, 2014; Stewart, 2007). This oversight is unfortunate, given the growing diversity of reli-gions in the United States (Pew Research Center, 2015). Moreover, stepfamilies are inherently bicultural in the sense that partners bring together two backgrounds that can differ with respect to family-of-origin experiences, racial and ethnic identity, and, as we explore in this chapter, religion.

Certainly, there are many ways of *doing* religion. Some simply claim a religious identity or affiliation. Others engage actively in religious life and rituals. Still others focus on espousing religious values or doctrines without a desire to practice religion in formal settings. Consequently, there is value in clarifying and distinguishing key terms when discussing associations between religion and family life—terms such as religious affiliation, religious salience, religious behavior, religious beliefs, religious commu-nity, and spirituality (Brown & Porter, 2013; Marks, 2006; Tanyi, 2002). This chapter focuses on three of these terms: *religious affiliation*, defined as the religious sect to which one reports belonging; *religious salience*, defined as the extent to which one views

There is little research on stepfamilies who practice non-Christian religions.

religion as a central and important facet of life; and *religious behavior*, defined as actions that emerge from or reflect a commitment to one's religious affiliation (e.g., attendance at religious meetings or services). Hereafter, the use of the term "religion" will generally refer to religious affiliation, and "religiosity" will generally refer to religious salience or religious behavior. Because the term "spirituality" has been defined as "a personal search for meaning and purpose in life, which may or may not be related to religion" (Tanyi, 2002, p. 506), it is not a focus in this chapter.

At this point, it is also important to acknowledge the growing prevalence of individuals who report being religiously unaffiliated in the United States (Pew Research Center, 2015). Some religiously unaffiliated individuals may identify as agnostic (i.e., the existence of deity being claimed as unknown or unknowable) and/or atheist (i.e., a lack of belief in deity). A declaration of no religious affiliation is not easily interpretable, so it seems wise to avoid making any firm assumptions about those in this category. I will return to this point later in the chapter.

In the following sections, I begin with an overview of theory and research that highlight the potential role of religion and religiosity in family life. I then focus on stepfamilies specifically, and present findings from descriptive analyses using data from the National Longitudinal Study of Adolescent to Adult Health (Add Health). Add Health is a nationally representative study of adolescents and their families who began participating in comprehensive data collection activities starting between 1994 and 1995. The data collected include information about religion and religiosity. The purposes of these analyses are to (a) provide context by highlighting religious dynamics in stepfamilies relative to other family structures, and (b) explore potential associations between religiosity and stepfamily functioning. The chapter will then conclude with a discussion of implications and directions for future research, recommendations for practice, relevant legal and policy issues, prompts for critical thinking and reflection, and additional readings and resources. When applicable, the content from the opening vignette will be used to illustrate various points made throughout the chapter.

The Intersection of Religion and Family Life

It would be inaccurate to say there is little to no research focused on linkages between religion and family life; however, religion in relation to diverse family structures and processes, and family transitions, is not well studied (Marks, 2006; Pryor, 2014; Stewart, 2007). Starting with a broad view, religion can be viewed as standing at the nexus of (a) family formation, (b) family transitions, and (c) family processes. Each of these topics is, in turn, discussed in the following sections, and each serves to build a conceptual foundation for the exploration of associations between religion, religiosity, and stepfamily life.

Family Formation

Family formation refers to when, how, and why social relationships are pursued and formed. From a life course perspective, developmental and relational trajectories unfold over time, and the type and timing of role transitions individuals experience are highly powerful (Elder, Shanahan, & Jennings, 2015). Religious beliefs can exert influence on an individual's relational beliefs, attitudes, and behavior, ultimately influencing the type and timing of relationship transitions, such as forming a committed romantic relationship, pursuing marriage, or becoming a parent (Bengtson, Copen, Putney, & Silverstein, 2009; Brown & Porter, 2013). Indeed, previous research has linked religion to one's propensity to marry, cohabit, or remain single over time (Bramlett & Mosher, 2001). For example, individuals affiliated with more conservative religions tend to exhibit relatively lower rates of cohabitation and higher rates of marriage, and express greater intentions to have children (Adsera, 2006; Brown & Porter, 2013; Pearce, 2002). Religion can also shape the dating pools from which individuals pursue romantic partners; some individuals seek to partner with others who share their religious affiliation.

Perhaps more influential than religious affiliation are indicators of religiosity, such as religious behavior and salience. For example, researchers have found that higher levels of attending religious meetings or services and religious salience (i.e., importance) are associated with stronger intentions to pursue marriage and bear children (Adsera, 2006; Becker & Hofmeister, 2001). Depending on the religion, high levels of religious participation can confer upon individuals more traditional attitudes about family formation (Lehrer, 2004a, b). Moreover, the teachings or doctrines of a particular religion can influence an individual's family attitudes by shaping perceptions about the costs and benefits associated with various family formation decisions (Lehrer, 2000; Lehrer, 2004a,b). More frequent attendance at religious meetings or services generates opportunity for such influences to be propagated and reinforced. Thus, religiosity is thought to

Religion can provide stepfamilies with tools that promote positive relationships. For example, families might incorporate religious principles emphasizing forgiveness, kindness, and respect.

be a more potent determinant of family attitudes and decisions than religious affiliation alone (Brown & Porter, 2013). Taken together, religion and religiosity appear to inform when, how, and why individuals move into and arrange various relationships. Turning to the opening vignette, consider how Rosa's religious experiences might have shaped her decisions about pursuing committed couple relationships and becoming a parent.

Family Transitions

Family transitions refer to when, how, and why social relationships dissolve or subsequent social relationships begin. Drawing from an exchange perspective, Levinger's (1965) model of marital- and family-system dissolution posits that one's propensity to maintain or dissolve a committed relationship is a function of the central attractions of the current relationship, the attractions of alternative relationships, and various barriers that might obstruct one's departure from a relationship. In many respects, features of one's religious experience and belief system can operate as barriers to dissolving a committed relationship. For example, turning back to the opening vignette, consider how Rosa's affiliation with Catholicism influenced how she appraised her past divorce. The view that divorce is religiously taboo very likely gave Rosa pause before ending her prior marriage, and most likely influenced any decisions about whether to pursue a relationship with her new partner, Jim.

Moreover, religious beliefs could represent a central attraction of a current relationship, particularly if both partners share the same or a similar belief system. Shared beliefs, principles, and behaviors rooted in religious tradition could unite partners and strengthen couple relationships by creating common ground and mutual purpose. Relationships in which religious beliefs are not shared between partners, however, can stir conflict and diminish a partnership's compatibility over time. These issues could render a relationship less attractive, and lean individuals toward the eventual dissolution of the relationship. Also, apparent associations between religion or religiosity and marital dissolution can be entangled with other sociodemographic factors, including education and financial resources (McDanieal, Boco, & Zella, 2013).

An individual espousing a religious belief that romantic partnership is religiously desirable could also prompt re-partnership following the dissolution of a committed relationship. Several studies have indicated that individuals affiliated with conservative or mainline Protestant religions, as compared with their Catholic or religiously unaffiliated counterparts, exhibit a greater likelihood and accelerated pace of remarriage following divorce (Brown & Porter, 2013; Wu & Schimmele, 2005; Xu & Bartkowski, 2017). In addition, more frequent attendance at religious meetings or services is associated with a greater propensity to remarry (Brown & Porter, 2013; Xu & Bartkowski, 2017). Findings related to religious salience are somewhat mixed. Some studies have found that greater religious salience is associated with greater odds of remarrying following divorce (Brown & Porter, 2013). Others have found a weak or null association between religious salience and the propensity to remarry (Xu & Bartkowski, 2017). Taken together, it appears religion or religiosity can inform when, how, and why relationships dissolve or new social relationships begin.

Family Processes

Family processes refer to what families do—and when, how, and why they interact. In many ways, family processes are the most operative feature of family life, and stepfamily life is no exception. Family processes are a primary mechanism that links family structure, stress, change, or transitions to various individual and family outcomes (Amato, 2000; Boss, Bryant, & Mancini, 2017; Hetherington, Bridges, & Insabella, 1998; Lippold & Jensen, 2017; Patterson, 2002; Sheeber, Hops, & Davis, 2001). Walsh's (2002) Family Resilience Framework (FRF) outlines specific family belief systems, organizational patterns, and communication processes that can foster family resilience, or a capacity to function well in the face of challenges or adversity. The three belief-system components outlined in the FRF reflect closely features of religion or religiosity, namely *making meaning of adversity, positive outlook,* and *transcendence or spirituality.*

From a resilience perspective, religious beliefs can provide families a lens through which to interpret and make sense of life adversities, including the death of loved ones, loss of a job, the

onset of health challenges, or in the context of stepfamily formation, stressors related to general changes and transitions in family
boundaries and roles. Religious ideologies also offer narratives
that can help individuals and families maintain a positive outlook over time. Affiliation and engagement with religion can also
extend families' opportunities to espouse a sense of transcendent
purpose that promotes growth, inspiration, and creativity (Walsh,
2002). Thus, the FRF highlights the protective capacity of religion
or religiosity for families, including stepfamilies.

The Family Adjustment and Adaptation Response (FAAR)
model (Patterson, 2002) is another theory that further highlights
the potential role of religion or religiosity with respect to family
processes. The FAAR model posits that a family's ability to adjust
and adapt well over time is a function of family meaning-making,
family demands, and family capabilities. Family capabilities generally take the form of tangible or psychosocial resources (i.e.,
what a family has) or coping behaviors (i.e., what a family does;
Patterson, 2002). Family demands can take the form of daily
hassles, acute stressors (i.e., discrete events of change), or ongoing strains (Patterson, 2002). Family meaning-making includes
appraisals of family demands and capabilities, perceptions about
family identify, and a family's world view (Patterson, 2002).

Perhaps linkages between religion or religiosity and family
meaning-making are the most intuitive. Consider how religiously
active individuals often imbue their lives and personal narratives
with religious or spiritual meaning, generating a lens through
which life events and the world around them are observed and
interpreted. Individuals can also imbue their family relationships and experiences with spiritual meaning. This phenomenon
is often referred to as sanctification (Mahoney, Pargament,
Murray-Swank, & Murray-Swank, 2003). Sanctification, in this
context, refers to a "... psychological process in which aspects of
life are perceived as having spiritual character or significance"
(Mahoney et al., 2003, p. 221). The sanctification of family
relationships—including couple relationships, parent-child
relationships, and step-relationships—can influence a family's
process of appraising family demands and capabilities (Mahoney
at al., 2003; Krumrei, Mahoney, & Pargament, 2009; Poston &
Turnbull, 2004), such that family experiences can be viewed as
being bestowed by a deity or higher power.

Consistent with the FAAR model (and FRF), features of religion or religiosity can also embody or generate various family
adaptive capabilities. When family relationships are imbued
with spiritual or transcendent properties, family members might

experience confidence and security in their relationships, exert effort and investment in their families, and experience a positive outlook in relation to family life (Brodsky, 2000; Mahoney et al., 2003; Mattis, 2002). Some research has found positive associations between family sanctification or parental religiosity and investment in marital relationships, harmonious couple interactions, and warm parent-child interactions (Clydesdale, 1997; Mahoney et al., 2003; Mahoney, Pargament, Tarakeshwar, & Swank, 2001; Tuttle & Davis, 2015). Moreover, some religions might confer upon families a set of capabilities that promote relational functioning. For example, families might incorporate religious principles emphasizing forgiveness, kindness, and respect (Mahoney et al., 2003)—principles that could be especially influential amid the transition to stepfamily life.

Additional research has indicated that among families with special-needs children, religion or religiosity can foster meaningful community connections and cultivate a repertoire of religious behaviors and beliefs from which families can draw in times of need (Poston & Turnbull, 2004). Other studies have shown how some African American families rely on religious behaviors and practices to cope with the stress and demands that arise from systemic manifestations of racism (Shorter-Gooden, 2004). Taken together, religion or religiosity appear to have the capacity to bolster a family's adaptive capabilities. This capacity for stepfamilies is illustrated in the opening vignette, particularly with respect to Rosa and Jim employing their religious beliefs and principles in ways that promote commitment to the stepfamily and the strengthening of new and extant relationships.

Religion or religiosity also have the capacity to generate or exacerbate family demands. Religiously derived demands include responsibilities, energy, and effort related to attending religious meetings or services and engaging in prescribed religious practices (e.g., prayer, reading religious texts). Religious activities require time—an often scarce resource for families. Families can also possess a set of religiously informed expectations about family dynamics and behavior (Mahoney et al., 2003). Indeed, religion often confers upon families prescriptive

Many stepfamilies must figure out how to merge religious traditions.

messages about wrong versus right, good versus evil, and sinful versus acceptable. These messages can generate social scripts that dictate what "should" or "should not" occur in the family system—issues that can become especially demanding and complex in stepfamilies while navigating the merging of two family backgrounds.

If social scripts are violated, greater demands could be placed on the family system, resulting in greater risk of family maladjustment and negative psychological reactions, such as anxiety, guilt, and defensiveness (Mahoney et al., 2003). In this way, religiously informed social scripts can exacerbate family demands to the extent that demands are perceived as religiously undesirable or involve behavior perceived as "sinful." Turning back to the opening vignette, consider how Selena's pregnancy was appraised negatively by Rosa and Jim, based on their assessment of whether God approved or disapproved of Selena's life choices. Selena's impending transition to parenthood already constituted a significant demand on the family system, and the added layer of religious interpretation very likely exacerbated the level of stress associated with it. Here it is worth noting that stepfamilies formed in middle or late life—an increasingly common phenomenon (Papernow, 2018)—might experience fewer religiously informed demands with respect to parenting, as children are probably older and no longer living at home.

Conflict in families can also emerge when members possess disparate religious interpretations and preferences with respect to family activities, gender roles, sexuality, and appropriate methods for conflict resolution, among other matters that influence family life (Mahoney et al., 2003). Navigating these differences can place notable demands on family systems, and such differences might be more pronounced in stepfamilies relative to nuclear families. Consider how Rosa, Jim, and Selena had misunderstandings and conflict surrounding Jim's expectation that the family attend religious meetings or services each week.

Researchers have noted the important bidirectional and transactional influences of religion and family life (Boot, Johnson, Branaman, & Sica, 1995; Day et al., 2009; Thornton, Axinn, & Hill, 1992). Put another way, family dynamics and religion exert influence on each other, such that features within a family can shape the religiosity of its members, and features within an associated religious context can shape family dynamics. For example, youth who experience higher-quality relationships with and between their parents might also report more frequent attendance at religious meetings or services (Day et al., 2009). Another study found that the dissolution of a parental relationship can generate shifts in religious commitment among youth over time (Denton, 2012). Moreover, some researchers caution that although reciprocal and direct family-religion links have been observed, they are often moderate to weak in magnitude (Booth et al., 1995).

Religion, Religiosity, and Stepfamilies

At this point it should be apparent that religion can be significantly entangled with family life in general, and stepfamily life in particular. Yet, turning to stepfamilies specifically, very little research has focused on the role of religion or religiosity (Marks, 2006; Pryor, 2014; Schramm, Marshall, Harris, & Lee, 2012; Stewart, 2007). Certainly, the empirical and theoretical work just reviewed could be extrapolated and applied to particular stepfamily contexts; however, a central proposition in this chapter is that more research is warranted. The content overviewed previously can serve as a useful framework for research moving forward. To further establish a foundation for research in this area, we now turn to some descriptive analyses that are intended to (a) provide context by highlighting religious dynamics in stepfamilies relative to other family structures, and (b) explore potential associations between religiosity and stepfamily functioning.

Drawing from Add Health data, Figure 7.1 displays information about religious affiliation, religious behavior, and religious salience across three family structures: (a) cohabiting or married biological, two-parent families;[1] (b) single-parent families; and (c) cohabiting or married stepfamilies (note that the term "fragile families" is often used in the literature to identify stepfamilies formed through cohabitation due to their higher rate of dissolution). For religious affiliation, parent respondents in the Add Health study were asked, "What is your religion?" Respondents then selected their affiliation, or reported having no religious affiliation. One indicator of religious behavior involves attendance at religious meetings or services. In Add Health, parent respondents were asked, "How often have you gone to religious services in the past year?" Response options included "once a week or more," "less than once a week, but at least once a month," "less than once a month," and "never." In terms of religious salience, parent respondents were asked, "How important is religion to you?" Response options included "very important," "fairly important," "fairly unimportant," and "not important at all."

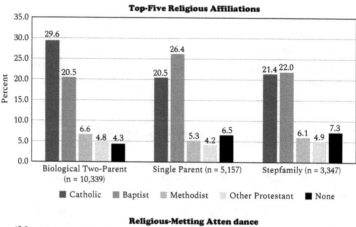

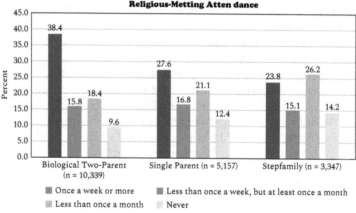

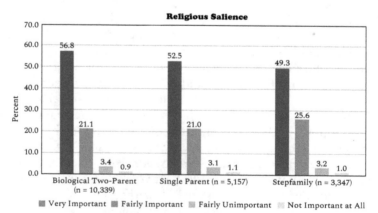

FIGURE 7.1 Proportions of Top-Five Religious Affiliations, Religious Meeting Attendance, and Religious Salience by Family Structure (Parent Reports). Note: Proportions differed significantly by family structure; $\chi^2(8) = 363.71$, $p < .001$; $\chi^2(6) = 350.46$, $p < .001$; $\chi^2(6) = 51.09$, $p < .001$, respectively. Note: Adopted children were not included in the analysis.

In terms of religious affiliation, 28 groups were represented in the Add Health data (including a large array of Christian sects, Islam, Judaism, and Buddhism, among others). Turning to the five most frequent religious affiliations (each representing at least 4% or more of respondents), there appears to be meaningful differences across family structures. Nearly 30% of parents in biological two-parent families identified as Catholic, compared with 20% and 21% of parents in single-parent families and stepfamilies, respectively. A greater proportion of parents in single-parent families (26%) identified as Baptist, compared with parents in stepfamilies (22%) and biological two-parent families (20%). Parents identifying as Methodist or as being affiliated with some other Protestant religion were fairly comparable across family structures. About 7% of parents in stepfamilies reported having no religious affiliation, followed by 6% of parents in single-parent families, and 4% of parents in biological two-parent families.

Also apparent are differences across family structures with respect to religious meeting attendance. As shown in the second graph in Figure 7.1, 38% of parents in biological two-parent families reported attending religious meetings once a week or more, compared with 28% and 24% of parents in single-parent families and stepfamilies, respectively. Attendance rates of less than once a week, but at least once a month, were comparable across family structures, ranging from a low of 15% to a high of 17%. Attendance rates of less than once a month were highest among parents in stepfamilies (26%), followed by single-parent families (21%) and biological two-parent families (18%). A similar pattern is evident among those indicating they never attend religious meetings. These rates were 14%, 12%, and 10% among parents in stepfamilies, single-parent families, and biological two-parent families, respectively.

In terms of religious salience, parents across each family structure appear quite similar. One notable distinction, however, is among parents indicating that religion is very important. About 57% of parents in biological two-parent families, 53% of parents in single-parent families, and 49% of parents in stepfamilies indicated religion as being very important in their lives. Relatively more parents in stepfamilies indicated that religion is fairly important (26%), compared with the other family structures (about 21% in both biological two-parent and single-parent families). In no way do these data suggest that family structure *causes* differences in religious affiliation, religious meeting attendance, or religious salience. Instead, these data reflect potential associations between religion or religiosity and individuals' decisions about family formation and transitions, as discussed previously.

Now we turn to religious dynamics within stepfamilies. As noted earlier, religion and religiosity can influence individuals' propensity to exit or enter committed couple relationships. Thus, we might expect to see greater religious diversity in family structures other than biological two-parent families (Schramm et al., 2012). This diversity could be indicated, in part, by greater mismatches between parents' and stepparents' religious affiliations. Data from Add Health seem to support this hypothesis. As shown in Figure 7.2, 63% of couples in biological two-parent families share the same religious affiliation, in contrast with 50% of couples in stepfamilies. Of note, religious-affiliation mismatches also differ across family structures in the context of parent-child dyads. Turning to Figure 7.3, 60% of parent-child dyads in biological two-parent families share the same religious affiliation, contrasted with 51% and 49% of parent-child dyads in single-parent families and stepfamilies, respectively. This finding is consistent with past research that suggests religious transmission from parents to youth is weaker in stepfamilies and single-parent families compared with biological two-parent families (Petts, 2009, 2015).

Also interesting to consider is the potential association between religiosity and stepfamily functioning. Two foundational components of stepfamily functioning are the quality of the stepparent-child relationship and the quality of the step-couple

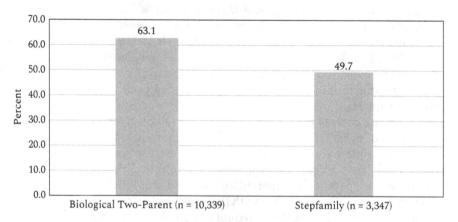

FIGURE 7.2 Proportions of Couples with Matched Religious Affiliations by Family Structure. Note: Proportions differed significantly by family structure; $\chi^2(1) = 243.52$, p < .001. Note: Adopted children were not included in the analysis.

Source: The National Longitudinal Study of Adolescent to Adult Health (Add Health), Wave I

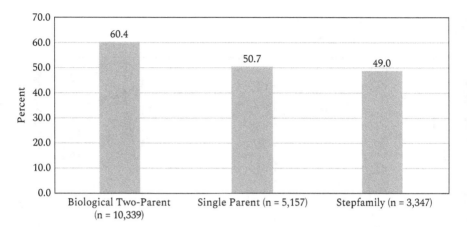

FIGURE 7.3 Proportions of Parent-Child Dyads with Matched Religious Affiliations by Family Structure. Note: Proportions differed significantly by family structure; $\chi^2(2) = 215.70$, $p < .001$. Note: Adopted children were not included in the analysis.

Source: The National Longitudinal Study of Adolescent to Adult Health (Add Health), Wave I

relationship (Coleman et al., 2013; Jensen & Howard, 2015). In what ways might religious behavior and salience among parents and youth influence these components of stepfamily functioning? To begin exploring this question, I again used the Add Health data. Figure 7.4 charts levels of stepparent-child relationship quality and couple relational happiness with respect to reports on parental and youth religious meeting attendance and religious salience.

Stepparent-child relationship quality was a composite scale, formed from the following five youth-report items: "How close do you feel to your stepparent?" "How much do you think she/he cares about you?" "Most of the time, your stepparent is warm and loving toward you," "You are satisfied with the way your stepparent and you communicate with each other," and "Overall, you are satisfied with your relationship with your stepparent." All items were coded such that higher values indicated higher relationship quality. Response options ranged from scores of 1 (strongly disagree/not at all) to 5 (strongly agree/very much). *Couple relationship happiness* was measured with one item that asked parent respondents to indicate, on a scale from 1 to 10, how they would rate the relationship with their current spouse or partner. A score of 1 indicated "completely unhappy," and a score of 10 indicated "completely happy"

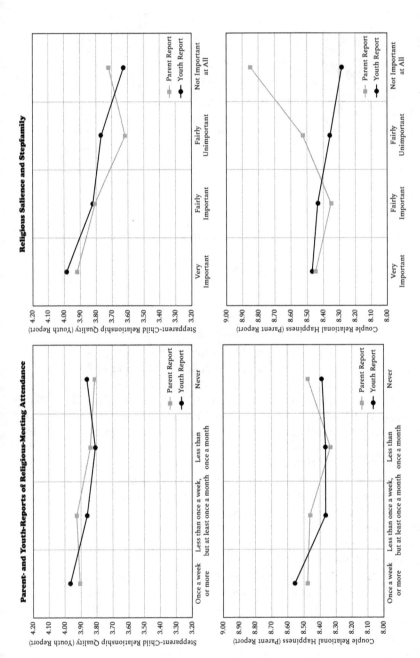

FIGURE 7.4 Parent and Youth Reports of Religious Meeting Attendance, Religious Salience, and Stepfamily Functioning: Stepparent-Child Relationship Quality (Youth Report) and Couple Relational Happiness (Parent Report). Note: Stepparent-child relationship quality ranges from values of 1 to 5; Couple relational happiness ranges from values of 1 to 10. Adopted children were not included in the analysis.

Source: The National Longitudinal Study of Adolescent to Adult Health (Add Health), Wave I

In terms of stepparent-child relationship quality, there appears to be only a weak association with religious meeting attendance. For instance, across both parent and youth reports of religious meeting attendance, stepparent-child relationship quality peaked at about 4.0 units for those attending once a week or more, and approached a low of 3.8 units for those attending less than once a month or never—a difference of only .15 units. A potential association between stepparent-child relationship quality and religious salience was slightly more pronounced. Across both parent and youth reports of religious salience, stepparent-child relationship quality peaked between 4.0 and 3.9 units among youth, indicating that religion was very important, and slightly decreased to around 3.6 and 3.7 units among youth, indicating religion is fairly unimportant or not important at all.

Turning to couple relational happiness and religious meeting attendance, a similar pattern emerged. Across both parent and youth reports of religious meeting attendance, couple relational happiness peaked at around 8.5 units among those attending once a week or more, and only slightly declined (and even rebounded) among those attending less than once a week, less than once a month, or never. A potential association between couple relationship happiness and religious salience appears more nuanced. In terms of youth reports of religious salience, couple relational happiness peaked at around 8.5 units among youth, indicating religion was very important, and slightly declined with each unit decrease in religious salience, with a low of about 8.3 units among youth, indicating religion was not important at all. Given the fairly stable levels of couple relational happiness across youth reports of religious salience, this could indicate the two variables are not meaningfully associated. In contrast, couple relational happiness is around 8.5 units among parents, indicating religion is very important; drops slightly to 8.4 units among parents, indicating religion is fairly important; increases to 8.5 units among parents, indicating religion is fairly unimportant; and peaks at around 8.9 units among parents, indicating religion is not important at all.

This trend stands in contrast to all of the others, though upon reflection, this phenomenon seems rather interpretable. Reconsider how many couples in stepfamilies have a mismatch of religious affiliations between partners. These mismatches could generate conflict within couples, especially when religious salience is high among one or both partners. Thus, when parent respondents indicate low levels of religious salience, they might experience higher levels of couple relational happiness because religious differences between partners do not stir up as much conflict; that is, if religion is not at the forefront of parents' lives, it might be less likely to generate conflict when parents navigate religious differences with new partners.

Taken together, the descriptive findings signal the value in exploring religious diversity, religion, and religiosity in the context of stepfamily life. Such explorations might be especially complex in stepfamily contexts, as the findings indicate that stepfamily subsystems might experience more mismatches in religious affiliation than subsystems in biological nuclear families (or even single-parent families).

Conclusions related to these data should be tempered by some limitations. For one, not all parent and youth respondents provided information about religion and religiosity. Thus, although Add Health contains a representative sample of adolescents and their families, missing data can mitigate the external validity of the analyses. Moreover, Add Health data at Wave I were collected between 1994 and 1995. Since then, there have been notable shifts in the general makeup of religious affiliation and religiosity in the United States (Pew Research Center, 2015). Reported associations between religiosity and stepfamily functioning are also cross-sectional, rendering ambiguous the temporal order of variables. In addition, much of the content of this chapter has been focused on associations between religion and stepfamily life in the United States. Thus, the descriptive findings are not well situated

Religious symbols and experiences have the capacity to bring stepfamily members together.
Source: https://pixabay.com/photo-1181864/.

to highlight religious nuances among stepfamilies in other countries with distinct religious and cultural landscapes. The findings also do not speak to potential differences across racial and ethnic groups in the United States. Ultimately, the analyses presented in this chapter are intended to be informative and illuminating, not conclusive and definitive. As noted earlier, research centered on religion and stepfamily life is limited, and, despite some limitations, the descriptive analyses presented in this chapter help form a foundation upon which future research can be conducted.

Implications and Future Research

There is a growing appreciation of religion-family linkages over time among researchers and practitioners. Although work in this area has expanded, research has largely neglected the investigation of religion in the context of stepfamily life and the transitions that precede it. The first half of this chapter overviewed a rich theoretical and empirical body of work that can inform emerging work in the area of religion and stepfamily life. The FAAR model seems especially useful as a guiding framework to explore the risk, protective, and promotive capacity of religion or religiosity in stepfamily life. Indeed, the FAAR model highlights how aspects of religion and religiosity can operate as a family demand, family capability, or meaning-making process.

At this point it seems important to note again that an increasing number of individuals in the United States identify as religiously unaffiliated (Pew Research Center, 2015). No part of this chapter intends to suggest that religiously unaffiliated stepfamilies possess any inherent disadvantages compared with their religious counterparts. In fact, the descriptive findings suggest that some stepfamilies might experience greater functioning when parents' religious salience is low; the question then becomes why and under what conditions. Again, the intention of this chapter is to explore and explicate the potential role of religion and religiosity in stepfamily life.

The analyses presented in this chapter highlight notable differences across family structures with respect to religious affiliation, behavior, and salience. Moreover, the analyses in this chapter highlight potential associations between religiosity and stepfamily functioning. These findings are solely descriptive, not explanatory. In that light, the chapter's content points to a number of promising sites for future research. For one, researchers should investigate the extent to which religious differences, both within couples or between parents and youth, exert influence on stepfamily functioning and individual well-being. Researchers should also investigate ways that stepfamilies manage religious differences and employ religious practices, behaviors, or beliefs to promote stepfamily functioning and well-being.

Researchers should also explore the nuances of specific religious groups in the context of stepfamily life. How do affiliates of specific religious sects employ religion in their day-to-day interactions and lives? In addition, what are the specific mechanisms and processes that link religion or religiosity to family outcomes (Marks, 2006)? There is much more research needed to uncover the risk, protective, and promotive capacity of religion or religiosity in stepfamilies. This work could examine links between religious features and stepfamily functioning within a specific religious group, or examine dynamics in stepfamilies across different religious groups. In other words, this work could incorporate a between-religion perspective or a within-religion perspective when studying religion or religiosity in the context of stepfamily life. Moving beyond the Unites States, which was the focus of this chapter, future research could also make efforts to investigate the religion-stepfamily intersection in the context of other developed and developing societies and cultures. Across the globe, religious affiliations and practices differ notably from the predominately Judeo-Christian tradition found in the United States.

Another important site for future research is among members of the lesbian, gay, bisexual, transgender, and queer/questioning (LGBTQ+) community, and among sexual and gender nonconforming couples and children. In the context of stepfamilies formed by same-sex couples, religious experiences and differences among partners could influence stepfamily dynamics in important ways, especially how one or both partners view religion having a notable influence on their experiences within the LGBTQ+ community. Moreover, the complex makeup of religion and religiosity in stepfamilies could shape or inform coming-out processes for LGBTQ+ youth. Thus, future research focused on religion or religiosity and stepfamily life should be inclusive of members of the LGBTQ+ community, whether focus is placed on LGBTQ+ adults or youth. In addition, whereas other chapters in this book focus on specific racial and ethnic identities in the context of stepfamily life, this chapter focuses more broadly on religion. Rather than viewing them as mutually exclusive, there is most likely value in acknowledging the intersection of religion and racial and ethnic identity in future research.

Future research should also incorporate a longitudinal and transactional perspective. Religious affiliation and religiosity are not static features of individuals and families; they are dynamic, and can exhibit continuity or change over time. Attending to the dynamic nature of religion or religiosity will be an important feature of future research in this area. Stepfamilies in particular will very likely experience shifts in religion and religiosity as they form new relationships, merge together different family histories and expectations, and negotiate new family norms. The descriptive findings reported in this chapter also highlight the value in capturing information from multiple informants, such as parents and youth (Mahoney et al., 2001). Researchers should incorporate conceptually rich measures of religion and religiosity that speak to the experiences of parents, stepparents, and youth.

Recommendations for Practice

In addition to religious leaders, many family therapists, family life educators, social workers, and other helping professionals will encounter religious dynamics among the stepfamilies with whom they engage. There remains a great deal of professional uncertainty about whether and how practitioners should incorporate clients' religion and religiosity in clinical or family educational settings (Carlson, Kirkpatrick, Hecker, & Killmer, 2002; Stander, Piercy, Mackinnon, & Helmeke, 1994). Moreover, a practitioner's willingness or hesitance to broach religious topics with families will most likely hinge on their his or her own religious background. In that context, practitioners should be mindful of how their own religious persuasions influence or bias their intervention efforts with families. Thus, practitioners should engage in continuous self-reflection and assessment. Seeking consultation and supervision might be advisable if one finds her or his religion (or lack thereof) exerting undue influence on clinical or educational decision making.

Ultimately, when working with stepfamilies, practitioners should consider incorporating information about religion when families deem it important to do so. Thus, it might be advisable for practitioners to assess the potential influence of religion on stepfamily dynamics at the outset of clinical or educational work. Extant tools might prove useful on this front, such as spiritual lifemaps, genograms, histories, eco-maps, and eco-grams (Hodge, 2015). A key strength of genograms and eco-maps is that they serve as visual aids for families, a feature that could be especially helpful for children who might struggle to articulate their feelings and perceptions. As appropriate, attending to religious matters when working with stepfamilies can be considered congruent with efforts to possess and practice cultural competence and sensitivity (Stander et al., 1994). Note that meaning-making is not strictly a religious enterprise. Practitioners working with stepfamily members who identify as agnostic, atheist, and/or otherwise religiously unaffiliated can draw on meaning-marking processes, insomuch as they are salient for the stepfamily.

Possible associations between religion and stepfamily functioning also have implications for professional training programs. For one, training programs for practitioners and religious counselors should include content focused on stepfamily dynamics (Papernow, 2013). In addition, it could be valuable for training program curricula to include discussions or courses on the role of religion or religiosity in family practice settings (Carlson et al., 2002; Stander et al., 1994). Such content could equip practitioners with at least a minimal level of exposure and comfort with the topic. It's hoped the content of this chapter will contribute to this cause, and encourage practitioners to be mindful of the ways that religion might influence stepfamily dynamics and functioning.

Relevant Laws and Policies

In terms of larger legal and policy contexts, a nuclear family bias continues to permeate society (Gamache, 1997); that is, biological, married, two-parent families are generally viewed as the gold standard to which other family structures are contrasted. Consequently, stepfamilies are often either ignored by society or treated as an inferior or stigmatized group (Ganong & Coleman, 1997), despite being increasingly common. Such cultural beliefs about families inform family policies and laws (Malia, 2005, 2008). Policy makers' and lawmakers' apparent bias toward nuclear family ideology has led to few substantial legal changes that explicitly benefit stepfamilies (Malia, 2005). For example, the *parental rights doctrine* upholds the primacy of biological parents as the sole and lawful decision makers with respect to rearing children, leaving little room for extended kin or stepparents (Skinner & Kohler, 2002). Further, *parenthood as an exclusive status* declares that a child cannot have more than two parents, both of whom have full parental duties and rights that are not shared with others (Malia, 2005).

Legal and policy barriers to formalizing stepfamily relationships could exert stress on individuals, especially those who adhere to religious views that emphasize formal or legally bound family ties. Consistent with a normative-adaptive perspective, future legal- and policy-reform efforts could advocate for a more inclusive legal conceptualization of family, and a stronger cultural shift toward acceptance of nonnuclear families (Kavanagh, 2004). A culture in which stepfamilies are more widely accepted and legally accommodated will also be facilitated by a collective avoidance of stereotyping stepfamilies and using the term "step" as a pejorative term (Claxton-Oldfield, 2008; Ganong & Coleman, 1983).

Also important are interfaces between stepfamilies and state-level laws regarding marriage and divorce (e.g., "covenant marriages," "no-fault divorces"). Such laws speak to the requisite conditions under which a marriage can be formed or dissolved, ranging from restrictive to flexible. Recall how religious beliefs can inform how individuals appraise marriage, approach the legal contract of marriage, and make decisions about when, how, and why a marriage should end. Local laws related to marriage and divorce can either help or hinder individuals' decision making in this respect. Moreover, the extent to which local marriage and divorce laws are restrictive could explain, in part, increasing rates of post-divorce cohabitation among stepfamilies, or the formation of "fragile families" (Xu, Hudspeth, & Bartkowski, 2006). Taken together, the intersection of marriage-related laws, divorce-related laws, and religion has implications for stepfamily life, both in the context of transitions that precede stepfamily life and transitions that might follow.

Family life and religion also intersect with immigration law. As of the writing of this chapter, there have been several attempts made by the executive branch of the U.S. federal government to impose restrictions on immigration and travel that disproportionately affect Islamic nations. Ethnocentric and nationalist attitudes, and their resultant legislative agendas, can exert influence on the religious makeup of the United States, and thus the religious makeup of families and stepfamilies over time. Such attitudes can also exert stress on families placed at the center of political debate and scrutiny due to their religious orientation, immigration status, and nation of origin (Peters & Massey, 1983).

Questions for Discussion

1. In what ways can religion or religiosity influence individuals' decisions about family formation, family transitions, and family processes or interactions?

2. Consider how stepfamilies might grapple with religious differences between stepfamily members.
3. Consider how your religion or religiosity (or lack thereof) influences you as a practitioner, researcher, and/or educator. How can you be more proactive and inclusive in your assessment and incorporation of religious dynamics in your work?
4. Reflect on the laws and policies that can further influence the stepfamily-religion connection.

Additional Resources

Carlson, T. D., Kirkpatrick, D., Hecker, L., & Killmer, M. (2002). Religion, spirituality, and marriage and family therapy: A study of family therapists' beliefs about the appropriateness of addressing religious and spiritual issues in therapy. *American Journal of Family Therapy, 30*, 157–171.

Mahoney, A., Pargament, K. I., Murray-Swank, A., & Murray-Swank, N. (2003). Religion and the sanctification of family relationships. *Review of Religious Research, 44*, 220–236.

Patterson, J. M. (2002). Integrating family resilience and family stress theory. *Journal of marriage and family, 64*, 349–360.

Pew Research Center (2015). *America's changing religious landscape.* Washington, DC: Pew Research Center.

Schramm, D. G., Marshall, J. P., Harris, V. W., & Lee, T. R. (2012). Religiosity, homogamy, and marital adjustment: An examination of newlyweds in first marriages and remarriages. *Journal of Family Issues, 33*, 246–268.

Stander, V., Piercy, F. P., Mackinnon, D., & Helmeke, K. (1994). Spirituality, religion and family therapy: Competing or complementary worlds? *The American Journal of Family Therapy, 22*, 27–41.

Walsh, F. (2002). A family resilience framework: Innovative practice applications. *Family Relations, 51*, 130–137.

For more information about the National Longitudinal Study of Adolescent to Adult Health see http://cpc.unc.edu/addhealth

Note

1 Due to their small numbers, adopted children were not included in the analysis.

References

Adsera, A. (2006). Religion and changes in family-size norms in developed countries. *Review of Religious Research, 47*, 271–286.

Amato, P. R. (2000). The consequences of divorce for adults and children. *Journal of marriage and family, 62*, 1269–1287.

Bengtson, V. L., Copen, C. E., Putney, N. M., & Silverstein, M. (2009). A longitudinal study of the intergenerational transmission of religion. *International Sociology, 24*, 325–345.

Bramlett, M. D., & Mosher, W. D. (2001). *First marriage dissolution, divorce, and remarriage*. Hyattsville MD: National Center for Health Statistics.

Booth, A., Johnson, D. R., Branaman, A., & Sica, A. (1995). Belief and behavior: Does religion matter in today's marriage? *Journal of Marriage and the Family, 57*, 661–671.

Boss, P., Bryant, C. M., & Mancini, J. A. (2017). *Family stress management: A contextual approach*. Thousand Oaks, CA: Sage.

Becker, P. E., & Hofmeister, H. (2001). Work, family, and religious involvement for men and women. *Journal for the Scientific Study of Religion, 40*, 707–722.

Brodsky, A. E. (2000). The role of religion in the lives of resilient, urban, African American, single mothers. *Journal of Community Psychology, 28*, 199–219.

Brown, S. M., & Porter, J. (2013). The effects of religion on remarriage among American women: Evidence from the national survey of family growth. *Journal of Divorce & Remarriage, 54*, 142–162.

Browning, S., & Artelt, E. (2012). *Stepfamily therapy: A 10-step clinical approach*. Washington, DC: American Psychological Association.

Bumpass, L. L., Raley, R. K., & Sweet, J. A. (1995). The changing character of stepfamilies: Implications of cohabitation and nonmarital childbearing. *Demography, 32*, 425–436.

Carlson, T. D., Kirkpatrick, D., Hecker, L., & Killmer, M. (2002). Religion, spirituality, and marriage and family therapy: A study of family therapists' beliefs about the appropriateness of addressing religious and spiritual issues in therapy. *American Journal of Family Therapy, 30*, 157–171.

Claxton-Oldfield, S. (2008). Stereotypes of stepfamilies and stepfamily members. In J. Pryor (Ed.) *The international handbook of stepfamilies: Policy and practice in legal, research, and clinical environments* (pp. 30–52). Hoboken, NJ: John Wiley & Sons.

Clydesdale, T. T. (1997). Family behaviors among early US baby boomers: Exploring the effects of religion and income change, 1965–1982. *Social Forces, 76*, 605–635.

Coleman, M., Ganong, L., & Russell, L. (2013). Resilience in stepfamilies. In D. Becvar (Ed.) *Handbook of family resilience* (pp. 85–103). New York, NY: Springer.

Cutrona, C. E., Russell, D. W., Burzette, R. G., Wesner, K. A., & Bryant, C. M. (2011). Predicting relationship stability among midlife

African American couples. *Journal of Consulting and Clinical Psychology, 79*, 814–825.

Day, R. D., Jones-Sanpei, H., Smith Price, J. L., Orthner, D. K., Hair, E. C., Moore, K. A., & Kaye, K. (2009). Family processes and adolescent religiosity and religious practice: View from the NLSY97. *Marriage & Family Review, 45*, 289–309.

Denton, M. L. (2012). Family structure, family disruption, and profiles of adolescent religiosity. *Journal for the Scientific Study of Religion, 51*, 42–64.

Elder, G. H., Shanahan, M. J., & Jennings, J. A. (2015). Human development in time and place. In R. E. Lerner (Ed.) *Handbook of child psychology and developmental science*, Volume 4 (pp. 6–54). Hoboken, NJ: John Wiley & Sons.

Gamache, S. J. (1997). Confronting nuclear family bias in stepfamily research. *Marriage & Family Review, 26*, 41–69.

Ganong, L. H., & Coleman, M. (1983). Stepparent: A pejorative term? *Psychological Reports, 52*, 919–922.

Ganong, L. H., & Coleman, M. (1997). How society views stepfamilies. *Marriage & Family Review, 26*, 85–106.

Ganong, L., & Coleman, M. (2017). *Stepfamily relationships: Development, dynamics, and interventions* (2nd ed.). New York, NY: Kluwer Academic/Plenum.

Hetherington, E. M., Bridges, M., & Insabella, G. M. (1998). What matters? What does not? Five perspectives on the association between marital transitions and children's adjustment. *American Psychologist, 53*, 167–184.

Hodge, D. R. (2015). *Spiritual assessment in social work and mental health practice*. New York, NY: Columbia University Press.

Kavanagh, M. M. (2004). Rewriting the legal family: Beyond exclusivity to a care-based standard. *Yale Journal of Law and Feminism, 16*, 83–143.

Jensen, T. M. (2017). Constellations of dyadic relationship quality in stepfamilies: A factor mixture model. *Journal of Family Psychology, 31*, 1051–1062.

Jensen, T. M., & Harris, K. M. (2017a). A longitudinal analysis of stepfamily relationship quality and adolescent physical health. *Journal of Adolescent Health, 61*, 486–492.

Jensen, T. M., & Harris, K. M. (2017b). Stepfamily relationship quality and stepchildren's depression in adolescence and adulthood. *Emerging Adulthood, 5*, 191–203.

Jensen, T. M., & Howard, M. O. (2015). Perceived stepparent–child relationship quality: A systematic review of stepchildren's perspectives. *Marriage & Family Review, 51*, 99–153.

Jensen, T. M., Lippold, M. A., Mills-Koonce, R., & Fosco, G. M. (2018). Stepfamily relationship quality and children's internalizing and externalizing problems. *Family Process, 57*, 477–495.

Jensen, T., & Shafer, K. (2013). Stepfamily functioning and closeness: Children's views on second marriages and stepfather relationships. *Social Work, 58*, 127–136.

Jensen, T., Shafer, K., & Holmes, E. K. (2017). Transitioning to stepfamily life: The influence of closeness with biological parents and stepparents on children's stress. *Child & Family Social Work, 22*, 275–286.

Krumrei, E. J., Mahoney, A., & Pargament, K. I. (2009). Divorce and the divine: The role of spirituality in adjustment to divorce. *Journal of Marriage and Family, 71*, 373–383.

King, V. (2006). The antecedents and consequences of adolescents' relationships with stepfathers and nonresident fathers. *Journal of Marriage and Family, 68*, 910–928.

Lehrer, E. (2000). Religion as a determinant of entry into cohabitation and marriage. In L. Waite, C. Bachrach, M. Hindin, E. Thomson, & A. Thornton (Eds.) *The ties that bind: Perspectives on marriage and cohabitation* (pp. 227–252). Hawthorne, NY: Aldine de Gruyter.

Lehrer, E. L. (2004a). Religion as a determinant of economic and demographic behavior in the United States. *Population and Development Review, 30*, 707–726.

Lehrer, E. L. (2004b). The role of religion in union formation: An economic perspective. *Population Research and Policy Review, 23*, 161–185.

Levinger, G. (1965). Marital cohesiveness and dissolution: An integrative review. *Journal of Marriage and the Family, 27*, 19–28.

Lippold, M. A., & Jensen, T. M. (2017). Harnessing the strength of families to prevent social problems and promote adolescent well-being. *Children and Youth Services Review, 79*, 432–441.

Mahoney, A., Pargament, K. I., Murray-Swank, A., & Murray-Swank, N. (2003). Religion and the sanctification of family relationships. *Review of Religious Research, 44*, 220–236.

Mahoney, A., Pargament, K. I., Tarakeshwar, N., & Swank, A. (2001). Religion in the home in the 1980s and 1990s: A meta-analytic review and conceptual analysis of links between religion, marriage, and parenting. *Journal of Family Psychology, 15*, 559–596.

Malia, S. E. (2005). Balancing family members' interests regarding stepparent rights and obligations: A social policy challenge. *Family Relations, 54*, 298–319.

Malia, S. (2008). How relevant are U.S. family and probate laws to stepfamilies? In J. Pryor (Ed.) *The international handbook of stepfamilies: Policy and practice in legal, research, and clinical environments* (pp. 545–572). Hoboken, NJ: John Wiley & Sons.

Marks, L. (2006). Religion and family relational health: An overview and conceptual model. *Journal of Religion and Health, 45*, 603–618.

Mattis, J. S. (2002). Religion and spirituality in the meaning-making and coping experiences of African American women: A qualitative analysis. *Psychology of Women Quarterly, 26,* 309–321.

McDaniel, S., Boco, A. G., & Zella, S. (2013). Changing patterns of religious affiliation, religiosity, and marital dissolution: A 35-year study of three-generation families. *Journal of Divorce & Remarriage, 54,* 629–657.

Papernow, P. (2013). *Surviving and thriving in stepfamily relationships: What works and what doesn't.* New York, NY: Routledge.

Papernow, P. L. (2018). Recoupling in mid-life and beyond: From love at last to not so fast. *Family Process, 57,* 52–69.

Patterson, J. M. (2002). Integrating family resilience and family stress theory. *Journal of marriage and family, 64,* 349–360.

Pearce, L. D. (2002). The influence of early life course religious exposure on young adults' dispositions toward childbearing. *Journal for the Scientific Study of Religion, 41,* 325–340.

Peters, M. F., & Massey, G. (1983). Mundane extreme environmental stress in family stress theories: The case of Black families in White America. *Marriage & Family Review, 6,* 193–218.

Petts, R. J. (2009). Trajectories of religious participation from adolescence to young adulthood. *Journal for the Scientific Study of Religion, 48,* 552–571.

Petts, R. J. (2014). Parental religiosity and youth religiosity: Variations by family structure. *Sociology of Religion, 76,* 95–120.

Pew Research Center (2011). *Pew social & demographic trends survey.* Washington, DC: Pew Research Center.

Pew Research Center (2015). *America's changing religious landscape.* Washington, DC: Pew Research Center.

Poston, D. J., & Turnbull, A. P. (2004). Role of spirituality and religion in family quality of life for families of children with disabilities. *Education and Training in Developmental Disabilities, 39,* 95–108.

Pryor, J. (2014). *Stepfamilies: A global perspective on research, policy, and practice.* New York, NY: Routledge.

Schramm, D. G., Marshall, J. P., Harris, V. W., & Lee, T. R. (2012). Religiosity, homogamy, and marital adjustment: An examination of newlyweds in first marriages and remarriages. *Journal of Family Issues, 33,* 246–268.

Sheeber, L., Hops, H., & Davis, B. (2001). Family processes in adolescent depression. *Clinical Child and Family Psychology Review, 4,* 19–35.

Shorter-Gooden, K. (2004). Multiple resistance strategies: How African American women cope with racism and sexism. *Journal of Black Psychology, 30,* 406–425.

Skinner, D. A., & Kohler, J. K. (2002). Parental rights in diverse family contexts: Current legal developments. *Family Relations, 51,* 293–300.

Stander, V., Piercy, F. P., Mackinnon, D., & Helmeke, K. (1994). Spirituality, religion and family therapy: Competing or complementary worlds? *The American Journal of Family Therapy, 22,* 27–41.

Stewart, S. (2007). *Brave new stepfamilies: Diverse paths toward stepfamily living.* Thousand Oaks, CA: Sage.

Sweeney, M. M. (2010). Remarriage and stepfamilies: Strategic sites for family scholarship in the 21st century. *Journal of Marriage and Family, 72,* 667–684.

Tanyi, R. A. (2002). Towards clarification of the meaning of spirituality. *Journal of Advanced Nursing, 39,* 500–509.

Thornton, A., Axinn, W. G., & Hill, D. H. (1992). Reciprocal effects of religiosity, cohabitation, and marriage. *American Journal of Sociology, 98,* 628–651.

Tuttle, J. D., & Davis, S. N. (2015). Religion, infidelity, and divorce: Reexamining the effect of religious behavior on divorce among long-married couples. *Journal of Divorce & Remarriage, 56,* 475–489.

van Eeden-Moorefield, B., & Pasley, K. (20130. Remarriage and stepfamily life. In G. Peterson & K. Bush (Eds.) *Handbook of marriage and the family* (pp. 517–546). New York, NY: Springer.

Walsh, F. (2002). A family resilience framework: Innovative practice applications. *Family Relations, 51,* 130–137.

Wu, Z., & Schimmele, C. M. (2005). Repartnering after first union disruption. *Journal of Marriage and Family, 67,* 27–36.

Xu, X., & Bartkowski, J. P. (2017). Remarriage timing: Does religion matter? *Religions, 8,* 160.

Xu, X., Hudspeth, C. D., & Bartkowski, J. P. (2006). The role of cohabitation in remarriage. *Journal of Marriage and Family, 68,* 261–274.

CHAPTER EIGHT

Studying Diverse Stepfamilies

CONCLUSIONS AND FUTURE DIRECTIONS

Gordon Limb, PhD, Brigham Young University
Susan D. Stewart, PhD, Iowa State University

AS WAS NOTED in the Introduction, this book has three primary purposes. The first is to increase awareness of the increased number of non-White stepfamilies of color and stepfamilies who are religiously, spiritually, and culturally diverse in an effort to stimulate research on racial, ethnic, and religious diversity in stepfamily life in the United States and the world. The second purpose is to provide new data on stepfamily life within different social and demographic groups within the context of an economically diverse and racialized country with Christianity as its primary religion, and one that perpetuates an idealized notion of the family, based on marriage and blood ties, that in reality represents a minority of all families. Third, each chapter included a vignette to deepen readers' understanding of stepfamily life as opposed to relying on hypothetical, theoretical, and empirical models. We follow the lead of the family discipline's leading scholar on stepfamilies, Dr. Patricia Papernow, who in her book, *Surviving and Thriving in Stepfamily Relationships*, effectively demonstrates the complex "architecture" of stepfamilies through the personal stories of real stepfamilies (Papernow, 2013). Thus, we wanted to build this edited book around core common themes highlighting the diversity, inclusiveness, and intersectionality of each group. Through vignettes, literature reviews, practical examples, and new information based on original data analysis, each of the authors addressed these complicated but important issues and provided their recommendations for future research. We applaud the authors for their painstaking efforts to deal with these complex issues.

Having examined stepfamily dynamics within a Native American context the past five years, I am well aware how difficult it is to tell that story. All research and writing has its biases and limitations and this book is no exception. I appreciate Dr. Stewart's leadership in trying to bridge some of these limitations as we try and find ways of inclusion and recognize that most stepfamilies are part of multiple categories. In my research, we often note that there are more than 550 federally recognized tribes (Bureau of Indian Affairs, 2017). While the word "different" is often used, I have found that Native American people have more commonalities than differences. And when social scientists tell their story, or that of any racial, ethnic, or religious group, our goal is to tell the story of the average, representative member of that community as opposed to the story of someone on the extreme ends of any spectrum. We also strive to recognize the differences within groups by taking a *strengths perspective* in telling that story, thus giving practitioners and clinicians a building block from which to help members of those groups in a way that shows sensitivity and humility. While this can be a challenge, it's something that academicians, practitioners, and others must promote as we encourage cultural competence, discussed in more detail in the following sections. As Papernow notes, "thriving stepfamilies face the same challenges as struggling ones" (2013, p. 24). The next section summarizes each chapter and discusses both similarities and differences for each of these groups.

Chapter Findings Including Differences and Similarities

In Chapter 2, Dr. Stykes provided historical context, detailing the changes and characteristics of contemporary stepfamilies, and discussed several theoretical perspectives commonly used to explain stepfamily dynamics. His analysis indicated that various definitions of what constitutes a stepfamily influence our understanding of their prevalence. For example, among all children living in stepfamilies, three in ten were not linked with a stepparent based on the household roster but through the report of a biological parent who indicated the presence of a live-in partner. He found that a broader definition of stepfamilies that includes cohabiting and same-sex partners and adult stepchildren resulted in a 163% increase in the number of children living in stepfamily households. Dr. Stykes found that recent scholarship advocating for a more inclusive definition of stepfamilies has received substantial attention and for the most part has been well received. Questions involving the quality of relationship ties with cohabiting stepparents and same-sex partners, however, were limited and we continue to struggle to embrace a more inclusive definition of stepfamily to improve our understanding of the specific dynamics occurring in stepfamilies. Finally, while he focused on stepfamilies in the United States, there are a number of considerations that apply to stepfamilies outside America. As a result, scholars and academicians can and should include more inclusive definitions of stepfamilies as they collect data and report on findings.

In Chapter 3, Dr. Bryant examined a number of stepfamily frameworks that are particularly useful for understanding African American stepfamilies, including the family solidarity model, family systems, family stress, and boundary ambiguity. She further explained the conceptual frameworks within which African Americans are situated, the demographic characteristics of African American stepfamilies, and findings from recent research. She noted that data indicate African American stepfamilies are more structurally diverse than those of other racial and ethnic groups, and nearly half of African American children will reside in a home that includes their biological parent's cohabiting partner. She also noted that the decrease in marriage rates among African Americans did not reflect a decline in the value of marriage or family as much as a result of other factors, such as education and income. She also noted that many African American families include "fictive kin," hence the term "stepchild" may have a broader definition than for many other racial groups. Finally, given the importance of extended family members who provide needed support, therapists should consider expanding family therapy sessions and intervention processes to include family or nonfamily members who are and can make a contribution to healthy stepfamily functioning.

In Chapter 4, Hoffman and colleagues suggested that from a direct practice vantage point, those serving Hispanic stepfamilies should listen carefully for indications that unique cultural influences may be sources of strength and, conversely, difficulty. They specifically mentioned that expectations from community members regarding adherence to culturally prevalent views of familism and gender roles may help explain interpersonal behaviors and decisions within the family. They suggest that practitioners be careful not to underestimate the influence of church and religious values and also those from extended family members and kin who may provide substantial emotional and material support. Another challenge facing Hispanic stepfamilies is that their members may have different *bicultural identities* (i.e., different levels of enculturation and acculturation) and different immigration statuses that can add to family stress. Finally, when working with more traditional Hispanic gender roles, helping professionals should be mindful of their own cultural values so that personal or mainstream ideals do not unintentionally influence their recommendations and services. Dr. Hoffman and colleagues conclude by providing five questions that researchers and helping professionals should consider as they seek to help this population.

In Chapter 5, Turner and colleagues state that American Indian stepfamilies share many characteristics of nonnative stepfamilies but have unique strengths such as collectivism and community; however, instead of conceiving relationships in linear terms, American Indians tend to think of relationships in circular terms, especially concerning the need to maintain balance and harmony among body, mind, and spirit. They note that many American Indians face challenges such as poverty, stigma, substance use, unemployment, and poor mental health. These issues are very likely at least partly responsible for lower quality relationships and well-being among parents, stepparents, and stepchildren among American Indians compared with those of other racial and ethnic groups, though more research is needed to pinpoint driving influences. American Indians with children who marry or partner with non-Indians have the additional challenge of figuring out how to merge traditional beliefs into the home. On the other hand, American Indians tend to be more accepting of nontraditional family forms and have larger networks of family and friends to rely upon for caretaking and instrumental support. Indeed, resiliency was also discussed as is an important part of a Native American heritage and lifestyle, particularly as it relates to historical trauma. Resiliency will become an increasingly important protective factor as American Indians face familial separation and stepfamily formation. They conclude by suggesting that one strategy shown to be effective is for practitioners to work closely with tribal leaders, and use community resources to encourage families to reach out and develop culturally appropriate support systems.

In Chapter 6, Dr. Nozawa notes that stepfamilies in Asia remain an "incomplete institution" and are often based on the "scrap and build" household model in which biological parents are replaced with stepparents upon remarriage. That stepfamily dynamic might have some universal ground in that parenting and stepparenting rigidly based on the scrap and build household model will most likely bring difficulties, and sometimes painfulness, for both child and adult members in the adaptation to stepfamily life. He found variation in stepparenting styles, stepparent-stepchild relationships, and residential parent-child relationships both in Japan and also other East Asian societies. Further, stepfamily dynamics in Asia can be heavily influenced by the values of extended family members, such as grandparents of stepchildren in the United States and other Western cultures. Finally, he noted that stepfamily dynamics are in transition under ever-changing revisions of family laws and family policy in Asia, and that there is growing support to move to the expanded network model of stepfamilies.

In Chapter 7, Dr. Jensen stated that it might be advisable for practitioners to assess the potential influence of religion on stepfamily dynamics at the outset of clinical or educational work. Overall, members of stepfamilies are less religious and attend services less frequently than married, two-biological-parent families, though more research is needed to identify factors underlying this association. There is also a greater mismatch between partners, and parents and children, in stepfamilies. His findings suggested that religious transmission from parents to children is weaker in stepfamilies compared with biological two-parent families, and that how religion affects relationship quality is highly complex. He noted that attending to religious matters when working with stepfamilies can be considered congruent with efforts to possess and practice cultural competency. He advocated that training and educational programs include content focused on stepfamily dynamics and discussions about the role of religion and spirituality in practice settings. Finally, he encouraged practitioners to be mindful of the ways that religion might influence stepfamily dynamics and functioning.

Similarities and Differences Across Groups

When considering similarities and differences among the groups covered in this book, there are a few notable findings. A number of authors noted that racially, ethnically, and religiously diverse stepfamilies often have more in common with one another than they do with their White, Christian counterparts. As increasingly more research is conducted with these groups, we anticipate that additional commonalities will emerge and become part of treatment. A similarity among many of the chapters is the recommendation to include extended family and others outside the immediate stepfamily throughout the process. In many cultures, non-blood relatives and influential people in the community or religion should be sought for input and support. This broader inclusive definition helps these stepfamilies receive the long-term support to overcome challenges and remain healthy. Further, a number of authors also noted a recent push for a more inclusive definition of what constitutes a stepfamily. Many studies in the literature impose restrictions on operational definitions of stepfamilies that exclude a number of stepfamily groups (e.g., same sex, cohabiting, and longer duration stepfamilies.). We encourage future research to not only utilize more inclusive definitions of what constitutes a stepfamily but also include broader resources (e.g., extended family) as they collect data and information.

On the other hand, as part of the intersectionality discussion, each of the authors noted that stepfamilies are complex and each group has unique cultural and/or religious influences that can be both positive and negative. As Turner and colleagues mentioned, service providers should approach each individual and family "where they are" and utilize culturally appropriate, evidence-based treatment strategies whenever possible. Each individual and family have unique strengths that can be tapped into as they progress down this path. In an effort to become more culturally competent, examining these often overlooked elements will help those working with stepfamilies to provide more effective services.

Culture-Specific Interventions

In many helping professions, accrediting bodies and professional licensure require demonstration of cultural competence. In social work, for example, the Council on Social Work Education (CSWE) has adopted a competency-based education framework for programs in order to receive and maintain accreditation. CSWE states that "competency-based education rests upon a shared view of the nature of competence" and is the ability to integrate and apply social work knowledge, values, and skills to practice situations (2015, p. 6). Specifically, of the nine required competencies, Competency Two includes "engaging diversity and difference in practice" with special mention of the "intersectionality of multiple factors" including many of the dimensions listed in each of this book's chapters.

According to an article written in the *Chronicle of Higher Education*, cultural competence "means an individual can work across cultural lines, can value and adapt to diversity, and can demonstrate such abilities in leadership and policy-making roles (Breslow, 2005, para. 2). While cultural competence has its place in higher education and professional practice, demonstrating competence across "cultural lines" and with diverse individuals can be difficult to achieve and measure. In my work, I've often heard clinicians say, "The more I learn about [insert racial, ethnic, or religious group or individual] the more I realize how much I don't know." Thus, while achieving cultural competence can be a challenge, a more recent term many researchers studying diversity and difference are using is "cultural humility."

Initially developed for physician training in multicultural education, one of the first studies that used cultural humility as an alternative to cultural competence was conducted by Tervalon and Murray-Garcia in 1998. This model was then adapted into the social sciences for child welfare and practice with immigrants and refugees (Ortega & Faller, 2011). Here, cultural humility suggests that individual and group cultural experiences are unique and should be honored rather than emphasizing or focusing on shared group characteristics. The downside of focusing on shared group characteristics is that it tends to give power to clinical expertise about a client or group's culture and creates power imbalances between clinician and client.

Cultural humility refutes the concept that clinicians can ever achieve "expertise" or competence about another culture, and requires the clinician to engage in a lifelong journey of self-evaluation and learning to develop "mutually beneficial and non-paternalistic partnerships with communities on behalf of individuals and defined populations" (Tervalon & Murray-Garcia, 1998, p. 123). As such, cultural humility originates from a position of honoring and utilizing the strengths and intrinsic values of different cultural approaches, at both the individual and group levels, rather than maintaining a Western/White model of understanding the world (Ortega & Faller, 2011). Therefore, as we look to the future, promoting cultural

Moving from cultural competence to cultural humility.

humility as we discuss cultural competence will enable us to better serve racial, ethnic, and religiously diverse stepfamilies.

Future Directions

As noted in Chapter 2, much of what we know concerning step-families involves research based on participants who were White, middle-to-upper-class, married, and Christian. While research regarding all stepfamily formations is important, this book calls for increased attention and focus on racially, ethnically, and religiously diverse populations. Since Stewart's 2007 book, *Brave New Stepfamilies*, there has been little specific focus on non-traditional stepfamilies, aside from Papernow's excellent and forward-thinking books (2013; see also Bonnell & Papernow, 2018) that include chapters on lesbian and gay step-couples, Latino step-families, African American stepfamilies, and later-life re-couplers. Indeed, in 2013, when we first began studying U.S. stepfamilies from American Indian tribal groups, there were few, if any, empirical studies conducted on this population. While stepfamilies are a growing family dynamic, and most if not all professionals will encounter and help them, the research is lagging in evaluating and demonstrating how to effectively help this important family group.

Thus, there continue to be major gaps in the stepfamily research literature. For example, the most common approach in research and clinical work with stepfamilies continues to be family systems (Jensen, Shafer, & Larson, 2014). While in many cases this approach has been found to be effective, other approaches need to be tested and compared to establish efficacy. Other gaps include families with disabilities, bereavement issues, effects of imprisonment and homelessness, and grandparents raising stepchildren. While there are a growing number of studies in the stepfamily arena, much more can and must be done to help this important population.

One of the purposes of each chapter was to provide new data on stepfamily life with different groups. For the most part, chapters in books only delve into research issues from a conceptual framework. We felt that this was not enough to move the work forward. Hence, we asked each author to utilize primary or secondary data to produce new knowledge in their respective areas. We believe this addition increases the application and usability of this book for academic and professional audiences. For example, in Chapter 2, Dr. Stykes found that two-thirds of children in stepfamilies were identified by linking the child to both a biological parent and also a stepparent living in the household. He also noted that White children and those whose parents are better educated are overrepresented among traditional stepfamilies as opposed to cohabiting stepfamilies, another challenge to conducting representative research.

In Chapter 7, Dr. Jensen noted that his descriptive findings underscore the value in exploring religious diversity, religion, and religiosity in the context of stepfamily life. While explorations might be especially complex in stepfamily contexts, stepfamily subsystems might experience more mismatches in religious affiliation than subsystems in biological, nuclear, or single-parent families.

As a final example of research challenges, in Chapter 5, Turner and colleagues used original data and found that Native Americans who grew up in a stepfamily reported more difficulties in relationships and lower individual and family well-being compared with respondents of other racial and ethnic groups. External factors such as low education levels, low socioeconomic status, and high unemployment rates are disproportionately present among these groups and also need to be accounted for.

Finally, from a research, policy, and practice perspective, each chapter gives readers important insights on what can be done with each group to effectively move these areas forward. In a changing political landscape, it is important to advocate for and give a voice to these often overlooked racial, ethnic, and religious groups. It is equally important to help diverse stepfamilies *themselves* anticipate trouble spots and develop a common set of tools to navigate their relationships within these contexts (an excellent resource is *The Stepfamily Handbook*, by Bonnell and Papernow). As readers apply the information within this book, they will more effectively learn about, advocate for, and serve these and similar groups. We invite all to join us in finding better ways to work with, respect, and honor all families.

Questions for Discussion

1. What have you learned about the intersectionality and inclusion of the groups covered in this book?
2. How is cultural humility similar to and different from cultural competence?
3. How are the groups covered in each chapter similar to and different from one another? What is one thing you learned about a group that you did not know before?

Additional Resources

Bonnell, K. S., & Papernow, P. (2018). *The stepfamily handbook*. Kirkland, WA: CMC.

Papernow, P. (2013). *Surviving and thriving in stepfamily relationships*. New York, NY: Routledge.

Stewart, S. D. (2007). *Brave new stepfamilies: Diverse paths toward stepfamily living*. Thousand Oaks, CA: Sage.

The National Stepfamily Resource Center (http://www.stepfamilies.info/) provides additional information on stepfamilies, including educational materials, support services, and research-based answers to common questions about stepfamilies.

References

Bonnell, K. S., & Papernow, P. (2018). *The stepfamily handbook*. Kirkland, WA: CMC.

Breslow, J. M. (2005, October 5). The problems of cultural competence. *The Chronical of Higher Education*. Retrieved February 15, 2019, from https://www.chronicle.com/article/The-problems-of-cultural/121350

Bureau of Indian Affairs. (2017). Indian entities recognized and eligible to receive services from the United States Bureau of Indian Affairs. *Federal Register, 33*. Retrieved February 15, 2019, from https://www.gpo.gov/fdsys/pkg/FR-2017-01-17/pdf/2017-00912.pdf

Council on Social Work Education. (2015). *2015 educational policy and accreditation standards for baccalaureate and master's social work programs*. Retrieved February 15, 2019, from https://www.cswe.org/getattachment/Accreditation/Accreditation-Process/2015-EPAS/2015EPAS_Web_FINAL.pdf.aspx

Jensen, T. M., Shafer, K., & Larson, J. H. (2014). (Step)parenting attitudes and expectations: Implications for stepfamily functioning and clinical intervention. *Families in Society, 95*(3), 213–220.

Ortega, R. M., & Faller, K. C. (2011). Training child welfare workers from an intersectional cultural humility perspective: A paradigm shift. *Child Welfare, 90*, 27–49.

Papernow, P. (2013). *Surviving and thriving in stepfamily relationships*. New York, NY: Routledge.

Stewart, S. D. (2007). *Brave new stepfamilies: Diverse paths toward stepfamily living*. Thousand Oaks, CA: Sage.

Tervalon, M., & Murray-Garcia, J. (1998). Cultural humility versus cultural competence: A critical distinction in defining physician training outcomes in multicultural education. *Journal of Health Care for the Poor and Underserved, 9*, 117–125.

Index

CPSIA information can be obtained
at www.ICGtesting.com
Printed in the USA
LVHW021054200521
687955LV00010B/178